BESSARABIAN NIGHTS

by Stela Brinzeanu

AUROCHS

To Helena

Acknowledgements

I'd like to start by thanking my friends and beta-readers who read the book prior to publication and made invaluable suggestions to it time and again: William Johns, Richard Blackwell, Veronica Pinon and George Stanica. Thank you for putting your valuable time into this story!

Special thanks must also go to Professor Dennis Deletant who kindly agreed to act as history consultant on this project. Să trăiți!

Further thanks are due to Lilia Gorceag and Nadejada Radu – psychologist and social assistant respectively – at the IOM (International Organization for Migration) Mission in Moldova. Your answers to my plethora of questions and information offered about victims of human trafficking have been vital to this project.

I am indebted to Paul Moynihan for his patient editing and elaborate proofreading. Your efforts have been phenomenal!

The publishing process wouldn't have been as smooth without the expert advice and help from the excellent team at Authoright, who amongst many other things, helped with the design of the book cover and website.

Many thanks to all my family and friends - your unfailing encouragement and support along the way was, is and forever will be greatly appreciated.

Once again - I thank you all!

Contents

"The breathing of our breed is on the brink of
bathos...comrades."
(Grigore Cojocaru – teacher turned labourer)

Prologue

Despite my almighty faculties as ghost of the country, I am in no position to interfere or in any way influence the lives and destinies of my people. That belongs to forces higher than myself.

It hurts to see them all leaving for places far from home and hearth, where the grass seems greener. The abject poverty sweeping through my land forces many to go abroad, willingly or unwillingly. Especially my daughters – for they are the ones who mostly bear the brunt of this harsh time in history. My beautiful girls are deserting in droves and only few come back, be it dead or alive.

This is a story from the enchanted land of Bessarabia in Eastern Europe – a dominion ruled by superstition and lore. Absorbed deeply into the psyche of those living here, these nebulous, ever-changing yet somehow permanent precepts confine the lives of the majority.

It is a genuine country, officially known as Moldova, but also as many others call it – "no man's land" – housing four million people and counting down each day.

Part of my people's psyche, I, the old ghost of Bessarabia, inhabit them all. This grants me the authority to start spinning this yarn. Unlike Scheherazade's 1001 tales, the following is an account of real-life stories from our modern times.

Part One

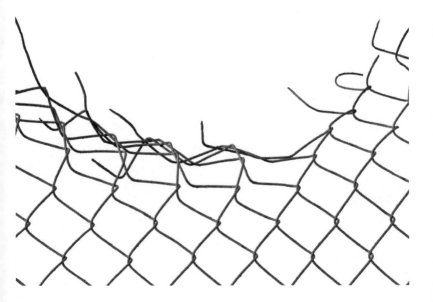

Stiletto Silver

Ksenia woke up in an alien kitchen, an awfully dirty alien kitchen. A huddle of grubby cups and glasses of all shapes and sizes crowded the sink. Overflowing, sooty ashtrays were scattered on the table in the middle of the room. The floor was littered with crumbs of food and dirt.

Her OCD affronted, Ksenia was filled with disgust.

"How on earth did I end up here, of all places?" She rubbed her forehead in an attempt to trace her moves of the night before.

The door opened with a sudden pull. A fake blonde in silvery stilettos walked in, heels clacking purposefully across the tile floor. Arms akimbo, she stopped in front of Ksenia.

"Good morning."

"Who are you? Where am I?" Ksenia asked the blanched lady, who was clearly older than she pretended to be – the thick slab of orange foundation cream only deepening her wrinkles.

"You don't remember me? We met at the Paradiso bar last night."

Ksenia frowned in confusion. She felt nauseous and her head was spinning.

"I didn't drink much...I don't understand...Sorry, what's your name again?"

"Galea," the fake blonde said through the blowing and popping of noisy gum bubbles.

"Can I have some water please? I feel dizzy. Where is Boris?"

"Don't know." Galea filled a filthy mug with tap water and handed it to Ksenia. "He abandoned you last night after your vicious attack on that girl."

Ksenia splurted her water.

"What attack on what girl?"

"You got jealous and set someone's hair on fire."

"I don't remember any of that."

"You were proper smashed."

"Oh my God. I need to talk to Boris. How do I get to Fantasma Hotel from here?" Ksenia tried to get up but her whole body ached. The feeling of sickness that had been lingering in her stomach rose to her throat.

"You can't go anywhere."

"What do you mean? Why not?"

"You owe us money."

"What for?"

"We had to pay the girl you assaulted and also 'fix' the bouncers not to call the police."

Ksenia was staggered.

"Where is my purse? I'll pay you back."

"Two thousand euros, please."

"What??? Are you kidding?"

"Does it look like it?" Galea displayed a cold, half smile and carried on with her loud bubble popping.

"What's going on?" Ksenia panicked.

"I don't have that much money. Let me go to the hotel and find my boyfriend. We'll pay the money back to you."

8

"He walked out last night after your *performance* and refused to have anything to do with it."

"Please – I need to speak to him."

"Look, you are not going anywhere, full stop. You work for us until you pay your debt," Galea threatened ominously. She even stopped chewing.

"I can't stay and work in Italy. I've just graduated…I've been offered a job as an Arts teacher in Moldova!"

"What we offer is much better. Don't you know how miserly-paid jobs are in that shitty country?"

"I am sorry but I can't stay here," Ksenia turned towards the door.

Galea barred her way.

"No one asked you if you can or not, darling. You owe us money and gotta pay it all back. End. Of. Conversation."

"I am getting out of here," Ksenia pushed past.

A long, narrow corridor with closed doors made it difficult to guess where the exit was and she headed blindly down it towards the other end.

Galea called out:

"Boys, we've got a li'l daffodil here. Can you sort her out?"

Like dogs answering a command, two rough looking men immediately appeared and, without saying a word, airlifted Ksenia back to the kitchen. One of them sat backwards on a high chair, lit a cigarette and eyed her indecently, lowering his gaze indulgently from Ksenia's chest, taking in her slim hips and down to her long legs.

"We met last night and you seemed a nice girl. Why are you causing such a fuss now?"

Ksenia barely identified Igor, the guy who was with Galea at the bar the night before. He looked stereotypically Eastern European, sporting a gelled-up fringe in the shape of a wide-teethed comb fixed horizontally on his bulbous forehead. A Roman nose and protruding ears did not help his case either.

"Listen carefully," he carried on, "this can be done two ways and two ways ONLY, trust me..."

Ksenia didn't. Fear arrested her.

"...One way is willingly and the other one is..." He lifted his head exhaling the smoke in ringlets "...unwillingly. You do what we say – you live. If you don't then...you suffer. It's entirely your choice but the only one you have. Is that clear?"

Ksenia kept blinking. This all felt unreal.

"I hope you are going to be reasonable – for your own sake. Now, all you have to do is serve customers for a few months until you pay off your debt – that's all. I will return your passport and you'll be free to go then. I suggest you don't waste your time – or ours – and instead get ready to work."

"Please let me go. I promise to pay you back as soon as I get to Moldova. I swear to God I will."

"That wasn't one of the options. Are you deaf or stupid?" Igor raised his voice. "I'll repeat them one more time – your choices are to do what we tell you, willingly or not."

"I can't do it."

Before Ksenia was able to say anything else, Igor swung his arm and applied a heavy blow to her left ear. She stumbled and hit the wall on the other side. Both ears started ringing and Ksenia detected a strangely familiar smell that reminded her of having her nose broken during a basketball match with the neighbouring village at the age of fifteen. The same peculiar scent filled her lungs now and turned her stomach.

But there was no time to dwell on it.

More heavy blows followed.

She fell to the floor.

Ksenia crawled under the kitchen table but its shield was kicked away.

"You fuck or you die, bitch." Igor pulled her by the hair and shouted in her face like a madman. "I mean it, do not test me."

Igor and the other guard, who had been silently standing in the shadows all this time, left the room.

Ksenia's body felt like a spiny ball of fire. It was far worse than anything she had ever had to go through.

Galea came into the kitchen.

"You need to take a shower and then we'll to do a bit of work on you to cover all those red marks. You should be OK to start working tonight. The sooner you pay us the money – the sooner you go home. How's that for a deal?"

Ksenia's mouth was full of blood and her tongue had swollen. Cringing, she spat into the bin and turned with pleading eyes.

"Please Galea, I beg you – do not force me into this. Let's talk and sort something out. I can't do what you are asking of me."

Galea said nothing and turned swiftly on her silver heels but this flicker of hope was quickly put out by the return of Igor and the other guard. His name Ksenia later learned to be Ghena, or the One-Eyed Monster due to total blindness in his left eye and his perverse and twisted attitude to sex.

This time, they didn't waste any time on chit-chat but proceeded straight to business.

"Please, I beg you.."

"Shut up, whore."

Thick leather belts came off and wild lashings measured up her body, head to toes. They kicked, spat, pulled fistfuls of her hair out and just when it felt like their fury subsided, they both mounted Ksenia like savages.

Delirious and sick, she knew no longer where she was or what was happening to her.

Goose-Grey

"You've been kept in this basement for the last three days," Ksenia was informed by a girl she did not know, "and you'll be here a lot longer if you carry on disobeying them. These brutes do not like wasting time or money and you can easily disappear, without a trace for all those who love you. Gone forever, do you understand? You won't be the first one. I've seen many come and many go. Get it? By the way, my name is Nadea, or Nadejda, if you like. What's yours?"

Through blurred eyes, Ksenia stared at the tall, slim stranger, trying to figure out where she was. Awful flashbacks filled the void of her mind. Ksenia could have sworn they were just horrible nightmares, if it weren't for the sharp pain needling her body.

"*It's too painful for a dream,*" Ksenia thought "*but then all sensations seem real in any dream. Perhaps I could ask this stranger to tell me if I am dreaming or not. How silly – of course she'll say it's real. She, herself, is part of the dream. It's best to keep quiet and not get involved. I might wake up from it any minute now.*"

The stranger, however, carried on talking:

"You have no choice right now. They can discard you like a cigarette butt at any moment and that will be it. Listen to me, darling – what you could lose, you have already lost in the last few days. There is nothing else you should think about protecting right now, other than your life."

The girl sounded genuinely concerned but Ksenia had already learned not to trust anyone in that house. Her bleary eyes prevented her from seeing Nadea properly.

"That's because she is a vision, a dreamy image, that's why."

Ksenia blinked again to get a better focus but the apparition was still there, getting clearer if anything. Hard, goose-grey eyes and a dark, potato-shaped birthmark on her left cheek were the first features Ksenia could distinguish. Thin, black hair dropped to the stranger's sunken shoulders.

Ksenia tried to look for more details to ascertain whether it was a real person or not but her eyelids felt heavy and sticky. She wanted to touch them but found her hands made of lead and impossible to lift.

Nadea picked up on Ksenia's intention.

"Your hands are tied together with a rope. It feels thick, huh? That's blood. Your blood. I know, this may all seem like a nightmare, but it's real. And dangerous. If you wanna survive it, you gotta play along and get well first."

The stranger fell silent and started applying compresses of damp, well-used kitchen towels on Ksenia's body. Shortly after, without a word, she disappeared as if she'd never been in the room in the first place.

With the ghost out of her view, Ksenia doubted all that had just happened. Only the rawness of those grey eyes and the intrusion of the birthmark lingered on, and something else, which before too long she'd be

14

well accustomed to – a whiff of cigarette smoke mixed in with the cheap, astringent perfume of a working girl.

A small lamp dimly lit the corner. Despite it, the space around felt dark and tight. All Ksenia could see were a number of blue bin bags with yellow draw-tape and stained cardboard boxes lined up near the barren walls. She wondered what they were full of.

Ksenia was cold. Lying on the ground with only a thin blanket on top of her, she became aware of a sharp chill cutting her to the bone. The eeriness of the basement was daunting.

Some time later Nadea returned with more compresses. It could have been hours or mere moments, Ksenia couldn't tell.

"How deceptive and distorted time can be in the realm of dreams," she thought.

In her obduracy to not be part of the nightmare, Ksenia refused to acknowledge Nadea's presence. She decided not to respond or in any way involve herself in what was happening or what she thought was happening.

But the stranger's voice persisted:

"You've not spoken a word. It's OK if you don't feel like talking. You don't have to but I just want to know that you can still do it, that you understand and can hear my voice. Just wink or nod or say something, I beg you."

The heartfelt plea caused Ksenia to stir involuntarily.

"Thank you," Nadea smiled and gave her a hug. "I'll go and get some food for you – won't be long."

The sincerity and warmth of that affection soothed the pain but it also broke the spell, causing harsh reality to fully sink in.

Raw Red

While Nadea was gone to bring food, Ksenia resumed the task of piecing together her scraps of memory. She was desperate to get her head round the events that led to that dark place.

"What happened?"

The question rang in her mind over and over again, its maddening echo seeking to unhinge her sanity.

"Boris, my boyfriend...We came to Milan together on holiday. Where is he?"

Ksenia could well remember the day they arrived, checking in at the hotel and having an afternoon of wild sex. The big wall mirrors reflected openly the intense, feral affair which left Ksenia more in love with Boris than ever before.

Both tall and slim, Ksenia was the attractive one. Her lean body and beautiful figure had been complimented many times and Ksenia was a confident young woman. The straw-coloured, wavy hair rained abundantly past her shoulder blades. Full, red lips stood out alluringly on the pale, Caucasian skin she had inherited from her Russian grandmother – Dasha Tyomkina – along with her steppe-deep-green eyes.

Boris was a former judo wrestler with a squashed nose. The narrow forehead and dark, thick stubble lent him a gloomy countenance, saved by a surprisingly goofy, open smile. Sheepishly, Ksenia loved his ripped body too. With big, powerful hands, he played with her like with a toy, bringing pleasure and flaring lust every time as if it was the last.

After dinner they decided to check out the nightlife in Milan and stopped at a bar they walked by on the main street. Ksenia liked the place, had a couple of elderflower martinis and enjoyed the dance floor.

She remembered meeting another Moldovan couple not long after they got there but her memory refused to cooperate beyond that. She didn't think she got drunk from two drinks but the mental blackout she experienced did not make sense and caused alarm.

Raw pain and fear still subjugated her breath.

She didn't feel hunger when Nadea left to bring food but her growling stomach started making urgent demands. The bitter cold in the cellar crept to the marrow of her bones. There was nothing on the floor to grab. Ksenia curled under the thin blanket, bringing her knees to her chest, and blew into her hands. The warm, late May weather was slow in reaching the basement.

She heard the door squeaking and thought Nadea was back with the food.

"Looks like our little whore is cold."

The male voice caused Ksenia to gag reflexively.

"We better warm her up."

Igor and Ghena returned and it wasn't to release Ksenia. The puke could no longer be contained and she threw up to the side of the mock-up bed.

"Ooooh, she likes it dirty," the One-Eyed Monster got excited. "My kinda girl."

They laughed and pulled the blanket off her.

"Hang on buddy. I wanna fuck something too. Get up, whore! Come here and get it!"

Praying for it to be quick and painless, Ksenia did not move nor did she open her eyes. Quick it wasn't and there was lots of pain.

They abused her on all sides and in ways she hadn't known possible. Her body had become a fleshy slab with holes, which they both filled in turn or at the same time.

Her shrieks of terror angered Igor and excited Ghena. However, both reacted equally by further abusing her already ripped and torn body.

The guards forced themselves into Ksenia's mouth.

She was out of breath and her face turned purple. Ghena released her head but before she had enough time to gasp for air, he wrapped her hair around his wrist and forced Ksenia's head into her puddle of vomit.

"Lick it, bitch. Open your filthy mouth and lick it all."

She coughed and choked.

The torment went on for over an hour, before Ksenia was left in tatters, mopping the floor.

"Think it over. We'll be back for more fun tomorrow – might bring the German Shepherd with us too. It's a well-trained dog and you'll like it. The more the merrier." The Cyclops spat in her face.

They left the cellar roaring with laughter.

Not able to move, Ksenia couldn't tell if it was because of pain and lack of strength or lack of will to do it. Wondering if that was what dying felt like, she was ready to go.

The door squeaked again and Ksenia's body cringed. The steps, however, were lighter this time. Nadea approached and kneeled beside the naked figure writhing in the dark corner, covered in raw red weals.

"I've got some warm water to clean you."

Nadea tended Ksenia's throbbing flesh, dabbing her open wounds with much care. She was silent in her work, apart from short snivels that couldn't be entirely suppressed at the sight of the new girl's plight.

Ksenia fell into a slumber. A tunnel of happy voices and laughter resounded all around and she recognised the place. It was the waterside where she had sealed in blood the sisterhood pact with her two best friends, Doina and Larisa, all those years ago.

She had returned.

The vivid colours of the grass, the sky and the pond, the strong smell of tree sap and fresh soil drew her in and she blissfully surrendered.

Cyan

Larisa was in the final year at the University of Westminster in London studying journalism. Looking more Dalston than Moldova, she sported a black bob and colourful trainers – a style she had embraced on day three after her arrival in the UK five years ago. The tight miniskirts and high heels she'd been used to wearing in Moldova – where everyone tried to impress everyone else – had been readily discarded without a second thought. Short of stature and temperament, Larisa knew her mind and usually spoke it too.

There were a couple more weeks to go before she could lay her hands on the much desired Western degree. Eager to forget her roots, she was planning on starting a new life as far away as possible from her land and from her people.

One spring day, a telephone call was going to change all that.

Immersed in dissertation work at the British Library, Larisa almost jumped when her phone started vibrating in her jeans pocket. Not wanting to be distracted, she ignored it but it kept on going.

Unable to reach somebody, most people usually resort to voice messages or texts, unless they are Bessarabian of course – my lot never leave voice or text messages – that's far too futuristic a method for their liking. Instead they call until, dead or alive, you pick up the phone.

Curious to see who was so eager to get hold of her, Larisa dug out her phone and saw Doina's name. She never answered her or Ksenia's appeals. They normally rang once or twice and she always phoned back – it saved them the astronomic costs that the Moldovan Telecom imposed on calls made abroad. Skype was still a long way away for the people of my land.

The phone kept on vibrating and Larisa left the library in order to check whether the world was on fire.

"Hi Doina, is everything OK?" she asked with bated breath.

"Well…it might be nothing, but I don't think everything is OK. I don't know what's happened to be honest."

"Happened what? To whom?"

"It's Ksenia…she's disappeared."

"What do you mean?"

"You know she went to Italy on holiday?"

"I didn't, but carry on."

"She went with Boris."

"She's still going out with Boris?"

"Yeah, it looks like it's getting serious now."

"Jeez…"

"They were only meant to be gone for seven days. When Ksenia failed to return, Maya – her landlady – alerted her parents. We've already informed the police but it's been more than a week now and we haven't heard any news."

A state of shock and confusion arrested Larisa's mind. Her heart pounded hard and loud, squeezing her breath into a shallow flutter.

She tried to think.

"What if she went with Boris to visit his friends or family or something?"

"They'd have dropped off Ksenia's luggage first. She had taken her painting stuff along with her – some brushes and paper, you know…It was a pretty heavy bag, definitely not one to walk around with. We laughed about it before she left."

"Maybe they didn't have time to."

"Also Ksenia promised to call as soon as they returned. She hasn't and that's not like her."

Larisa still harboured a ray of hope.

"Have you contacted his family?"

"We don't know where to find them. Boris lives in Chisinau but I believe he comes from somewhere up north. Ksenia mentioned the name of the town once but I don't remember it. I hope his parents will also contact the police to report him missing."

A million questions flooded Larisa's mind. Doina said something else but, in her turmoil, Larisa only heard the last bit:

"Let's talk more tomorrow after I've spoken to the police again, OK?"

"OK," Larisa replied automatically.

Ravaged by the impact of the news, her senses went haywire and she could not focus. Her vision blurred and ears rang while she stood still and frozen under the sunny, cyan sky.

Larisa couldn't go home immediately upon hearing the bad news. It wasn't until a few weeks later, after submitting her dissertation, that she was able to fly out.

Not keen on homecomings, this was a time when she could not avoid it. Ksenia was one of her blood sisters and she had to go back as soon as possible.

Soggy Burgundy

Larisa – daughter of Silvia and Trofim Bulat – was born in the village of Marani, a small community in the southern part of Moldova. Her surname betrayed her Tartar family roots, reaching back to the Golden Horde that swept across Eastern Europe in the thirteenth century.

A descendant of the fierce tribes, Larisa had gleaming skin that was a living legacy of the yellow tents used by her ancestors. High cheekbones and vulturine, dim-tawny eyes reinforced the impact of her lineage but the inky hair threw her into a totally different kin, albeit just as nomadic. Her friends nicknamed her – what in translation from Romanian would be: the Gypsy-lassie.

Her mother was the doctor of the village and her father taught science in the local primary school. However, Trofim Bulat's true passion was music, but, like many other men in the village and beyond, he too had let his dreams and talents drown in alcohol. His artistic yearning of his younger days now only stretched to singing at weddings and christenings to earn extra money as head of the family.

In their spare time, both Silvia and Trofim worked the land like the rest of the people in the community, intellectuals or not. Larisa was older than her brothers – Oleg and Slavic – by two and three years respectively and had never felt close to them. Her own universe from her earliest memories rested on a trinity: Ksenia, Doina and herself. Born in the same neighbourhood and of a similar age, the girls bonded in many ways, forming deep connections that would last a lifetime.

From early on they had sensed the powerful attraction between them and called themselves best friends. But that wasn't enough. Wishing to strengthen their bond, they decided to mark it with blood.

It was during the summer holidays when time seemed timeless.

The girls decided to perform the sisterhood ritual as soon as they reached their habitual summer haunt by the village pond. It wasn't a matter of urgency. They were just eager to have it over and done with before getting on with playing in the mud, chanting to snails or chasing after the dragonflies.

Unfortunately what was expected to be a simple affair proved not so simple after all. None of them knew how to go about it, apart from the fact that they had to mix their blood. However, all three had stick-thin frames and the veins on their wrist protruded menacingly. Inclined to bend the rules from an early age, Doina suggested cutting the skin on their palms instead. It was easier and not as painful.

They were still at primary school but their hands already displayed signs of rough, country living. Dried blisters from manual work could harden the skin to such a degree that it was possible to hold burning coal without flinching.

The three of them carved a small cross on their right palm and held hands together, enough for the blood to mingle. They felt some stinging but pain was not an issue. They were used to it like the English are used to the rain. It was part of daily life: fighting with boys, falling from trees, riding horses without saddles, getting on the wrong side of a drunken father – sources of pain were an inexhaustible river spring that, somehow it seemed, had nothing better to do than adjust its course to always come their way.

At the end of the village and far away from prying eyes, the secluded pond was the perfect place for such intimate and risky affairs. It was an isolated sanctuary and provided the perfect escape for the likes of them and Zuzu – a young man in his late twenties who was deemed to be mentally disturbed. His birth name was Serghei but everyone called him Zuzu – 'the crazy one'.

Zuzu and the wildlife around them were the only witnesses to the ritual and oath taking. The girls didn't mind him. Their special spot was also his hideaway from the rest of the world. Often he was beaten and abused just for crossing someone's path – or as sport – and the poor soul withdrew to where he was embraced fully and accepted for what he was or wasn't. The waterside was his kingdom, his home, even before the girls made it their playground. He wasn't bothered by their presence.

Zuzu usually met them with a wide grin and had fistfuls of mud, which he handed excitedly to Ksenia to paint his face with, turning him into a *haiduc* – a *'warrior of the woods'*. Taking a shine to her, many times he brought Ksenia cups of honey stolen from his grandparents' apiary. Almost completely ignoring Doina and Larisa, he was drawn to Ksenia – either for her art skills or perhaps he sensed she would one day share his fate.

Zuzu called her 'Oosha' – unable to pronounce 'Ksiusha' – the term of endearment and affection Doina and Larisa used for her occasionally. However, 'oosha' in Romanian translated as 'doorway', a nickname

Ksenia was never happy about. Consequently, her friends also called her 'Oosha' when they wanted to annoy or tease her.

Following the mud make-up session, Zuzu carried on with his usual business – blowing up frogs. It sent him into hysterics for hours on end. Walking along the shore, he picked one frog at a time, sat cross-legged and blew into its anus with a straw as if he was playing the pipe. Swollen to the point of popping, they were then released back into the pond. Unable to swim any longer, the tortured animals drifted with the ripples. His happy laughter was that of a madman. Everybody in the village said he was crazy and the girls just went along, without once questioning it.

In their small community of thirteen hundred people, Zuzu was perceived as a medieval monster with long, thick nails. The rumours had it that his mother used an axe to cut them off.

To be fair, that would happen to anybody – mad or not – if they never washed their feet and – except for the scant protection of some rubber galoshes regardless of weather – walked barefoot all the time.

Zuzu always wore the same outfit – sporting a naked torso and a pair of old, washed-out, ragged pants. Never dressing any differently, he seemed to have been born that way.

The other characteristics for which villagers abused him were his eyes, which danced as if on ice, and the fact that he never spoke. Zuzu was not mute. He sang joyfully to birds and trees at the waterside but he categorically refused to speak to people. Many years later, he'd start talking again, trying to save Ksenia's life. Other than then, no one ever heard him utter a word.

All in all, Zuzu was no less normal than Doina, Ksenia or Larisa. Drawing the line at exploding frogs, they had enough of their own odd fixations. Had anyone in the village caught wind of it, they would have been put in Zuzu's gang and excluded from the orderly life of the village.

Ksenia loved drawing in mud on the wet shore of the pond. Using any stick or stone she could lay her hands on, she marked the canvas of the earth with a variety of shapes and forms. Her artistic endeavours, more often than not, ended with her being covered in dirt or getting stuck in silt.

Doina liked to climb the highest trees and came down swinging from branch to branch in a bid to outstrip the wind. Falling into the pond or crashing on hard ground did not deter her from such risky ventures. She loved the thrill of danger even in those days and it only increased with age. Tobogganing on steep hills in winter times, she used to grease the sleigh's blades with pork fat so that it went down faster. Her love of speed was taken even further when as a teenager she was allowed to ride her brother's motorbike.

Larisa was also after sensations, albeit of a different nature. She liked to explore and experiment with the tactile feelings of allowing dozens of snails to roam free on her body, watching them criss-cross sticky trails on her legs, thighs, tummy and neck. Physical pleasure was at the heart of it all. It tickled and made her laugh.

Later, in adolescence, due to a puritanical upbringing, this entertainment took on a less innocent form – one pertaining to the province of sensual delights. As a child, however, Larisa could not have guessed the peaks of joy the snails would take her to.

The day the sisterhood ritual was performed, there wasn't much horsing around and they went home early. Larisa's cut went deep and the blood flow wouldn't stop. She planned on entering the house unnoticed and accessing her mother's medical cabinet for bandage dressings. But that was not possible as long as Silvia was at home – she had the eyes of a hawk. The moment Larisa entered the house, her mother appeared from nowhere, with the stealthy step of a sneaking cat. Spotting her daughter's contorted face, she asked:

"What happened *this* time?"

Larisa didn't like the way the question was posed but it wasn't the right time for such observations. Her palm was stinging badly. She had wrapped it in a few layers of burdock leaves. Previous blunders and mishaps had taught her the way around nature's first aid kit. Burdock leaves were a great place to start, due to their antibiotic properties, very similar to penicillin. Regardless, blood still showed through and the light green of the leaves had long turned into soggy burgundy.

Larisa explained the noble cause behind the injury but her mother wasn't impressed.

"You silly girls – that was quite unnecessary."

"I love Doina and Ksenia. They are my best friends and from now on we are blood sisters," Larisa protested.

"You went through all this pain for something that had already been sealed at the time of your christening."

"What do you mean? We weren't cut open during the christening ceremony, were we? I definitely didn't have any cross marks on my body before I etched this one myself an hour ago."

"There are two ways by which people can become blood siblings: being christened together or by choice when they are old enough to do so. And by the way, you are not old enough to do it."

Larisa pretended she didn't hear the last remark. Something else bothered her more:

"How then, were we made blood sisters at our christening? By what means if we haven't been cut open?"

As far as she knew until that moment, the sisterhood ritual was a pact between all parties involved, who had a special connection and were happy to mark it officially with a small cut in the shape of a cross and the mingling of blood.

"To become blood siblings, it's not necessary to have blood exchanged. Blood siblings are also called *Siblings of the Cross*. Those who are christened together become so involuntarily. They get blessed by the priest with the same cross and chrism and the pact is done."

"But that's crazy," Larisa burst out, forgetting all about her pain. "That way you don't have a choice and can end up being sister or brother with somebody you may want to avoid your entire life. I was lucky to have Doina and Ksenia but it could have been Rita or Christina, then what?" she almost choked trying to say it all in one breath.

"What's wrong with Rita or Christina?"

Rita and Christina were two classmates who sat right behind Larisa, who always copied her homework and never shared the delicious wet, sugared bread their grandmothers packed for lunch.

"What's *right* with them? Don't even get me started."

Silvia washed her daughter's wound with a marigold tincture and Larisa blew on her palm to alleviate the sting. Once the cleansing was done, her mother brought a fresh leaf of aloe plant from the veranda and split it in two. The plant performed its magical wonders and the cooling gel soothed Larisa's raw flesh. The size of the fire-ball she felt she was holding decreased considerably.

Without saying another word, Silvia stood up and left the room. Larisa, curious about what happened at the christening ceremony, waited for a couple of minutes before following her mother to the kitchen.

Silvia was conscientiously kneading the dough for the morning bread. She had her back towards the door but sensed her daughter's presence.

"How's it feeling?" she asked without turning.

"A lot better…"

"Too bad. I hoped the pain would last longer and teach you a lesson."

Larisa decided to keep quiet for a few moments. She carried on observing her mother toil with the lifeless dough, which she always kneaded for an extremely long time, too long, in her opinion. But she never dared say so.

There is no bigger insult to the Bessarabian women than criticise their cooking. Silvia believed that bread had to be prepared with lots of love and it was her habit to massage the dough for an eternity. Patience was one of the qualities her daughter reproached her with many times for not passing down.

When Larisa thought enough time had passed to stress her penitence, she swallowed audibly to make it obvious and returned to the previous subject.

"How come we ended up being christened on the same day?"

Silvia didn't reply immediately, perhaps scouring the chamber of her memory for more details.

"It just happened so. There were five children in the church on that Saturday night in late October: you three and two boys, Marcel and Adrian. By tradition, the boys were supposed to be christened first but the established practice was disturbed that day. The priest commenced the ceremony as usual. He approached the boys but didn't get anywhere near them. Ksenia started crying straight away in a deafening, high-pitched voice, as if she was being slaughtered. The priest could hardly hear himself above her screeches and none of his chants

30

calmed her down. In fact, it seemed to make it worse. Perhaps she sensed the injustice about to take place. Anyway, she cried her lungs out like a possessed child and infected Doina and you shortly after. Like a chorus of wild birds, all three of you screamed so hard that your navels had swollen and you were all the same shade of blue. The priest had no other choice but to christen you first and get you out of the church as soon as possible."

That must not have come easy for the clergyman, given that all the rituals of the land prioritise men, with women always left to follow.

"As soon as your ceremony was over, the priest changed waters before proceeding with christening the boys."

Larisa was aware of the Church's view that women were sinful due to the *"whole apple incident in the heavenly gardens"* – as her grandmother referred to it – but that was a long time ago, she thought: *"Doesn't Jesus preach forgiveness?"*

"The waters in the holy cauldron always get changed after one gender is christened. Otherwise it would automatically make them all *Siblings of the Cross* and sinful should they marry each other later on in life."

"What a waste of time that was. There is no one in this world I would want to marry less than Marcel or Adrian." Larisa scuffled and turned on her heels.

Such talk made her impatient even as a child. She had her palm to deal with and wasn't prepared to allow absurd traditions give her a headache too.

Pale Caramel

By the time Larisa arrived in Moldova, the police investigation was in full swing. They had already interviewed Ksenia's relatives, friends and community members. Unfortunately, still no inquiries had been made from Boris's side and the details Doina and Larisa could provide were not enough to track down his family.

"I can't believe we don't know anything about Boris apart from his name and age. Not even a picture of him – nothing," Larisa was frustrated.

"We didn't really need to, did we?"

"We should have got to know him better when we met him last summer."

"We would have, had it not been for your reaction, Gypsy-lassie."

Larisa remembered the scene very well. Ksenia had invited them to meet her boyfriend for the first time. They had dinner at *Vic's* pizzeria in Chisinau city centre but neither of them got to talk much to Boris as he kept going outside to take phone calls.

"I only asked why he had three mobile phones on him, that's all. It was just a joke. You don't find that in

London where people can afford it and I certainly didn't expect to see it in Moldova."

"He said he was into grain export. I guess his business justified having more than one."

"I didn't mean to insult him, you know. It was just an observation," Larisa's voice betrayed guilt. "I hope he is not upset with me."

"Don't think so."

"Have you seen him since?"

"Nope..."

"I promise I'll make it up to Boris but I am more worried about Ksiusha right now. We've got to find her soon, Frizzy."

"Will you guys ever stop calling me Frizzy? We are not kids any more and if you haven't noticed, I am curly and not frizzy."

Doina tossed back her pale caramel hair, which rolled into natural curls down to her shoulders. One of her great-grandfathers had been Jewish. He had never married her great-grandmother, though. In the aftermath of the first Chisinau pogrom against the Jewish people in 1903, he immigrated to Argentina unaware his sweetheart was pregnant. Doina was the only one in their family to have inherited his hair genes. The blue eyes from the other side of the family offered a stunning contrast and everyone said she was attractive, except Doina herself, who thought her nose was too big.

Ignoring Doina's complaint, Larisa carried on.

"Hopefully some news of Ksiusha will reach us any day now."

'Missing' posters were displayed near the airport, coach and train stations in Chisinau city, the capital of Moldova. Police officers assured Tamara and Petru Robu that they were working with Interpol – the global police organisation – and any developments in their daughter's case would be communicated straight away.

Week followed week without any breakthrough. Ksenia's family and friends grew ever more frustrated and anxious. Embers of hope grew dimmer by the day until they were totally extinguished at the end of summer. An official letter from the police said the case of Ksenia's disappearance was being closed due to lack of information to pursue it any further.

"I have no other leads, evidence or witnesses to follow up with." The officer scratched his head and shrugged his shoulders when Larisa and Doina went to the station.

"Yet there are no bodies either and that's good news. It means they are alive somewhere and we've got to find them." Doina's eyes lit up, sparkling with hope.

"I'm afraid there's nothing else we can do." He spoke slowly, lowering his head, all the while staring at the girls.

"But we can't give up, officer. Ksenia means a lot to us – she is our blood sister," Larisa pleaded.

"I know that from my investigation and I didn't mean you should also give up. All I'm saying is that the police can't justify dealing with this case any more. That doesn't stop you from carrying on."

He opened the door for them.

Larisa instantly latched onto this idea and started hatching a plan.

Burnt-Umber

L eaving the police station, Larisa and Doina headed straight home, each of them wrapped in a thick veil of silence. Despite the apparent disconnection, their thoughts channelled in one common, angst-ridden prayer: that of finding Ksenia as soon as possible.

The dejected girls reached their village with the onset of twilight. The only sounds to be heard were those of barking dogs, croaking frogs and annoyingly loud cicadas.

Approaching their neighbourhood, a different kind of sound joined in the descending night, one which was music to the Eastern soul – the accordion. Only one person in the village could play that instrument with such passion and skill. It was Valentin – Doina's older sibling.

"He's out on the razzle again, that good-for-nothing brother of mine."

"Come on, he is a true artist."

"He'd be better off finding a job."

Despite having a girlfriend, Valentin liked to boast he cared only for three things in life: his wine, his motor-bike and his accordion. All of them were dangerously inseparable. He drove everywhere, carrying the accordion on his back at all times with a bottle of wine stashed in his bosom.

"*Life is for celebrating,*" he used to say "*and I want to be able to do it whenever I feel like it.*"

Valentin's intense passion for music was well known in Marani and beyond, hence his frequent invitations to play at various social gatherings.

Neither Doina nor Larisa was in the mood for any partying but the accordion had a way of soothing the soul. Like moths drawn to light, the girls headed towards the luring melodies.

The round table in the middle of the veranda was surrounded by a handful of people: Valentin – completely oblivious, was deeply absorbed in his Gypsy Rhapsody; next to him sat Anastasia – his girlfriend, followed by Valentin's best friend, Andrei, and his girlfriend – Rodica.

A burnt-umber clay pitcher, traditionally adorned with a strand of fine, white field flowers painted with the tip of a goose feather, was almost half empty – the wine drained fast. Home-made snacks were scattered across the table – pickles, cheese, maize cakes and vegetables. The deeply etched tannin marks on the shabby tablecloth betrayed the household's way of life.

Doina and Larisa greeted the gang and made for the ragged divan in the corner of the room. Barely waiting for them to sit down, Andrei grabbed the glass, filled it to the brim with wine and offered it to Doina. She refused it but he would not take "*no*" for an answer:

"Try it – this is the proper stuff! Home made, healthy and delicious. You'll live a thousand years!" Despite his young age of twenty-seven, the voice was hoarse from smoking and drinking.

"I said – no, thank you." She pushed his hand aside.

A stranger to the use of multiple glasses, Andrei then turned towards Larisa, offering the same glass of wine.

The customary routine is that the host or the person serving alcohol hands it to everyone in the same glass. After each drink, the glass is turned upside down to empty it completely before the next person is served. Overlooking such a small but important detail may put the next drinker at risk of having babies with a stutter – so the lore of my land goes.

Larisa realised there was no point in pretending she didn't see the glass held right in her face. It was wiser to do what Doina did and refuse the offer instead. But Andrei, it seemed, was on autopilot:

"Try it – this is the proper stuff! Home made, healthy and delicious. You'll live a thousand years!"

"No, thanks, I don't want to live that long. You can have my thousand years."

Andrei grinned from ear to ear baring a string of tawny teeth, shrugged his shoulders and downed the glass in one breath. He nibbled on some pickles and then proceeded to fill the glass again.

It was Valentin's turn.

At the end of the song, he took off the accordion, stretched his legs and rubbed his hands with excitement:

"This is all just warm-up. Wait till I am well oiled – then you'll hear what I call music."

He raised his glass high and toasted loudly:

"To us and our health."

Doina couldn't help the jibe:

"Your health would be much better if you didn't toast it so often."

Her brother chose to ignore the comment and, like Andrei, he reached for the pickled cucumbers.

At first glance there was nothing special about Valentin and his accordion: a usual squeeze-box and yet another Moldovan young man who, owing to life's hardship, looked older than his age. The lanky build, hump and short fringe were not in his favour but his handsome face made up for it. Despite their dreaminess, his black eyes could be intense and charming. With an open smile, he gained favours from many girls from many villages.

Yet none of that made him stand out, until he picked up the accordion. What happened then was nothing short of magical. In the heat of the performance, the two of them – man and object – became one. They were beauty, harmony and joy, stirring everyone in proximity. An extension of each other, it was hard to say where one ended and the other began. Valentin's fingers flew up and down the keys in what seemed to be chaotic movement but which produced the most accomplished sound. Those who happened to be around were transfixed. An unearthly spirit, unleashed through the enthusiastic play of a passionate soul. The ease of his performance was rimmed with effortless concentration and on many occasions people wondered if he was in the same room with them or not.

Valentin entered a trance every time he reached for his beloved instrument. Guided by a force from beyond, he brought flares of worlds unknown. Currents of energy and powerful vibrations transported listeners to spheres afar, seeking resonance and peace.

They were mesmerised.

The spell was broken by a belch from Andrei, whose physiology, dense with alcohol yeast, was too heavy for that kind of flight.

"Comrades, I wish to make a toast in honour of this great artist. Long live Valentin!" – and he dispatched the nth glass as speedily as frogs swallow their prey.

38

Valentin carried on playing. He himself was far away, perhaps nothing more than sampling music from the spheres and transporting some of it, he cued release to the soul's aches.

The group listened to him for hours, each lost in their own thoughts. When Larisa rose at last, Andrei was fast asleep on the floor with his head in his girlfriend's lap, which she stroked languidly with her eyes half closed.

Doina too was lost in thought but stirred as soon as her friend stood up, calling her to follow out on the veranda.

"We are on our own and can't give up on Ksenia. The good thing is that she is still alive. Dead bodies do not go unnoticed and had that been the case, we'd have found out about it by now."

Larisa's exposition sounded good but that was no certainty.

"What if it's just wishful thinking?"

"I have a strong feeling that Ksiusha is alive and until that flame is burning, we have to keep on searching for her," she tried to sound bold. "We have no choice...actually, we do – our choice is to keep searching."

Desperation circled them on a regular basis, like a hungry wolf waiting for the moment they crumbled so that it could pounce without delay and devour every morsel of their hope.

"The question is, how do we go about it? Where do we even start?"

Larisa spoke of her plan:

"Italy. I thought about it – with my Romanian passport I can travel free in the EU zone. Until you get yours, it will be good to help the search from here."

"What chance do we have to find her abroad if Interpol didn't?"

39

"A big one. Ksiusha's just another missing Moldovan as far as they are concerned. She doesn't mean to them what she means to us."

Doina looked towards the horizon. The first glimmers of dawn fondled the sky and she watched it intensely as if to decipher some kind of distant clue or read into the future.

Ksenia and Larisa used to joke that, despite the lore dictating that true beauties were born out of the sea's foam, Doina must have been born out of the horizon light, as she enjoyed looking into the distance so much. There seemed to be a mystic connection between the two of them.

As to the traditional wisdom, the girls weren't willing to give it any credence.

Moldova is landlocked.

If they were to go by the lore, they'd have to accept the logical conclusion that there were no beauties in the country. None of them, of course, was prepared to do that.

After giving it some thought, Doina agreed the plan was worth trying.

"Fine, you go abroad and I will get in touch with all the local NGOs from here to see if they can help in any way."

"As soon as I get back to London next week, I'll make arrangements to travel regularly to Italy until we find her, one way or another."

Having graduated, there weren't many engagements waiting for Larisa, apart from the part-time interpreting work she still did to pay for her London life. The work assignments were flexible enough to offer a lot of free time but she still needed to keep the employment agency informed as to her availability.

Insipid Mint

With purpose and perseverance, Doina and Larisa put their plan to work. Without much encouragement from the outer world, they sailed ahead with only hope and inner faith. To them, death was not an abstract concept floating far away, seen only in movies or read about in books. Witnessing it so often when growing up in the small village of Marani, they were too well versed in how fragile the human condition was. Nonetheless, both carried on with one wish in their hearts – to find Ksenia alive.

As total commitment to honour the friendship pact the three of them swore to all those years ago, Doina and Larisa had run over the cross sign with tattoo ink – cherishing and charging it with talismanic value.

Doina regularly visited local NGOs in Chisinau who provided assistance to Moldovans deported from abroad as illegal immigrants or rescued from the sex and trade slavery. Those organisations helped victims with counselling and reintegration into society. Doina did voluntary work in the evenings for a couple of them. That offered the opportunity to inquire about Ksenia with all those returning home.

"*Someone will have seen her,*" she thought and showed Ksenia's picture to everyone coming though the door.

Larisa, on the other hand, made plans to travel to Italy on a regular basis. She informed the interpreting agency that she wouldn't be available for jobs at weekends any longer. That meant she'd have to take more work during the week but it wasn't the end of the world. She hoped for more hospital assignments at the insipid mint, maternity wards – they took care of her bank account.

The influx of Russian, Romanian and Moldovan mothers into the UK needed an interpreter during their deliveries. Not many other translators were keen on those jobs due to all the blood. Larisa didn't mind it. Having grown up with a mother-doctor, their household had doubled as the village hospital and she had grown accustomed to seeing viscera under the kitchen table from an early age. More importantly, the long work engagements were going to be supporting her search for Ksenia and for that she was grateful.

Larisa started going to Italy every other weekend and the first thing she did was to inform the police and fill in a missing person's report. Following that, she liaised with Bessarabian communities from different cities: Milan, Rome, Naples, Verona, Bologna, Padova, Reggio Emilia – many different cities where she found the same haunted faces of her people.

Larisa established a routine, which she carried out devoutly each and every time she travelled to any city: visiting churches where immigrants gathered, charity centres which fed them, parks where they liked to drink and spend time off, in the case of those who had it. She spoke openly with them all, showing Ksenia's picture and talking about her plight.

The summer flew by and the rainy autumn caught Larisa doing the same thing. One cold November day she was in Milan again doing the usual rounds. She stopped at a welfare centre, which offered hot soup to homeless and hungry immigrants.

The winding soup queue reminded Larisa of the ones she had witnessed as a child in Marani in the early 1990s, after the Soviet Union's collapse, when all villagers systematically lined up at the only shop in the village, coupons in hand, waiting patiently for rationed portions of bread or flour, sugar, salt and whatever else was available.

Larisa spotted a few people carrying plastic bags with a calendar imprint – fashionable in Moldova – and approached, greeting them in her mother tongue. She recognised the man sporting a heavy Eastern European moustache, Grigore Cojocaru – a teacher of Romanian language and literature, who had left his wife and two children at home in Moldova and come to find work in Italy.

"Still no work, Mr Grigore?"

"It's like I've been cursed or something, I tell you."

"You just need to get rid of that horrible facial hair, man, and you'll find a job," Larisa thought to herself but did not interrupt Grigore.

"No choice but to carry on looking because there's no way back – I've borrowed a lot of money and the interest is going through the roof. Are you still searching for your friend?"

"Yes, I am."

He shook his head with empathy and introduced Larisa to the other Moldovans in the queue. There were more than a dozen of them but she only retained the names of the two closest to Grigore: Zinaida – a nursery assistant from the countryside working as carer for the aged in Italy, and Ichim – a surgeon turned labourer, whose blistered hands full of dry paint would never hold the scalpel again.

"Show them your friend's picture."

Larisa pulled out Ksenia's photo and more people gathered around her. Some of them had been in Italy for months, others for years but no one was able to help.

"What a shame that not only the middle generation is abroad but now the young ones leave the country too," Grigore sighed with grief.

"What are you talking about?" Zinaida cut him off. "As if you don't know – folks have been leaving Moldova in droves for years. In my village and many neighbouring ones there are only children and grandparents left behind. Everyone else is gone."

"I think a lot more are getting ready to leave, to be honest." Larisa pointed out her recent observations. "It's funny to see people absorbed in dictionaries as if they are the latest best-sellers. I've seen women weeding crops during the day and swapping their hoes for books at lunchtime. They devour entire word lists in different languages: Italian, Greek, Turkish. Looks like the entire country is cramming for an exam, I tell you."

"I don't think publishers can keep up with the demand for dictionaries. Two of my sisters-in-law searched all over Hincesti to buy them but weren't able to find any." Zinaida kept nodding to reinforce the truth of what she was saying.

"I blame the Communists – they've messed us up completely," Ichim the surgeon–labourer commented. "You are probably too young to know what I am talking about." He fixed Larisa with intense eyes that bored into her. "But it's a legacy that unfortunately has a big impact on your generation too and who knows how many more to come."

"Passing the buck is exactly why our country is in such a mess." Grigore made no effort to hide the disapproval in his voice.

"What's the point in pretending there was no harm caused by the totalitarian regime? You can hide your head in the sand but I am being honest here, for the sake of these kids. They need to understand where it's all coming from."

A short, uncomfortable pause followed and the two men lit cigarettes.

"During the Communist era," Ichim carried on between puffs, "Moldovan people were forced to adopt a slave mentality. The Communists created a nebulous mass of people by fixing big chips on our shoulders and developing massive complexes amongst us. The end result?" – he inhaled conclusively.

"We are all in deep shit now," Zinaida hurried to offer her opinion.

Ichim nodded.

"That's one way of putting it. The truth is that it left us perfect to be manipulated and taken advantage of. That inertia unfortunately still lingers on and it's best to get out of there. Moldova is going to be a mess for a long time to come yet."

"Don't put nonsense into their heads. The young generation has nothing to fear. They are our only hope if things are to change."

"The Communists taught us the individual didn't count and did not hold any value, which is why so many seek financial recognition," Ichim persisted.

"That's precisely why we have to nurture character, talent, creativity, and inventiveness – that's what's going to save us. We've got to especially encourage these skills among our children so that they have a different fate."

"Why are you here then and not teaching back home?" Ichim asked mockingly.

"For the same reason you aren't treating patients," Grigore gesticulated, waving his hands in agitation. "What I'm saying is that we should be the only generation sacrificed for life in exile and servitude abroad. *Capisci*? Our children and these young ladies and the rest of the new generations should not have to go through this ordeal."

"It's already happening but my point is that not everybody is going overseas due to lack and that people have a choice…"

"Speak for yourself, Doctor," Zinaida interrupted. "Hunger and desperation – that's what drove me out of my home."

"I am not disputing the fact that many are driven to work abroad because of poverty, that's true – but just as many do it out of greed, because they want more."

"That's not me, I keep telling you."

"Generally speaking, Moldovans measure their worth with possessions. Our confidence has been destroyed at national and individual level and in order to find and define ourselves, we latch onto acquiring more and more earthly things. The perception of self-worth has completely been destroyed, that's all I am saying."

"Our miserly status abroad doesn't help. I'd be a totally different person had I been able to work by profession and be a teacher." Grigore twitched his moustache.

"That's where it all stems from. Because our self-worth is at ground-level, we trade ourselves low."

"Ain't doing it willingly, are we?" Zinaida was heating up.

"We are certainly not under duress."

"Under what? Never mind. Like I said – I did not leave my children behind for the sake of adventure, you know?"

Grigore finished his cigarette and lit another.

"The tragedy is that we are a starved nation. We are starved for food and like you say, Ichim, we are starved for assets too, slaving away blindly without a vision whatsoever beyond the immediate betterment of our material situation."

"We work so hard and despite it all, we are still poor – the poorest people in Europe, according to some sources," the surgeon–labourer hurried to add.

"That's because in the wild scuttle to silence the stomach, heap up goods and compete with the neighbours, we cater solely for personal, petty needs, feeding the monster of consumerism instead of investing in our future. That's the problem – not investing what we earn. Because of that our children may end up going through the same hell as us. Inaction – that's the devil, if you ask me."

"Oh shut up." Zinaida looked away. "What do you two know about hard work, Mr Professor and Mr Soft-Hands?"

"Not so soft any more," Ichim scrutinised his scratched and swollen palms.

"…How much of it have you done in your lives? Has either of you ever worked the land? Now, that's hard work and don't you start preaching me about it."

Totally ignoring Zinaida's comment, Ichim turned to face Grigore:

"I don't think it's anything to do with inaction. In fact – it's a flawed argument. You see, we Bessarabians are busy people. Over here people greet each other with *How are you?* Back home it's *What are you doing?* Everyone seems to always be doing something and if that's the case, things will inevitably have to change for the better, isn't it?"

"But the fact is that our country doesn't seem to evolve despite the vortex of activities." Grigore began pointing his finger, perhaps thinking he was back in the classroom. "That's because our attitude to what we do and how we deal with things is short-sighted."

"I know what you are saying but as much as I'd like to believe it's an individual responsibility for what's happening to and with us, I can't help blaming our government, families and schools for their failure to provide assistance and guidance." Ichim was unyielding.

"If I didn't know the reality better, I'd definitely say the fault lay primarily with our schools. However, being a teacher myself, I know them to be unpaid people, who are frustrated, unhappy and, quite frankly, insufficiently trained in matters of psychology. For example a future doctor, in order to become an expert, learns about the human body for seven or nine years, right, Ichim? A teacher on the other hand does psychology at university enough to fill a module. Human nature is complex and diverse. We know how different children are and how differently they assimilate knowledge. In my own experience, I've witnessed teachers in their ignorance telling pupils how stupid they were. Many parents do the same thing. The results are not hard to guess. We end up with the kind of society we live in. Whose fault? Ours. I'm afraid it's back to us – it's our own responsibility for what we get and the blame rests with us primarily."

"I can't believe my ears. You have gone bonkers. Our nation is being robbed and lied to and you say that's our own fault too. Never heard such nonsense in my entire life. And you call yourself a Professor! Pah!" Zinaida hissed.

Grigore dragged deep at his second cigarette, exhaled at length and then in true Eastern European fashion, spat out in the street through his incisors. Relishing the opportunity to talk, the frustrated intellectual was eager to put his linguistic dexterity to use – something which he didn't get to do often these days.

"The breathing of our breed is on the brink of bathos, that's what I say, comrades. What's even worse is that this order of things suits our leaders perfectly.

The more of us leave the country, the less internal pressure. Let the hot steam out so that the lid doesn't leap. We break our backs to send money home and the amount of remittances earned with our sweat and tears sustains the economy of the country by saving the value of the currency. This of course leaves them with not much else to do than yawn and go on about their private business of increasing personal fortunes in deranged engorgement. But you and I are directly responsible for that – yes we are – just by the mere fact that we have opted for the easy way out."

"Easy my arse," Zinaida barked.

"In the sense that we are looking to treat the affliction rather than go to its root and cure the causes. That's precisely why it will take a long time to change things and many more generations may suffer because of it."

Larisa couldn't fail to observe the bitter irony of the circumstances. Hailing from such different social circles, these three people would never have had the *pleasure* of such conversations in Moldova. Yet, here they were, all in the same boat: hungry immigrants queuing patiently to be fed at a charity centre in Milan.

Their turn came to be served and Larisa left them to eat in peace.

"See you soon."

"Hopefully, in our country next time. Good luck with finding Ksenia," Grigore waved goodbye as he entered the building.

The heated discussion Larisa had witnessed stirred deep emotions within her. Even though she shared the view that the national and individual identity crisis was the root-issue causing havoc to her nation, she saw no harm in choosing to get out. Yet the closest people to her – Doina and Ksenia – thought differently and like Grigore they were against emigration. Larisa's decision to go overseas caused a rift between her and her blood sisters, which threatened their sacred vow but she thought she had her reasons. The desire to go to far away places had long been playing on her mind. She couldn't tell exactly when it had kicked in but the earliest memory revealing such a longing went back to when she was nine years of age.

Eerie Black

Bessarabia is a superstitious land, where a black cat crossing people's paths can spoil their day – only for it to be saved later by happening upon someone with a bucket full of water.

Despite the fact that Larisa came from a virtually secular household, or, as she liked to say *"religious as, when and how it suited them"*, her family, like many others, feared the practice of putting on spells and charms, so common in that part of the world.

Her mother was not afraid of anything or anyone apart from Baba Vera, who, she assured everyone, was worse than Death.

"At least Death can be fair and take you away peacefully if she has some sense," she argued. *"Baba Vera, on the other hand, doesn't have any and – bang!!! – can curse or cripple you without warning."*

The term *'Baba'* means an old woman and *'Mos'* an old man. Baba Vera was indeed the oldest in the village. No one knew or could have guessed her age. Even the most senior people in the community said she was older than them. Short, dry and brittle, she moved quickly despite the burden of her years. The skin on

51

her face and limbs, wrinkled and speckled by time, hung in layers like a turkey's wattle. Notorious for practising sorcery, the villagers spoke of her in the same breath as Baba Yaga – a supernatural character in Slavic folklore.

Baba Yaga, also called Earth Mother, is usually portrayed in stories as a witch. Flying around in a mortar with a pestle as a guiding tool, she sweeps her tracks with a broom. Known to possess all answers to life and death, Baba Yaga is sought by fairy tale heroes for her wisdom and advice but not all are granted them. Spiders, bats and black cats keep her company in her lonely hut – and on the stove, magic brews boil perpetually. Her hut stands on giant chicken legs and is guarded by hungry dogs or evil geese.

Contrary to the children's rumours in the village, Baba Vera's hut did not stand on chicken legs but the hungry dogs and evil geese were present and correct.

Silvia generally avoided Baba Vera but there were times when she had no choice. Working as a community doctor, she couldn't reject the old woman's call for help when she'd broken a leg. Silvia had to bite the bullet and go to treat the patient she feared most.

"Larisa, get ready. You are coming with me." She spoke in a tone of voice which didn't brook negotiation or excuses.

Her daughter hesitated for a few moments, checking on her own fear and concern. The fine line between those states and actual excitement meant she was confused enough to agree to it.

"OK."

"Make sure you put your worst and oldest clothes on," her mother commanded from the other room, while she prepared the first aid kit. "We'll have to burn them afterwards."

"But I'll look like a scarecrow."

"It's dark outside. Nobody will see you, Miss Moldova. C'mon, let's get over and done with this business. It's already giving me the heebie-jeebies."

Larisa wondered what kind of a strange ability Baba Vera possessed to be so widely feared.

"*Such a cool skill to have,*" she thought and asked her mother:

"How can I become like her? Is there a school where they teach those spells and curses?"

Silvia hushed her on the spot.

"Don't talk nonsense. People playing with the occult die terrible deaths. The forces of nature they fiddle with turn against them sooner or later, destroying those fools and their families."

"What's the *yokult*, Mother?"

"Stop all these silly questions and let's go."

They left the house in a rush and headed towards the other end of the village, where Baba Vera lived with her daughter, son-in-law and their four children.

Walking purposefully under the night's black mantle, mother and daughter couldn't see each other and only their steps were heard. It was a starless sky and pitch black all around, as if the entire world had gone back to its cosmic womb.

The village streets were lined with lamp-posts, albeit all bulbless. Soviet town halls had been highly efficient at installing lamp-posts; post-Soviet town halls less so at replacing their bulbs.

Despite the Cimmerian darkness, they advanced speedily and skilfully. The light of memory and habit was guiding them effortlessly in the nocturnal journey.

"Listen carefully, Larisa. Do not touch anything in that house and don't let anything touch you. If they offer you food or drinks, refuse politely but categorically. Do you understand?"

Larisa didn't. None of this made any sense to her and she felt genuine fear starting to creep in. Apart from Baba Vera, she now worried about something else called the *yokult*, which she didn't even know the look of let alone be able to protect herself from it.

"Why are you taking me with you if there are so many things that can go wrong?" She looked over her shoulder, considering whether she should abort the mission and go back before it was too late.

"Just so that you can keep an eye on me. I'll be busy helping the old witch and may not be aware if she tries to harm me in any way. If you see me acting strangely, leave the house immediately and go seek help from the neighbours."

Larisa thought her mother's behaviour was already strange and they weren't even half way there. She really felt like sprinting back home but couldn't bring herself to do it.

By the time they reached Baba Vera's hut, her mother had made the sign of the cross what seemed like a hundred times, or maybe more – Larisa couldn't keep up the count. It was enough to keep them both immune to all the spells in the world. Silvia pushed the shabby willow wickerwork gate open with one hand and grabbed her daughter's with the other. Although there were only about ten steps to the door, Larisa felt sweat in her hand and couldn't really tell whose it was.

Dogs were barking loudly and there were no geese in the yard – too late in the evening for their liking. In any case, Larisa wasn't scared of them. She'd learned the trick to deal with their aggressive streak – by grabbing the long, soft necks and swinging them around and over the fence each time they charged at her. The frequent attacks of those belligerent birds throughout Larisa's childhood helped her master the technique pretty quickly.

Baba Vera's daughter appeared on the threshold and showed them in. The whole house comprised just two rooms. Larisa saw a blue door with greasy patches

– more so around the knobs – on each side of the meagre corridor.

They entered the one on the right, which turned out to be sparsely furnished with two beds alongside the walls and a bare, wooden table near the window. It wasn't possible to say whether the table was crooked or the window was at an angle. Maybe both. The fact that the only light in the room was coming from a weak earthen lamp didn't help and Larisa had to strain her eyes to make sure she was alert, in case of an emergency.

She decided to scan the room inch by inch and assess the situation thoroughly. Her mother was busy with fixing the witch's leg and she felt utterly responsible for the safety of them both.

Larisa stood erect by the door and continued her observations. To the left, there was a stove on which a cauldron was simmering. Because of her not so generous height, she attempted to rise on her toes to see what was boiling, but with not much luck.

"Is the witch getting it ready to throw us in there?"

Studying it over and over again, Larisa decided it wasn't big enough to fit them both.

"Actually," she thought, *"if anything, the smouldering pot is probably too small even for Mum on her own and there is no way the witch can throw me in there first. I swear to God – not even on a supersonic mortar or a broom would she be able to catch me."*

She carried on inspecting the room.

"But where is that yokult? I better spot it before it gets to me or else I and my entire family will die a terrible death. Don't really care about my brothers but my parents and I should really be spared."

Larisa eyed warily every object in the room.

"What does it even look like? Does it fly, crawl or jump?"

Unable to detect anything strange or uncommon, Larisa concluded there was no immediate danger coming from secondary sources and decided to turn her focus on Baba Vera herself.

The old woman was lying on one of the two beds in the room, almost completely buried under a pile of cloths.

"She looks pretty harmless but then isn't that what the witch wants me to think?"

The adjacent bed looked neat and pretty, with a hand-embroidered, colourful spread hugging it from side to side. Five pillows tucked in meticulously crocheted cases were arranged on top of each other – at the corner of the bed – in traditional East European countryside fashion. Everything seemed to be quite normal, when all of a sudden, from the corner of her eyes, Larisa saw shadows coming off the sidewall and running towards her. They were the grandchildren who must have been playing on the *lejanca* behind the stove.

The *lejanca* is a traditional and very common piece of furniture in Bessarabia. A direct continuation of the fireplace and stove – it's an in-built, perpetual hot bed, and pure bliss in winter time. The name derives from the Russian '*to lie down*'.

Larisa was aware that children usually loved piling up there to play or sleep but, because it happened unexpectedly when she was tense and concerned with spotting the *yokult*, her composure snapped under pressure. Silvia warned her not to touch or be touched by anything in the house but those little devils were suddenly all around, poking and pulling at her.

She was seized by horror and scrambled out of the house as if bitten by a snake. The fear that she might have to be burned along with the clothes, drove her to despair and she cried hysterically. Distressed, she totally forgot about her mother's safety and ran all the way home without once looking back.

When she returned, Silvia found Larisa in the kennel, sleeping curled up to Belka – their scruffy mongrel – and her puppies. She knew of her daughter's usual refuge in times of crisis. After helping her into the house, Silvia didn't wait long before she asked:

"What got into you to scamper away like that?"

Larisa explained her fears, her voice still shaking.

"Don't be silly, how could you think of something like that?" Silvia came round to give her a hug but Larisa sensed there was something else to follow. "We won't burn you," her mother assured her "but that doesn't mean it's over yet."

"*Anything you want,*" Larisa thought to herself, "*as long as you don't set me on fire.*"

Instead she asked open-eyed:

"What do you mean?"

"Nothing bad. You just have to wash your face with urine before going to bed, that's all. Not because of those kids – it's just a preventive measure and for our own peace of mind. That house is full of spells, my dear, and we need to disable them in case any caught on to you."

"You might as well burn me. I am not going to wash my face with pee."

Silvia knew that was that. Her daughter was the embodiment of stubbornness and made donkeys seem easy to deal with. Yet she had never forgotten or forgiven it. Larisa was left feeling as if she had the devil inside her. She started dreaming of foreign lands devoid of witches and spells.

The desire to live in a world unconfined and unrestrained by such beliefs and inclinations was deeply sown. Like a convict guilty of a crime, Larisa knew the only way to prevent further punishment would be to escape as far away as possible.

She was astonished to realise that stories of spells and eerie black magic affected even her mother – a doctor – who openly admitted those practices involved working with life forces still out of science's grip and were therefore to be feared.

The thought of a life tethered to the impassive posts of superstition and folklore was daunting and Larisa vowed to use the first opportunity and escape such a fate.

The lucky break came years later, when she and Ksenia applied for a cultural exchange programme in England. Larisa sensed on a deeper level that it was the beginning of something bigger.

She recorded the message in her dream diary she had kept since childhood.

Blue Yonder

I dreamt that my grandfather had died in a wrestle with a big brown bear. He would have won over the beast had it been a common one. But the bear had three hideous heads and spat rivers of fire. Unable to fend off the vicious creature, Grandpa disappeared in its wild fur. The beast let out a shattering roar which shook the ground.

I woke up in a fright. Longing for some fresh air, I was ready to spring out of bed but stalled. It was still dark outside and I didn't fancy running into any ghouls, which Grandpa said haunted the world at night. The unmistakable cock-a-doodle-doo of our rooster – Gatlung – came to my rescue and announced the break of dawn. Along with it, the ghouls would ebb away and I was happy to dash outside and greet the new day.

My parents were fast asleep and would not wake up until much later, way after the sacred change of guards between night and day took place. Dressed only in my cotton gown, I didn't feel cold at all. It was a hot summer and the fresh mornings were a blessing. From the porch I could see Gatlung, who perched on top of the gate, was announcing the time to the world with utmost pride and dedication. The rooster's silhouette was getting more and more defined since the day was advancing steadily and the night was slowly and gradually pulling away, over the crest of the woods, surrounding our village of Marani. I was mesmerised: more birds and animals were waking up, insects were already in search of food and the first rays of the sun were emerging boldly through the thick brush of the lofty trees.

I watched the effortless harmony unfolding around me while I breathed in deeply the fresh and moist country air. My being was light but my heart was heavy. I couldn't shake off the dream. Grandfather could not have died – not even in a dream. I loved him too much, both of my grandparents. They would never die. Never.

Mother suddenly appeared and even though I had stopped crying, she saw the fresh traces my roving tears had left on both cheeks.

"What's up? What are you doing up so early?"

"I had a bad dream in which Grandpa died."

"That was only a dream. It's not true, come here." Mother knelt down and gave me a hug.

"I'd like to visit them today, Mum. Can I? Please…?"

"Of course you can but make sure you are on your way before the sun gets too high. It's going to be a broil today."

Mother handed me a knapsack with cheese, bread, spring onions and tomatoes for the road.

"Have a safe journey and try to get to your grandparents before midday. The sun won't take any mercy on you if you get delayed. Take the route where there are wells so you don't have to carry water with you."

Our home was at the edge of the village and it took an hour and a half to reach the adjacent village of Pripeni, where my grandparents lived. It was a journey stretched with golden fields of sunflower, followed by cornfields, measured by wheat-fields and ending in a plum orchard where the village of my grandparents started.

I followed the river which connected the two villages, offering a wide variety of entertainment: frogs, which I liked to chase, fish, which I sought to catch, ladybirds, which I wished to sing to, snails, whose horns I liked to poke, bell flowers, which I loved to smell, bumble bees, which tickled my palms with their furry coats, and colourful dragonflies, which joyfully followed me all the way to Pripeni.

Taking breaks in the shade of the trees, I generously shared my cheese with the birds of the fields. Rolling and tumbling down the fresh grass, I was drawn to the cooling moisture of the earth while my gaze took me up and I observed closely the game of the clouds. Moments later I was up there, flying amongst the heaps of mist. Despite my presence, the fluffy shapes remained aloof. They carried on moving in effortless fashion, laced with mystery and purpose which had neither a beginning nor an end.

Drifting merrily through the clouds, I caught on to a familiar scent – the pungent, spicy-citrusy, yet earthly smell of the walnut tree from my grandparents' garden. Wrapped in it, I hurtled through space silently and dropped by my grandpa's side. He was busy decorticating maize under the large shade of the mighty tree.

I hugged him like I had never done before.

"How is my treasure?" he asked in a husky, deep voice.

"I miss you, Grandpa."

"Do you want to give me a hand with the corn?"

The spider's web of his wrinkles was somehow tighter on his face than the last time I saw him. Nonetheless, he was still the same strong giant I'd always known and I sighed with relief.

Slowly, in the all-embracing shadow of the old tree, from the bosoms of his foretimes, Grandpa started whistling a melody, lightly under his breath.

"That is a beautiful song, 'Pa. I would like to learn it," I chirped when he took a short break.

"I can teach it to you, my girl, but it will not sound the same. This song tells my life and only I can sing it. You have to find your path, live your life and sing your own song, Larisa. Everyone has got their own, unique song which only they can sing."

"I don't have a song, Grandpa. What is my song?"

His squinting eyes betrayed a wide smile behind the heavy, hoary beard.

"Nobody knows that apart from you. It's right there, in your heart and only you can hear it."

"But I can't hear anything."

"You will. When the time is right. First be on your journey and that will create your song along the way. It might take more or less time but you will always know it when you've found your tune. You will feel it right here, my girl," the old giant said, raising his bony fist to the left side of his chest, "and your song will tell your journey."

"What journey, Grandpa?"

"Journey is Being and therefore we are all Journeys. I am a unique journey and so are you. Find your path and celebrate it, my darling, sing it to the whole world! When you have found your path and have travelled it with passion and feeling, you will have a beautiful song to sing, which in turn will inspire other beautiful songs out there." Grandfather smiled from ear to ear, winked under his willowy eyebrows and then burst into a long, hearty laugh, which erupted from the deepest recesses of his massive belly and went on to echo into the wild blue yonder.

Bright Ruby

The strength of that phantasmagorical laughter caused Larisa to wake up in a state of utter confusion. Her grandfather had passed away a while ago but his presence and words felt more than real. She sensed a critical shift in the alignment of her stars because her grandfather had always been a man of deep wisdom and right timing. Not the type to rattle easily, he'd only give his advice when strictly necessary.

Floating between the worlds of dream and reality, Larisa observed their perpetual dance: merging and reflecting each other incessantly. Despite their deceptive differences, the two dimensions of life remained two sides of the same coin. Immersed in the dilemma of distinguishing between the two states, the rooster's crowing outside came to her rescue. Other roosters in the neighbourhood responded instantly. They started singing their songs as night became day. That magic spell of time responsible for the creation of the world eons ago, with every dawn – still remained pregnant with a world of possibilities.

Eager to know on which side of the coin her senses dwelled, Larisa left her warm bed and stepped outside. A gust of fresh, cool air stirred her to life. It was a light waft, which could only be found in countryside in the early hours, before the agents of the day intoxicated and spoiled it.

She inhaled deeply a few times, allowing the bracing current to touch her core and invigorate it anew. Standing on the porch, she couldn't see the rooster in its full glory of bright colours and hectic activity but she spotted its silhouette perched on top of the gate, just like she had seen it in her dream.

The early hour rendered the day a realm of fairytales – a surreal world made of mysterious contours and whispering shades. Larisa was part of it and felt just as much an observer as the observed. It spoke of secrets that no other part of day, or hour, was willing to disclose. The meeting point between two realities when changing guards upon humanity provided a unique window of opportunity for the open eye to see the un-see-able.

Standing still, she witnessed the sacred ceremony of the start of a new day.

Orange flares brushed up the skyline. Larisa descended the porch and went for a stroll in the garden. Behind the house, there were a few patches of yellow chrysanthemums, peppermint striped carnations and dense rows of cornflowers, all of which were followed by vegetable plots and vineyards.

She took off her slippers and walked barefoot through the dewy grass towards the flowers. All of them, one by one, were adorned with glitters of moon droplets. Larisa knelt and sank her face into their sweet-smelling embrace. Each time at the end of those passionate encounters, she emerged with beads of nocturnal moisture stroking her face and hair. Sliding idly, they dropped onto her creased cotton gown, cooling off the intense heat of a virginal body on the brink of sin. She licked her lips with fondness and supped the rest of the dewdrops from her hands. Facing the rising sun one more time, she returned to the house happy and peaceful.

It was the day of the English test for the cultural programme abroad, which offered first year undergraduate students the opportunity to improve their English at a college in Brighton, Great Britain. Not wanting to tempt fate, the girls decided to keep the exam under their belts until they knew the test results. Doina didn't apply at all due to lack of funds but she intended to travel to Chisinau and support her friends during examinations.

They all agreed to rise with the sun and meet at seven o'clock for the hitchhike to the city. The test was not till ten o'clock but the importance of the event called for extra care and they allowed more time than usual.

Larisa was ready to sneak out as per their plan but her father started cooking pancakes and cajoled the truth out of her. She was vague, hinting at taking some sort of tests, and promised to tell all in the evening.

Ksenia and Doina called at the gate and Larisa invited them in. Silvia had already gone to work and they were safe from any grilling.

"Good morning," Doina saluted from far away. "How are you feeling?"

"Tops...no more, no less." Larisa smiled and punched the air with enthusiasm.

"What foot did you climb out of bed on this morning?" Ksenia was being her superstitious self.

"Don't you start with the abracadabra questions..."

"No really – tell me." She pulled at her friend's sleeve.

"Right one of course." Larisa confirmed the observance of the unwritten law. "Hurry up and let's have some breakfast before we go."

She didn't have to say it twice.

Trofim laid the table with steaming, aromatic linden tea and a bowl full of golden pancakes.

"I can't believe you were planning to go for this test sneakily like that, without telling us about it." He shook his head emphatically, pretending to be offended.

Larisa cut him short, denying him the pleasure of acting.

"Father, we are running late and do not have time for justifications. Besides, you are in the minority. I don't think you want to start a debate with the three of us. Imagine me, multiplied by three."

"Well, my dear girls, I wish you all the luck today and my advice to you is: focus on your tasks. Concentration is the key to success. And eternity for that matter. Someone else, wiser than me, said it and I couldn't agree more."

"It's too early in the morning for such wisdom, father."

"I will say no more, but mark my words. Take them on board, young ladies. This certainty is one of the very few I still believe in after all these years." Trofim looked each girl in the eye, seeking silent assurance his message had hit home.

The three of them nodded quickly, if only to tuck into the scrumptious, sugar-coated, lemon sprinkled pancakes without any further delay.

It must have been too early for any nerves. They polished off the whole plate and only then started for Chisinau. In fact, they always finished whatever was put in front of them because the lore predicted ugly husbands otherwise.

The girls reeled off towards the highway for the hitchhike. Shortly before reaching it, a scraggy black cat crossed the road. You don't have to be a Moldovan to know what that means. In this respect my people are not so strange – they take the same fearful stance towards black cats as the rest of the world.

The three of them stopped in their tracks and looked at each other.

"I can walk past it and take the bullet…," Larisa offered.

"No, you can't," Ksenia stopped her anxiously. "Not worth taking the risk on such an important day."

"But I can," Doina said. "I'm not taking any tests…"

"You can't either. We are travelling together and the bad luck might rub off on us." Ksenia was having none of it.

"OK, then, we'll wait. There's got to be other people coming up the road."

"We may be here for hours," Larisa growled.

"This village may be a hole but it's not a desert, you know." Ksenia looked from under her eyebrows. "Somebody is bound to venture this way soon."

"I can see someone walking up. It's Teotea Frosea."

Teotea is a Russian term equivalent to a non-blood related auntie, as *Deadea* is for uncle. Many youngsters still use these Slavic terms to this day.

Another reason why Larisa wanted to emigrate was to avoid growing into a *Teotea*. She dreaded ending up looking like one: short and swollen like a barrel with legs, wrapped in a soiled apron and wearing a washed-out headscarf. With eyes which once pried joyfully into the wonders of the world long having lost their twinkle. Body and soul, once full of possibilities, becoming lay-land: a desolate soul in a desolate body, with hairy legs and a furry moustache.

"We can't let her take all the bad luck upon herself," Doina opposed. "She's had enough of it lately with the theft of her cow. You know how much grief she's had because of that whole affair."

***

Everyone in the village remembered the incident due to the mystery surrounding it. One morning Frosea woke up to an empty barn – the cow was gone. There were neither hoof-prints nor any signs of its being slaughtered. All that could be found were the unknown shoe-prints of three people, but that didn't explain how the cow had disappeared. It was a big animal and one certainly could not have lifted and carried it out. What happened to the cow? That was the burning question. People, apart from Frosea of course, were thrilled – finally something unusual happened in their world, disrupting the lethargic routine they wallowed in.

A lot of mind-bending and brain-storming took place but to no avail. No one could tell how the cow had vanished and Frosea decided to make contact with the spirit world. Only one person in the village was able to access the realm of the ghosts and off she went to visit Baba Vera.

"Invoking those creatures of light is not a simple thing and should only be done as a last resort. I'll do a Tarot reading instead. That'll answer your question, woman," winked Baba Vera.

Frosea nodded.

"While I set up the altar, go get a rooster and seven new candles. You have to bring some offerings or the cards won't reveal much."

While Frosea went to fetch the sacrifice, Baba Vera decorated her magic corner with all sorts of witchery paraphernalia. She covered the small, low table with a rabbit skin which displayed images of the sun, the moon and the stars painted in a unique bright ruby she herself prepared – many years ago – from a

69

combination of bugs, tree barks and vegetable roots, all mixed with a splash of blood. At the time, Baba Vera had personally slaughtered a lamb precisely twenty-one days old, to prepare the magic dye whose formula she kept a secret. She had learned it from her grandmother and was only going to share and pass it on to one of her own granddaughters, whom she would designate as her successor prior to her death.

A wooden carved statue, the size of a farmer's palm, was placed in the middle of the table. It resembled the figure of a woman – the goddess whom Baba Vera prayed to for gaining access to other dimensions of existence. A thick cluster of dried basil flowers was carefully laid next to a bowl with fresh water. Once everything was set up, the old witch drew a circle in chalk all around the altar to keep the energies pure and potent. All those observances had to be carried out with maximum caution and focus in order to channel the called-upon spirits and create the necessary fertile grounds for the magic ritual to follow.

As soon as Frosea brought the gifts, Baba Vera lit the seven candles and started chanting, whispering and spitting all around her. She mixed the cards for some time with more chanting, whispering and spitting. With eyes half closed, the witch then spread the Tarot cards on the rabbit skin and turned them up slowly, one after the other.

"The cards are showing only one person to have been involved in the whole affair."

"This can't be true…"

"Don't insult my powers or they'll stop working for you."

"One person could not have carried the cow out of the barn."

"I'm telling you, the King of Spades stole your animal, woman."

"Who is that? I wanna know."

"A wicked, wicked man. Only one type comes up as King of Spades in my readings and they tend to be of dark complexion usually."

"How is this helpful, Baba Vera? I still don't know who robbed me."

"You asked for a Tarot reading, Frosea. If you want more information, we'll need to do a scrying session over a bowl of blessed water. Come back tomorrow with seven new candles and a turkey."

"Aren't the offerings I brought today enough? The rooster is quite big – I fed it good corn for more than a year."

"What are you talking about, woman? The gifts were not for me but for the spirits which helped you today…"

"You said you wouldn't bother the spirits today…"

"All my work is aided by spirits of one sort or another. It's just a matter of which ones I summon at any given time. They have their own hierarchy, you see…I'll have to contact the top brass tomorrow if you want better results and you can't offer your presents twice. They are feisty creatures, I tell you, and not to be played with or, worse, taken advantage of. Otherwise they'll avenge for your greed."

"It's not out of greed, Baba Vera, but poverty and you know it."

"I do but they don't and, to be frank, they don't care. If you want a service from them, you have to reward their efforts accordingly."

"Do they eat turkeys?"

Baba Vera paused a little but managed to recover before too long.

"Listen to me, Frosea. You can't haggle with these forces. If you want to find out who's got your cow, bring the turkey and I'll do the scrying. I want to help you but you are being difficult."

Not happy with the minimal disclosure the Tarot cards offered, Frosea sought to delve further into the matter. The following night, she slaughtered one of the two turkeys left in her household and with high hopes she laid it before the village oracle.

At the sight of the plump bird, Baba Vera decided she needed to put on more of a performance. She fetched a shabby, wooden truck from the attic, its age only to be gauged by the work of weevils. The rusty hinges struggled to keep the creaking chest together.

The old witch knelt beside it and after whispering a string of incantations she opened it ajar. She unloaded fistfuls of chicken beaks and with the caution of someone holding dynamite, placed them in a certain order on the rabbit skin cloth. Sweating and with a barely perceptible sigh, Baba Vera dug out a batch of stones of different size and colour and immediately dotted them along the chalk line which circled the altar. She then threw a pinch of salt in one of the clay pots next to her and stirred it exactly thirteen times.

When the chants over a small cauldron to her side were over, she poured the blessed water into the other empty pot and carried on with more whispers. The seven candles placed at different angles flickered actively and gave birth to a retinue of moving shades, chasing each other on the four walls of the room.

Frosea was nervous and impatient but didn't budge out of fear of interfering with the energies at work.

Determined to unveil the greatest mystery of the village, Baba Vera assumed her half-closed eyes posture and watched the bowl of consecrated water with the fixed gaze of a lizard.

After precisely thirty-three minutes, she let out a faint smile.

"It shows the same King of Spades I told you about yesterday…"

"But that's not of much help…" Frosea cradled her head with both hands, on the verge of crying.

"Shhh! Be quiet."

Baba Vera kept watching the bowl.

"The King of Spades…right…? He had fitted your cow with humans' boots and they both walked out in orderly manner. That's what happened, Frosea. Now thank the spirits for their willingness to help." The kneeling sorceress bowed and touched her forehead to the ground three times.

"But who did it? I want to know who stole my animal."

"I'm afraid the waters are too cloudy to reveal the face of the villain."

Frosea was left poorer than ever. A bitter sense of loss dried her throat while the tantalising aroma of poultry soup rising from the witch's stove tickled her nostrils and caused her stomach to grumble.

***

Frosea was slowly approaching the girls, breathing heavily. The steep hill riddled with potholes was taking its toll on her.

Doina called to the middle-aged woman and informed her of the '*road closure*'.

"Oh dear, there are too many of them these days." Frosea waved her hand dismissively.

She sat on a log by the side of the road and with one corner of her flowery shawl she wiped the running sweat off her face.

Ksenia began biting her nails while Larisa tutted impatiently. There was still some time to spare but not much. She squinted querulously down the road and before long, the swaying figure of Mos Avram – one of the town's many drunks – appeared in sight. Weaving from side to side he was heading up the hill.

"Here's our hero."

"Let's just hope he doesn't slump before he gets here."

Singing and whistling merrily, Mos Avram reached them, eventually, and crossed the road. As soon as he passed the spot where the black cat had run across, they all dashed after him and headed towards the highway.

Quarter of an hour later a car stopped to pick the girls up. The journey was about forty-five minutes and they decided to use the time efficiently and practise with the cameras.

A previous experience with the educational authorities taught the girls it was worth recording their submissions. When Doina had handed in her entry exam papers at university the year before, she had no idea that her work would be tampered with. Confident she had passed the tests, Doina had been shocked to receive the official announcement that she hadn't reached the highest score and therefore could not benefit from free education.

The university had budget places for the top two students with the highest scores. For all her school years Doina studied hard, aiming to be the best. It was her only hope of getting into higher education, given that her family had no means to help her whatsoever.

Upon investigating the exam results, she was able to discover that her work had been manipulated with bits taken out and other bits added in. The institution apologised and blamed it on administrative errors and misplacing of students' work. Fortunately Doina's score was recognised after all and she did get in for free.

That incident's happy ending, however, did not reassure the girls and this time they decided it was safer to record their work in case it happened again. Living in a world of seismic activities on many levels of society, they were well used to watching their own backs.

The whole country was going through major turmoil and all state affairs were in disarray. Bribery was the door opener and the ice-melter in education just like it was in the health sector, security, local government...and the list goes on.

To avoid any mix-ups or misinterpretations of the English test they were about to take, Doina had the brilliant idea of borrowing cameras from Pintilie – the photographer of the village. Digital gadgets and mobile phones were still a long way away for many Bessarabians. Pintilie's devices were Soviet-style cameras – *Smena* and *Chayka*. He would only lend them if the girls learned how to handle and operate them properly. They were his sole livelihood and he could not afford to have them broken.

As the smallest, Larisa chose the *Smena*. Despite its bulky design, it wasn't too heavy. This left Ksenia with the *Chayka*, which was a lot more compact but all metal and a nightmare to carry around, but then she was taller and stronger.

At the end of the test hour, before handing in their paperwork Ksenia and Larisa took pictures of it in silent warning.

Whether it was because of the cameras and the girls' efforts or due to heavenly exertion, they both passed the test and the world began to change.

***

Many years later, in hushed tones, Doina was to inform Larisa of Mos Avram's tragic demise while attempting to coax his Kurilian Bobtail from the path of an oncoming tractor. Had he been only slightly more sober, he'd have realised it was in fact his neighbour's moggy, a lousy rat-catcher who frequently stole food from Mos Avram's kitchen.

It was an episode Larisa outwardly attributed to a statistical anomaly, although she was to approach black cats with a discernibly increased reverence for the rest of her days.

Grungy Ginger

On the way back from the city, having passed the English exam, the girls were singing out loud.

"The time is ripe to spread the wings,
Forget the past, forget the stings,
Let's soar high and follow dreams,
Today, tomorrow and for all springs..."

Doina quickly switched songs.

"You are going faraway,
And are leaving me behind,
Don't forget your country's bouquet,
Don't get used to foreign grind..."

Ksenia was delighted with the opportunity to study abroad only because it meant she'd improve her English and bring back lots of presents and pictures for Doina.

To Larisa the trip to England meant a lot more – she sought freedom and a new world.

"Now, I hope you don't get cheeky and decide to stay there for ever," Doina warned. "Don't abandon me."

Her teasing hid a note of uncertainty. In order to hide it, Doina carried on jokingly:

"Larisa, your boyfriend – Ruslan – will wilt away if you fail to return."

"Exactly, it's her you should be worried about not coming back, not me," Ksenia raised her eyebrows.

"Forget about Ruslan. Things aren't the same with him any longer. Anyway, do you know what? Maybe I won't come back – I've had enough of you two," Larisa deadpanned before the other two jumped on her back and they all tumbled to the ground.

By the time they returned to Marani – their nest and cradle – the girls were floating high above the ground with excitement and anticipation.

Silvia was shelling walnuts on the porch, carefully picking the nutmeat out and storing the shells away in sacks. Used as biofuel, they provided a cheaper and greener alternative to coal during the long wintry nights. Silvia didn't trust anyone else in the household to determine how much of it went into the fire – with good reason.

A couple of years previously, after a few too many pitchers of wine, Trofim unloaded a whole basket of shells all in one go. The generous dose caused the stove to explode shortly after, showering the house with walnutty shrapnel. Fortunately no one was hurt. The children were not back from school, Silvia was still at work. Trofim was in the safest place possible: in the cellar fetching more wine. Ever since the accident, the walnut shells were kept under lock and key, just like the wine was for most of the year.

The girls decided to all go into the yard and break the good news. Belka ran and jumped to greet them, wildly waving her grungy, ginger tail.

"You three! Looking so dandy. What's the occasion, pray tell me?" Silvia asked, hammering away at the flinty shells of the walnuts.

"We've got some news, but where is Father? I'd like him to hear it too."

"Where do you think? In his office of course." Her mother gestured towards the cellar with a resigned nod.

Every rural household has a cellar where winter supplies and barrels of wine are kept. The Cellar and the Church are the Yin and Yang – the pillars of my people, which hold them together by keeping them apart. Women take to the Church for weekend liturgies and masses while men gather in the cellar, where they sing and dance to their own Lord – Bacchus. Their ultimate reasons are the same though – to celebrate life, gossip, pass the time, complain about their spouses and get unfittingly intoxicated, the former with prayers and the latter with booze.

Larisa headed to the cellar to find her father drinking and playing *Seca* with two neighbours, as happy and content as Adam before Eve.

Seca is the Moldovan take on Poker and a popular card game, confined to male enthusiasts of all ages, up and down the country.

"Hi Father, I've got some news for you!"

"Hello, darling. I'll finish this game and be right up."

"This game will turn into more games, which won't finish till the crack of dawn. Please come with me now."

Being bossed around by a woman like that usually ends up in domestic violence amongst the people of my land. Trofim, however, was a gentleman and a gentle man – quite a rarity in that Eastern territory.

Larisa returned to the porch and said her father would follow shortly.

"You'll live and learn – their drunken words don't cost a dime," mother warned daughter.

However, before long, the doors of the cellar were kicked open and Trofim emerged. His smooth gait belied the many hours he'd spent keeping the wine barrels company.

"Good evening, everyone." He grinned widely and spoke carefully.

Quite a change from the man who served the girls pancakes in the morning.

"Father, you said you were going to finish pickling the watermelons today. They've already started to rot and you are drunk again. How you'll crave them in winter time to cure your hangovers."

"You have to tend to your soul before anything else, darling. How can I bypass my inner urges and act like a robot? Nurturing the self is the most important thing in the world, oh dear, oh dear…" Trofim winked.

The girls chuckled.

"How can you say that drinking wine with your buddies equals nurturing your soul? That's the most ridiculous claim I've ever heard, Father."

"Don't jump to such categorical conclusions before hearing out my arguments."

"Oh, Trofim," his wife sighed, "why do you always try to sound like a lawyer when you are drunk? Stick to what you do best – sing songs and drink wine."

He carried on.

"Ladies – nothing happens on the dry, not even weeds grow on barren land. Those that do are usually prickly or poisonous, displeased with life. Everybody knows the difference between a desert and a lush forest. If you want a plant to grow, you have to wet and nurture it, except plants grow with water and humans with the help of wine. Each to their own."

His face lit up.

"I tell you, when I am under the influence of this miraculous drink, I am in tune with the whole universe. Only then am I able to defy the physical laws and feel the pulse of life and the incessant rotation of our planet. Only then I can see the world move as it really does."

Trofim paused to steady himself and search for the right words.

"You seem to be struggling with the incessant rotation of this courtyard, Father."

"Because I surrender to its force, I feel dizzy and seem to lose my balance but that's only because planets never travel in a direct line. They change direction fairly often. I should know this stuff – I've been teaching it for almost twenty years."

The girls couldn't stifle their laughter any longer.

"Just how quickly do you think they change direction, father? According to your tipsy theory it would happen non-stop because when you are drunk, you don't walk in a straight line but are all over the place. You try to walk on seven roads at the same time."

"I'll tell you where you are wrong," Trofim retorted just when Larisa was convinced her father realised the flaw of his arguments.

He might have been slightly drunk but Trofim was still the village's science teacher.

"You see, this world is all about energy – if you believe that wise, old Jew. Energy by definition is not static – it moves constantly, right? Only the most sensitive of us – in certain states of mind – can feel its dance and it's such an honour, I tell you."

"I'm pretty sure inebriety is not one of those states, Father…"

He winked charmingly and began to say something but Silvia interrupted.

"Stop this rubbish for God's sake."

He didn't.

"I'll tell you something else. Just like the water and sunlight have miraculous powers for the plants – a process which scientists describe in many books and attempt to explain but will never be able to understand – for there is a fundamental difference between the two, my girls – in the same way red wine in combination with moonlight has a similar effect on humans. It certainly has on me."

"Moonshine rather then moonlight, more likely," Larisa teased.

"If drinking does anything to you, then it's certainly making you delirious." Silvia glared Gorgon-like at her husband. She then turned towards her daughter and melted. "Let's change the subject, darling. Did you not say you had some good news?"

Larisa cleared her throat.

"Actually we have two pieces of news: one good one bad. Which one shall I start with?"

"Tell us the good one first. After that no bad news will be bad." Trofim staggered on his feet.

"Ksenia and I passed the English language test and have been selected to go on a cultural programme in England for two weeks."

"This is extremely good news, perfectly justifiable to have a few more drinks." Her father snapped his fingers. "Those pancakes must have done the job," he whispered into Larisa's ear.

"Well done, girls," Silvia followed with her praise. "I think I can guess what your bad news is." She rubbed the tips of her fingers with her thumb, gesturing for money.

"It won't be a lot, Mother, I promise. We'll be hosted by an English family and the only expenses are going to be for travel and some pocket money for when we are there."

"I don't have it all – I'll have to check with friends and neighbours. Let's hope that amongst us we can scrape enough cash for you."

"It's a once in a lifetime opportunity, Mother, and I won't spend all the cash – I promise to bring some of it back."

The girls gave Silvia a hand with shelling the nuts. They all chatted on the porch until the night forced them indoors.

The porch, in Bessarabia, is where all life's dramas unfold. It is a community open stage where families, friends and neighbours gather to laugh, cry or just put the world to rights. The long, clay veranda adorning the front of most rural houses is sacred and viewed by all as the heart of every home.

Acid-Green

A month later Larisa and Ksenia landed at Heathrow airport. Not used to being pampered, they were surprised to find not one, but two college representatives waiting for them, advertising their names high above the crowds.

The warm greetings and wide smiles made them uneasy. Accustomed to sour faces and knotted brows, they didn't know how to react to this new way of being.

Such naturalness was unnatural to them.

The contrasting reality of the two opposing worlds was overwhelming. However, the informality and ease they were treated with soon helped Larisa and Ksenia to relax.

The organisers said the host family was looking forward to meeting them and they headed straight to the car – a Phantom Black Metallic Jeep – something the girls had never seen in their lives, let alone travelled in. USSR jalopies were all they got to experience in their home country.

"Mr and Mrs Anderson are lovely people, you will love them and they don't live too far from the college either."

It was early October. While the whole of continental Europe was still enjoying balmy temperatures, Brighton was cloudy, cold and whipped by extreme winds. Despite the weather, the city conquered their hearts instantly. The beautiful English houses with their immaculately trimmed and impeccably designed gardens were nothing short of picture-perfect postcards.

Ksenia and Larisa were used to seeing wild, unkempt, natural beauty, where the only designer and master was Nature itself. Chaos, therefore, was an indispensable element of the landscape patterns they were familiar with. Their families did tidy the gardens and looked after them assiduously but the only decorative aspect was whitewashing the tree trunks in springtime. Even that job wasn't carried out for any aesthetic reason but for a very pragmatic one: it helped to keep away parasitic bugs and stopped the trees from premature vegetation. It was logical and served a certain, practical purpose, like everything else had to in the country they were born.

What the girls witnessed in Brighton, on the other hand, was all man-made beauty, created only to please the eye. Ksenia and Larisa thought they had landed in Wonderland and even though it was an unfamiliar feeling in their experiential repertoire, they fully embraced it.

"Wow, this is incredible." Larisa looked around, mouth gaping. "Are their gardens for everyday use? Do people sit on the grass here? It looks too pretty for that."

"They are the ultimate gardens, if you ask me."

"Of course they are. For someone with unreasonable demands for orderly arrangements like you."

The girls were thrilled when the car stopped outside their temporary home: a two-storey semi-detached house, surrounded by the lush greenery of exotic giant trees and vibrant coral roses decorating the front garden. While under no illusion about the permanence of their stay, the girls envisaged spending more time in the gorgeous house than the five minutes that transpired.

One of the organisers walked ahead and rang the doorbell. Mrs Anderson, a well-kept lady in her early sixties, opened the door and with a cold glance measured up the foreign girls from head to toe.

The look on her face wasn't welcoming.

Asking them to wait in the hallway, she went to fetch her husband. After ten minutes the hostess returned, followed by her spouse.

"We are terribly sorry but we won't be able to accommodate these students."

"Why not?"

"They are not the twelve to thirteen year old girls we were expecting…"

"Well, darling, since they are here now…" Mr Anderson also measured the girls from head to toe but his wife looked daggers at him and cut him short.

"I'm afraid we won't be able to accommodate these two…young ladies because we are not sure they came here for the purpose of studying," she spoke nasally and nudged her husband.

Coming from a world dominated by machismo, the girls were stunned to witness something they didn't think existed – the phenomenon of the henpecked husband.

The organisers asked to have a word with the Andersons in private and they all disappeared into a side room at the end of the corridor.

Ksenia and Larisa were left standing in the hallway.

They looked around, intimidated by the foreign décor. A grand staircase coiled up and around the corner, leading to the second floor. Grey, stripy wallpaper with flowery patterns lined the walls from floor to ceiling, exuding an air of cold refinement. Standing by what they later learned to be a lowboy, the girls admired the quirky piece of furniture with its long legs elaborately carved. Right above it was propped up a no less impressive gilt-wood mirror, lending the house a period ambience. The solemnity of it all made the girls nervous.

"What do they mean they can't host us any more? What else are we here for, if not education?" Ksenia whispered.

"Maybe the organisers are not from the college as we thought. Do you think we've been duped and kidnapped?"

"Don't be silly. All our paperwork is in order…"

"But why were they checking us out like that? I know we are good looking." Larisa turned to look at their reflections in the grand girandole glass. "Well, you more than I am, even though with the right make-up I can pull it too. Is that what they were thinking?"

"Not so loud…They may hear us and then we'll definitely be kicked out."

"So what? I don't like their home anyway. It may be beautiful and expensive but I find it somehow creepy. Don't you?"

"I know what you mean, Gypsy-lassie, but that's because you are not used to seeing grandeur."

"Whatever…but it still it makes me uncomfortable." Larisa shook her shoulders. "And I think I know why we are getting booted out."

"Keep your voice down, for God's sake…"

"They don't like your short skirt, Oosha. You and your amazing pins."

"It's ridiculous. They can't turn us away because of that."

"Our dress code is the issue, I tell you."

"What's wrong with it?"

"Perhaps ripped jeans and short skirts imported straight from the bazaars of Istanbul aren't exactly right for this type of introduction."

"They are in vogue."

"There's no way they are aware of the fashion season in Moldova right now. They are probably not aware of the fashion season for eighteen-year-olds in the UK, let alone in a former USSR country."

"Shhh! They are coming back."

Everyone returned to the hallway and by the look on their acid-green faces, the verdict was clear. Without exchanging a word, the girls picked up their bags and headed towards the door.

The weather had turned and it started pouring down. They ran to the car. One of the organisers picked up her phone, desperately trying to find an alternative host family. The other went to great lengths and pains to make sure the girls were OK. She explained there was nothing to worry about.

"The couple changed their mind and opted out of the hosting programme. It's not your fault. They were expecting, umm…younger students, that's all. A misunderstanding, but we'll sort it out for you."

A couple of hours later, Ksenia and Larisa were welcomed into the home of Florence and James Harvey. They and Alex, their daughter, all came out into the courtyard, despite the rain, to greet the foreign students and immediately invited them into their living room.

The eclectic furniture was harmoniously arranged on wooden floors and oriental rugs. Pleasantly cluttered, the décor leant towards the traditional style. Soft and cushy chairs were casually placed to face the long sofa in the middle of the room. The bay windows looking into a jungly front garden were adorned with floor length drapes, loaded with gathers, matching the light-pink flowery patterns on the upholstery. Cupboards with traditional china and bookcases stood tall guarding the wider walls.

The whole room was a pleasure to the eye but the jewel in crown was the mantelpiece: embellished with candlesticks, family photos and a beautifully carved wooden clock, it enhanced the vibrant painting hanging right above it – an Impressionist depiction of country life and a field swirling with wild, crimson poppies.

The warm and intimate space provided such a lovely atmosphere, the girls thought, that rainy weather could never be a bother in such a house.

James switched on Classic FM and Florence treated the guests to a lavish spread of afternoon tea. She brought in various sandwiches, raspberry cakes and chocolate chip scones while Alex served aromatic Earl Grey tea.

Florence was what Ksenia and Larisa grew to call *a trendy mum* and she connected well with the girls. They shopped and cooked together, exchanging beauty tips and food recipes. Both Florence and Alex did their best to accustom Ksenia and Larisa to the new world in which the girls felt like female versions of Mowgli.

The first culture clash happened when Florence cooked the first meal. Neither of the girls could eat it, not because the hostess was a bad cook – all the meals were half ready anyway – but because they were not accustomed to English products.

In shop windows and on the shelves, everything looked ripe and mouth watering yet upon tasting those fruit and vegetables, the girls found them devoid of all taste.

"Give me a good old Moldovan apple with a wormhole any day," Ksenia grumbled.

The most challenging, however, was the bread situation. In rural Bessarabia nearly everyone bakes their own loaves. Ksenia and Larisa were addicted to bread – they used to have it even with rice and pasta. The thin, white slices – paltry and apologetic – offered in England, could not substitute what they were craving for and not much else agreed with their stomachs.

The other major jolt concerned grooming.

Running water is a foreign luxury to most rural Bessarabians. Instead, rain water is collected and regularly stored in wooden barrels due to its beneficial components. Freshly descended from the skies, it carries positive electrical charges, which care greatly for the body and the mind. Especially healthful and invigorating is the ozonic rain that comes with thunderstorms and lightning.

The water from the wells, though potable, is usually avoided at bathing time. Due to its calcareous nature, it can dry out the skin – especially the scalp – and is therefore branded *hard water*.

While using a shower for the first time in their lives was exhilarating for Ksenia and Larisa, they soon found out that Sussex was a *hard water* area. Larisa emerged from the bathroom with her hair so badly knotted that she thought she'd have to shave it all off.

"Did you use any conditioner?" Florence examined her hair.

"What is that, some sort of vinegar brand?" Larisa had no clue what she was being asked.

The only thing she knew would help untangle hair was vinegar. Occasionally, when rain was scarce during summer months, she'd bring water from the well to bathe in but due to its high calcite composition, it jumbled hair beyond redemption. The lore taught to mix vinegar with the water in order to avoid such disasters.

Florence – a true English lady – refrained from laughing at this medieval beauty tip and suggested Larisa try some conditioner instead.

After some time in the bathroom, Larisa came out again with hair just as entangled. Her scepticism of western products intensified.

"Your method doesn't work. My hair is just as bad. I think using vinegar is the way. Honestly, with it the hair is so smooth and shiny…"

"…And smelling of chips," Florence teased.

"To be honest, I'd rather have stinky hair than none at all."

"It doesn't look like you've used any conditioner at all."

"Of course I have. I had it on for more than ten minutes and washed it off thoroughly with more shampoo."

"You did what?" Florence broke into a jingling laughter.

After she cleaned off the running mascara on her cheeks, the host mother gave the girls a very comprehensive explanation about what conditioner was and how to be used. Shower times as a result, became a lot more pleasant.

Technology and online communication were other modern wonders the English family introduced the girls to for the first time. Larisa and Ksenia stared in disbelief at the miraculous face-to-face calls and SMS a computer could perform via Skype – something they'd never heard of before. Alex used it regularly to communicate with her cousins in Australia.

"England really is," Larisa thought, "a country from the future. Shame about the food."

Scarlet

Ksenia and Larisa were very nervous on the first day of the programme, constantly adjusting and readjusting their clothes all the way to the college, a ten-minute walk from the Harveys' house.

Just before reaching the destination, they stopped in front of a glass building to appraise themselves one last time before making an appearance at the school. Unfamiliar with how deceptive glass walls could be, they stopped to use its wall as a mirror. A sequence of adjustments followed: tucking shirts in, pulling bras and tights up and other things young ladies do when privacy is assumed.

Larisa leant closer towards the glass to apply her glossy lipstick and had the shock of her life: a big group of people was gathered and watched them, laughing from the other side. She was startled and drew away from the window.

"They must think we're a right pair of rustic halfwits..." was all Larisa could mumble, face and ears turning scarlet.

"What's wrong?"

Speechless, Larisa could only pull a puzzled Ksenia away from the beguiling building.

After such an embarrassing start to the day, the closer they got to college, the more nervous Larisa became.

"I think I've forgotten how to speak English."

"At least no black cats crossed our way this morning. I'll tell you what, Larisa – let's walk by the street cleaner spraying steam on the pavement over there. It's the same as having a bucket of water poured at our feet and it'll bring us luck."

They got to college half an hour before the appointed time and were shown around the building. Health and safety regulations were explained thoroughly – something they'd never heard of in their entire lives and which they instantly put down to a charming, if bothersome, English eccentricity.

The class started and the teacher introduced the girls to the rest of the students. She asked them to say a few words about themselves. When Moldova was mentioned as their country of origin, somebody asked:

"Aren't you a bit pale for somebody from the Maldives?"

"Maldives?" Larisa laughed. "I wish. We are from Moldova – an ex-Soviet country."

"So you are Russian."

"No, we are Moldovan," Larisa stated again.

"What language do you speak?"

"Romanian and Russian."

"Hang on a second, you speak Romanian and Russian but you are Moldavian. This is very confusing..."

"*Moldovan*, thank you very much..."

However, this assertion gave Larisa pause for thought. It was a sore issue back home. Lots of answers flocked to her head but none of them were straightforward. The true answer would demand some explanations and historical background, which were neither simple nor brief.

"Who exactly am I?" she thought to herself. *"This is the question that I ask myself all the time? Who am I? What am I? Am I Moldovan or Romanian? Both or neither?"*

Ksenia came to Larisa's rescue:

"We've got a complicated history and authorities – to this day – cannot agree on what to call our language. Some say it's Romanian and others swear it's Moldovan."

"Why's that?"

Questions from the students came raining in and it was as flattering as it was frightening. The history of their country, language and identity was confusing to themselves, let alone to a bunch of foreigners.

"Historical legacy and political agendas have turned us into brain-washed zombies with tumble-dried perceptions." Larisa tried to put into words what she felt about her breed.

"Really?"

"It's not that bad," Ksenia scowled at Larisa who carried on unabated.

"Ever since Bessarabia was ceded to the Tsarist Empire after the Russian–Ottoman war of 1806–1812, we have been forcefully alienated from our Romanian and Latin roots."

"Bessarabia? What is that? I thought we were talking about Moldova." The English audience was getting ever more confused.

"You see, originally Moldova was a Romanian principality consisting of two regions: the Higher and Lower Lands. The Eastern region of the Lower Lands was also known as Bessarabia, which incorporated much of present day Republic of Moldova and a small piece of southern Ukraine. According to some sources the name of Bessarabia traces back to the Cumans migration, which arrived in the area some time in the eleventh century. Other experts maintain that it comes from the Basarab Dynasty, who established the first Romanian Principality in the fourteenth century."

Larisa took in a deep breath and looked around the class. An unexpected fear that she might get lost in too many details seized her and she thought of cutting it short.

"In any case, when the Russians occupied the eastern part of Moldova in 1812, they kept its name of Bessarabia on the pretext that they were going to respect the region's heritage."

"Didn't they keep their word?"

"You don't know Russians, do you?" Larisa jeered. "A massive wave of russification followed. Local customs and traditions were banned, the Romanian language was replaced with Russian in all schools and it became the official language in administration. All sorts of clerks and officials arrived from Russia in hordes to replace the locals. Russian priests were appointed in rural churches to '*work* on' the peasants and farmers. In short, it was a very intense process of brainwashing, denationalisation and identity distortion."

"When did it stop?"

Larisa smiled in undertone and looked at Ksenia, who wasn't going to intervene. Not happy with Larisa's passionate views, she decided it best to keep quiet to prevent the English strangers from laughing at their disparate opinions.

She had warned Larisa many times about her overly critical and prejudiced attitude towards Russians. It offended her memories of her beloved maternal grandmother, Dasha Tyomkina.

Dasha, a feisty peasant girl with mischievous green eyes from the Pervomayskiy Rayon in Rostov Oblast, was caught in the wave of the migrant workforce of the thousands of Russians, Belorussians and Ukrainians, which the Soviet government *encouraged* to populate the new Soviet republic of Moldova after the Second World War. It was an agenda to compensate for the demographic loss caused by deportations, political arrests and other forms of Soviet persecution of the local population.

Dasha Tyomkina married a talented Bessarabian potter – Ion Robu – and had two daughters, Svetlana and Tamara – the latter Ksenia's mother.

Hearing Larisa talk like that in front of strangers, Ksenia grew increasingly frustrated.

"What's wrong with her? Why is she washing our dirty linen in public like that? Can't she keep it shut?"

"It hasn't stopped, that's the trouble. The Russians are still controlling our country."

Larisa carried on talking about Moldova's history but kept it brief, aware that she could easily alienate the English audience with such a convoluted subject.

Bessarabia was controlled by the Tsarist Empire until 1918, when it declared its independence from Russia as the Moldavian Democratic Republic and united with the Kingdom of Romania. But then, in 1940, Bessarabia was occupied by the USSR in the wake of the Molotov–Ribbentrop Pact with Germany. Despite the fact that my land got its independence again in 1991 after the Soviet collapse, the damage had already been done on so many levels.

"...The last two hundred years witnessed the destruction and distortion of the national identity, rendering it in tatters, especially during the Communist era. Weak, confused and polarised, we've become a pliable mass vulnerable to any abuse and manipulation. Let's hope things will change for the better soon," Larisa concluded and looked over at Ksenia – who was red with rage and unable to hold her feelings in any longer:

"It's actually nowhere near as bad as Larisa makes it sound," and then she faced her friend – "You make us sound like a bunch of idiots."

"I am only stating the facts. Please don't take it personally," and then turning towards the English students, Larisa obliged: "Ksenia is a quarter Russian, you see…"

Facing Ksenia again, she continued:

"Look, honey, I have nothing against the Russians, trust me, but I have the right to have my say about their expansionist agenda on our country, history and identity and the consequences of it all."

"Why can't you leave the past alone? The present is what we should be concerned with."

"And I am. It's the present I am talking about. We – Moldovans – have ended up living in a state of haze and dizziness, which has become a second nature and where responsibility is an alien concept to us. You refuse to see the causes and the background of our status-quo."

"That's very presumptuous of you."

"It's my opinion, my informed opinion about the world I've been born and raised in. Doesn't that give me enough credence?"

"You can't speak on behalf of the entire country. Opinions can and do vary, you know…"

"It's true that many Moldovans run away from, ignore or simply refuse to see things for what they are. What's worse – many more prefer to withdraw like turtles under their shell and let others make decisions concerning their lives."

"Where are you driving at, for God's sake?"

"The fact that it all boils down to our low self esteem and lack of confidence at national and individual level. And do you know what the icing on the cake is? This state of affairs is encouraged in Moldova, aided and maintained by authorities because it suits certain forces in the country and outside, not too far away."

"Don't tell me…That's the Russians' fault too?"

Larisa raised her left eyebrow in silence.

Ksenia opened her arms in ever-growing frustration and gesticulated despairingly.

"Everything's just a big Russian plot to you, isn't it? C'mon…reconstruction from the Communist era is already happening. Get over it!"

"I'm not totally denying that. But it's a very slow and sporadic process because our confidence has been so badly damaged."

"Hello – we all know it's going to take time…What did you expect? Overnight magic of some kind?"

"But you are missing the point. What I am talking about is that the identity and psyche of our people have been fragmented. They have been destroyed and insidiously reinvented through brainwashing and cunning manipulation of the collective memory…"

"Can I stop you right there…?"

"No Ksenia, you can't. Stop interrupting me all the time and let me finish…"

"Don't you point your finger at me like that."

By this point, the English students were looking from Larisa to Ksenia and back, as if following the rally at a tennis game. The two girls seemed to have forgotten they had an audience.

"I've lost my train of thought now. Where was I? Right – the collective memory I was talking about is the very pool of information that forms the basis of any national, social and cultural identity: our history, traditions, folklore and customs which date back hundreds of years, if not more. And our own collective memory – this tremendous instrument of power – has been tampered with and grossly altered by parties and outside forces according to *their* interests and bluntly used to daze our people. Do you get me?"

Despite the question asked, Larisa didn't let Ksenia answer and instead carried on.

"You know just as well as I do that many holy days, ceremonies, important dates, art and crafts, et cetera have been either banned, replaced or changed completely. Many people of our grandparents' generation were deported to Siberia. Although actually, in your case – your grandmother…"

"Leave my grandmother out of this…May she rest in peace!"

"I'm just saying – she was amongst the Russians who were brought in to replace those who were forcefully removed from Bessarabia. Either way, we can't pretend these things haven't happened. Look at the two of us arguing right now – we are living examples of those deliberate agendas to mess up our coherence about who we are and where we belong. What other proof do you want?" Larisa took a deep breath, finally.

"I just don't see the point on dwelling on all this. We can't change it and being stuck like that is not helpful, in fact – it's sterile."

"Precisely, but we can only move on if we first understand where we are at right now. This is the sum total of what happened in the past, especially the relentless Sovietisation, which moulded us the way we are today on all levels."

"Identity is not just memory, is it? It's also about aspirations and hopes. We've got to look forward, Larisa."

"Absolutely, but what are aspirations?"

"Listen, I think we better stop this…"

"You started it…Aspirations rise because of discontent. Every wish, hope and goal springs from a current need, which in turn is a result of past events. These of course do not control or command this striving but can offer a solid point of reference and a good view of the journey, right?

Ksenia decided to keep quiet, hoping it would shut Larisa up.

It didn't.

"What you want for the future can't be plucked out of the void and it's not random, created out of a vacuum. It grows organically from your history and background, Ksiusha. It does. I mean – it has to. Think about it – we've got to analyse and understand these things if we are to move forward and embrace the new, haven't we?"

"Jesus, you won't stop, will you? I should really know better than argue with you on this subject."

For the first time in a quarter of an hour, the flushed girls became aware of the total silence in the room.

Only the sound of street traffic permeated the air.

The English students were motionless.

"I guess you're right," Larisa mumbled and turned to face the class again. "I am sorry, we must have bored you to death…"

"Not at all. It was fascinating to watch." Then in a lower voice the student whispered to the girl next to her: "I'd hate to see those two fall out over a boy…"

The class carried on. Larisa, however, felt scattered and unable to focus.

The debate with Ksenia had picked at some sore issues. She recognised that any homecoming required piecing these things together. However, so many parts of the puzzle were falsified and filled with controversy, it was impossible to find a way through the dazzling mesh of artificial reflections of facts and fiction. Those intentionally placed historic and social mirrors depicting various angles and perspectives overwhelmed and discouraged the quest for truth, for either history or identity. Hence the state of limbo encouraged in Moldova – as much an orphanage as a country – booted around Eastern Europe by successive empires, due to its critical place on the map. For centuries it had been an invasion route from Asia to Europe, starting with the Cumans and the Golden Horde in the eleventh and thirteenth centuries, followed in turn by the Ottomans. More recently it acted as the gateway for Russia into the western world.

Still irked with each other, Larisa and Ksenia didn't speak for the rest of the morning. They interacted separately with other college students and learned much about England, the English language and culture. Everyone was very polite, making the girls feel welcome in the new country.

In the afternoon the students took the guests on a tour of Brighton city, after which they all stopped at McDonalds for fries and ice-cream. While the rest of them queued up to be served, Larisa and Ksenia went to wash their hands. Due to her irrational hygienic demands, Ksenia refused to take their bags into the bathroom and in their naïvety, the girls left them on top of a free table not too far from the counter.

Utter shock and total dismay seized them upon coming back to realise one of the bags was missing – Ksenia's bag. Both were fuming, albeit for different reasons: Ksenia was unhappy that her bag had been singled out and Larisa was upset that their favourite lipstick was in the stolen bag.

"At least you didn't have your passport in the bag. Don't worry, we will get another rouge," Larisa spoke first in an attempt to make it up with her friend.

Ksenia nodded in silence.

The rest of the day didn't go any more smoothly. On the way home, they stopped in a shopping mall. Not having enough spare money to buy anything, the girls resigned themselves to just looking around and trying on clothes in the fitting rooms.

Ksenia saw a pair of turquoise suede shoes with a kitten heel. Without thinking twice she headed to the exit, wishing to try them with the long dress she had spotted in the shop next door. The alarm went off and a burly security guard with hairy tattooed hands detained them.

"Sorry girls, I'm going to have to call the police."

"Why? What's happening?"

"We caught you stealing."

"Stealing? What? When?"

"These shoes you have in your hand. You tried to walk out with them."

More used to open-air markets than shopping centres, Ksenia was indignant.

"No I didn't. I was only going next door to try them on with that dress over there. The polka dot one hanging up by the counter – can you see it?"

"You intended to leave the shop without paying for them. That's called theft."

"I wasn't leaving any shop. This is a huge mall you've got over here."

The store manager was called, but worn down after two hours of facing the girls' obdurate refusal to admit any wrongdoing, he released them without charge.

"Western shopping…," Ksenia laughed nervously. "That will teach us."

The two weeks in Brighton flew by very quickly but it changed the girls, especially Larisa, in a powerful way. She was faced daily with vital questions from her western peers which helped her dig deeper and unravel more of her country's social, historical and cultural make-up. Even though they were not new issues to her, exposing and explaining them to somebody who was unbiased towards the truth caused a lot of upheaval in her heart.

"It's all gone so quickly. I hope you enjoyed yourselves here." Florence gave the girls a long, warm hug.

"Yes, we have. Thank you so much for being such an incredible host family." Ksenia felt gratitude filling her heart and reflected:

"English people aren't as cold as we've been warned."

"We will miss you," Alex said. "Make sure you stay in touch."

"Absolutely." Larisa was already hatching a plan to return.

She had fallen in love with England and the western way of life. It was a world so removed from the one she was used to that Larisa secretly vowed to become part of it.

Florence handed them a goodbye gift, smiling mischievously. It was a collection of English teas and two big bottles of hair conditioner.

Livid-Purple

Ksenia and Larisa returned to Moldova even though one of them had left her heart behind in England.

Back at university Larisa swiftly lost interest in pursuing her studies, spending more time thinking about how to make it to the UK again. Having tasted a different kind of life, she was keen on sampling more.

The crux came when one of the senior lecturers sheepishly admitted that Moldovian degrees were not recognised anywhere else in the world. Pursuing any further studies in her home country therefore was a waste of time – something Larisa thought should have been pointed out to the influx of male Arab and African students coming to study agriculture. But, she reflected, given the hungry way they looked at her and her friends, perhaps it wasn't agrarian interests they were pursuing in Moldova after all.

At the end of the first academic year, Larisa informed her parents she was dropping out of university, knowing exactly the seismic effect her words were going to have on them.

Silvia and Trofim held higher education in an esteem bordering on fanaticism and were not going to take their daughter's decision lightly. Not only did they want Larisa to carve out a good future for herself, but much more importantly – they didn't want to be the talk of the town. In a world devoid of privacy, anything that would attract attention had to be carefully considered.

"What are you planning to do if not study, pray tell me?" Silvia's face and neck went livid-purple. "Do you intend on working the land instead? After all our sacrifices to see you live a better life, don't tell me you want to revert to farming."

"No, I don't. I am happy to carry on with my education, just not in Moldova."

"What do you mean? Where else?"

"I want to do it in London."

There was an incredulous silence, then Silvia broke into a forced laughter.

"Where?"

"You heard me."

"Is this some kind of a joke?" Trofim didn't take his eyes off his daughter.

"It's not. I really mean it. You either let me do it London or I won't do it at all."

Silvia stopped laughing.

"How are you going to do it in London?"

"I only need you to help me with the first year and I will pay for the rest myself."

"How?"

"I don't know yet but I'll work it out."

"But I don't think we can help at all, my dear." Trofim was confused and hurt and Larisa felt a pang of guilt. "You know our circumstances very well. It's not like we've got hidden treasure buried in the garden or anything of the sort."

"Father, I already thought about it long and hard and there is a way to do it."

Larisa hesitated. Her idea had potential and could work just enough to get her to London but it meant a huge sacrifice for her family.

Her parents waited.

"How about selling a few acres of land?" she whispered with contrition.

Silvia forced another laugh.

"Our daughter is really funny."

"Larisa, darling, what you are asking for is far-fetched. That's our main source of income and we can't manage without it."

"You've got the farm too." She stood her ground but hearing her own words, Larisa realised the enormity of her request. "I will pay you back in time and will certainly not let you starve but I need your help to get me going."

"What is it that you really want?"

"Father, I'm suffocating here…I feel trapped…"

"If it's just more space you are after, I promise to build you a bigger kitchen."

Larisa sighed, exasperated by Trofim's well-meaning but typically Moldovan male response.

"That is the last thing I want, Father. Besides, I've already been accepted at University of Westminster in London." Larisa dropped her final bomb.

Her parents stared at each other, knowing Larisa's stubbornness would make this a pointless stand-off.

After further talks, more negotiations and lots of sleepless nights, they finally agreed to help their daughter go to London. They had little choice.

Larisa had held off telling her blood sisters about this major decision, reluctant to cause too much pain.

In the meantime, she tended to the easier task of releasing the bond of her first love.

Ruslan could not do anything to make her change her mind. The strong sentiments she once felt for him had long withered and Larisa was ready to part.

They met one last time at their usual rendezvous –
in the walnut tree grove on the school grounds.
Though in the middle of the village, it was a secluded
spot where not many people ventured in the evening,
let alone at night.

Silent spectators standing tall and always alert, the
mighty trees watched over all that happened under
their shadow, storing memories of many generations.
Their leaves sheltered enamoured students from the
rain; abundant blossom fed the buds of young ardours,
nurturing more promising but unfulfilled desires and
dreams.

Larisa was early and lay down on the cool grass to
wait for Ruslan. She watched the crowns of the trees
above with branches waggling to a purpose known
only to them and whispering to each other non-stop.

*"I wonder, how many secrets do you hold, beautiful
walnut trees?"* she thought. *"Marking the school years of
many generations of lovers, there is probably lots of gossip
you could tell. Goodbye my dear old friends – I'm going far
away. I know you don't mind for you've captured my heart
and soul. Your grip is such that no human or inhuman,
social or unsocial bug would ever destroy it. Like a Matrix,
you've embedded them carefully in a matter beyond the
conscious.*

*"I wonder – what does the world look like through your
eyes? Does it even exist? More importantly – do you also
have a quest, you – whispering walnut trees?"*

Larisa pondered over their grace and mystery. She
had barely moved by the time Ruslan arrived and lay
down next to her. His warm breath flowed towards the
apex of her neck causing her entire body to shiver and
ripple in response to the electric wave. She knew what
was coming – alluring kisses which usually instigated
stormy yet unfulfilling sessions right there on the hard
ground.

Despite her recent feelings, Larisa threw herself into it with the fully ardent passion of a fire about to die. They burned on the cool, earthen floor for more than an hour, doing everything except the act of penetration. Not because she didn't want to, but because the shame and guilt towards sex before marriage instilled at a very young age prevented her and many others from satiating their youthful impulses. Her parents, like the rest of the adults in the village, maintained a strait-laced moral education, totally oblivious to the greedy law of over-compensation and the havoc it can wreak upon repressed adolescents in later life.

In their passionate encounters of the last few years, Larisa got to learn the number and size of all the beauty spots on Ruslan's entire body. She knew how all his muscles tensed and moved under the tight, moist skin. Eagerly absorbing the taste of his body, she forgot about hers and abandoned it to his explorative fervour. Larisa knew how many vertebrae he had on his spine just like she could tell the number of throbbing veins on his manhood. Certain it was that if left to her own devices, she'd have eaten him alive like a praying mantis and most likely ended up in prison for post-coital cannibalism.

Locked in another one of those dry yet passionate encounters, she was painfully aware of how the intensity, which not so long ago transported her to other worlds, had decreased inexplicably.

Ruslan was oblivious to those thoughts and feelings besieging Larisa. He was a simple Moldovan man concerned only with having food to eat, a wife to bear his children and a cellar to get drunk in.

The intrusive flash of a torch brought their heated encounter to a premature end and they sneaked out of the park.

Fiodor Stepanovici, an old teacher of about sixty-five, was in the habit of spying on his students. As soon as night descended, he prowled the village up and down in order to prevent young people from falling into the sin of drinking, smoking or having sex. Any misbehaviour would be reported to parents, if there were any around, and trenchant remarks dished out in class the following day or at weekly school assemblies.

With so many families riven by alcoholism or parents working abroad, he felt a huge chunk of the younger generation was going off the rails and in need of guidance and support. Hence his self-appointed role of guardian, which he performed so diligently as if to carry out contractual duties sworn under oath. It had become his *raison d'être* and exceeded all reasonable, moral standards, save those of Eastern Europe.

During their school years, Larisa and Ruslan used to arrange their rendezvous in the village cemetery. It was probably the only place the tutor did not suspect. Or perhaps he consciously chose to avoid it out of fear that it could retain him there forever. Whatever the reason, all students knew that it was the best place for young lovers to meet without having to worry about the nosey teacher and his inquisitive torch.

After graduation, Larisa and Ruslan started meeting in the walnut tree grove, closer to home – it was more convenient despite the occasional disturbance from the well-intentioned yet impertinent teacher.

After Larisa broke the news to Ruslan, they parted, leaving him to bear the hefty weight of her impending farewell.

Doina and Ksenia took the news much more badly.

"Education is not the only reason you are going there, right? You harbour different plans, don't you, Gypsy-lassie?" Doina saw right through her friend's smoke-screen.

Larisa smiled sheepishly.

"I'll never abandon you if that's what you are worried about. We'll keep in touch regularly, I promise."

"That's not the point. You know our stand on this whole trade-migration business." Ksenia shook her head with disappointment. "Soon there won't be anyone left in this country. People are leaving in hordes to work elsewhere, all the while complaining that the country is in shit. Well guess what, it will be, until everyone returns to clean it."

"Ksiusha, I don't think we can blame those who are in dire need and who choose to work abroad temporarily. The difference is, I don't think Larisa has any intention of ever coming back and that's what's worrying." Doina did not study psychology for no reason.

A short pause followed, almost as if her blood sisters waited for Larisa to confirm or deny the assertion.

The majority of Bessarabians seek work in foreign countries with the hope of making enough money to return home sooner or later and enjoy a better life. Larisa on the other hand had no such desire. On the contrary – her wish was to get as far away as possible from home and hearth. Money played no role in her decision. Feeling trapped in what she regarded as an old-fashioned world, Larisa longed to fulfil much stronger urges – freedom of thought, choice and action.

"If that's the case," Ksenia sounded dejected, "you are betraying who you are."

"Rubbish, I'm doing this because I want to stay true to myself."

"You can do that here."

"The mentality I've grown up with and which I believe underlies the general psyche of our people is limiting and robs us of will power. The result is that we get victims of life by the wheelbarrow. I want to take control of my life and not spend the rest of it worrying about my day being spoiled by an encounter with a black cat."

"You are naïve to think that other countries are superstition-free. Remember Mr Harvey and that lucky blanket he wrapped himself in every time Brighton & Hove Albion played?"

"Yes but that's an individual's own beliefs. I am talking more about the general conventions relevant to an entire country."

"Pretty much everyone we met in England, *touched wood* and *crossed fingers* at one time or another." Ksenia took obvious pleasure in contradicting Larisa.

"It can't be wrong to assume that all societies have their own superstitions despite the growth and development of their civilisations," Doina took sides. "Don't think that if you leave Moldova you will escape irrationality."

"At least it won't be as paralysing as here. Don't you see, our lives revolve around unfounded fears and leave no room for taking charge or being accountable."

"Control-freak," Ksenia concluded.

"You baffle me." Doina cocked her head. "Why, for example, do you believe in dreams if you are so against traditional wisdom?"

"Dreams have nothing to do with superstition. They belong to the wonders of the subconscious mind."

"An unseen, irrational force nonetheless which you choose to believe in. You like recording dreams to interpret and foretell the future. That's not exactly a scientific process, is it? Dismissing traditions and lore just because they don't suit you is unfair and hypocritical."

"All I am saying is that they don't serve me. I don't think they serve any of us, to be honest. Why follow them? I'll go even further and say that some of them are even damaging to our psyche, stripping us of one of life's most important values – responsibility."

"You are so cold and practical, ready to un-root yourself, to abandon your culture and customs just because you are short-sighted and too rigid to perceive their insights."

"There is nothing for me to see because I don't wish to live my life around them. Staying in a country where the majority of people do isn't very appealing or favourable. I'm seeking a world which will not impel me to go against my nature. Besides, you never know – you two might also end up abroad one day."

"Never." Ksenia shook her head vehemently.

"You know what they say in England, Oosha: 'Never say never'!" Larisa was quick to remind her friend of Florence Harvey's favourite sayings.

"Never, never, never. I will always stay here and carry on with my art. Beauty will save the world, remember? And stop calling me *doorway*, will you?"

"Why, Oosha? It's better than a doormat!"

"And definitely better than what your classmates call you," Doina added, laughing.

Many other friends called Ksenia by her surname – Robu, much to her annoyance. It translated as *the slave* and she wasn't thrilled with such a denomination.

"Stop it, both of you."

The girls fell silent. No amount of teasing or joking was going to change the desolate mood of the impending departure.

"Look, I'm not flying to the Moon. I'll be back to visit you." Larisa chewed at her lower lip.

She was just as nervous about the whole thing as she was determined to undertake it.

Doina crackled her knuckles, nodding, unconvinced, and Ksenia looked the other way, averting her eyes and biting her nails.

Despite the fact that they were the two people she was closest to in the world, Larisa wanted and was ready to leave the country.

Freckled Saffron

In her travels around Italy searching for Ksenia, Larisa often recalled that fateful conversation which had caused a major rift between them for the first time. She saw her blood sisters a couple more times after that, but things weren't the same. Larisa wanted to find Ksenia safe and alive, in order to strengthen their connection and revive the happy trinity they'd always been.

Arriving at Termini train station, Larisa intended to go to the usual spot, in the car park, where Moldovan emigrants mingled and gave jobs to each other. On the way there, not far from the exit, she spotted a group of five women eating sunflower seeds and spitting shells out. They could not be anything else but Bessarabian – this peculiar habit is so ingrained in their psyche that it follows them everywhere so their travels across Europe could seem to be marked by a trail of black and white seed husks.

Larisa introduced herself to the women and began chatting about work and life in Italy. The deafening siren of a passing ambulance silenced them for a couple of minutes, after which the oldest one, Eugenia, a fifty-six year old food inspector form Leova, Southern Moldova, remarked:

"There you go – another Moldovan's lost their job."

"Tell me about it. The death of an Italian causes more grief to us than to their own families," Tasea, a midwife from Ungheni, on the Eastern border with Romania, replied while making the sign of the cross.

The rest followed suit.

"May they rest in peace!"

The sadness on their faces was genuine and Larisa couldn't tell whether it was due to their essentially kind nature, which she knew to be common of her people, or whether it actually was because somebody lost his job.

Finding work in Italy had become progressively difficult with the number of immigrants arriving daily. Caring for the elderly was the main job available to Moldovans and they all prayed the older Italians they looked after would live to a hundred years and beyond.

When Larisa mentioned Ksenia, the women all shook their heads, apart from the youngest, Alina, who said she'd been in Italy for many years and asked to see a picture.

With hands shaking, Larisa managed to finally get the picture out of her wallet. The tall, frail woman looked closely at the photo and then handed it back.

"Sorry – don't recognise her. Have you searched for her on the *streets*?" she asked, emphasising the last word.

"What streets?"

"You know…'*the streets*'…"

Larisa gulped.

"Don't be offended, I was only asking."

"Ksenia would never do that."

"Not many of us would do that willingly, you know."

"Still, I don't think…"

"It won't hurt to try your luck. Even if you don't find her there, somebody might know something. Those people and places hold many secrets. The girls may not even be willing or allowed to talk to you but there's nothing to lose." She resumed her seed eating and shell spitting.

Their shadows were growing long. Larisa left the women chatting in the freckled saffron of twilight and headed towards her hotel, befuddled and restless. It had never crossed her mind that Ksenia might be caught in the foul web of sex tourism. Such a possibility was frightening.

Puce

Another night passed, where broken sleep and sweat ensured an unwanted check-in with reality. It felt bearable while she slept – there was neither pain nor choking despair. Ksenia dreaded their return and startled when she heard the squeak of the door. However Nadea's light step came as a relief. She brought in another candle and some hot tea, which were laid on the floor next to Ksenia's motionless body.

"I'd like to show you something," she said. "Ksenia, please open your eyes for just one moment."

At the mention of her name, she looked up.

Nadea bore a slight, sad smile then turned her back and lifted her top.

"Can you see that little scar on my back?"

Ksenia could but did not react.

"The puce coloured mark on the bottom left of my lower back? C'mon, it's pretty obvious…"

Not getting a reply, Nadea carried on:

"I have been forced into this *business* with threats and violence just over a year ago when my godmother sold me to a trafficking gang in Turkey. She said she had found a cooking job for me at a rich person's house in Istanbul. I took the ferry from Odessa and a friend of hers met me on the other side of the Black Sea. The woman did take me to a rich home but it wasn't cooking that was required of me. I refused, rebelled and defied them hoping they'd get tired and eventually release me. Instead they carried on with the abuse and assaults till I ended up in hospital."

Nadea stopped briefly to check Ksenia's reaction but there was none.

She continued:

"Shortly after, I was taken to a clinic under the pretext of further treatment until I woke up one day under a drip. They told me I had fallen ill during some tests and had to be treated urgently. Nothing else was mentioned and I was taken back to the brothel a week later. The pain in my back was horrendous but they dosed me up with painkillers and applied heavy make-up before bringing troops of clients to the house. I was held captive with seven other Moldovan and Ukrainian girls. Not long after, I discovered the scar on my backside. I've been robbed of a kidney, Ksenia, but at least I am alive. After Turkey, I was then sold to Macedonia, Albania and now Italy."

Nadea spoke slowly and in a low voice.

"You remind me of myself and I don't want you to have to go through any more unnecessary pain. They won't release you, Ksenia, understand this! Instead they will destroy your spirit and body with alcohol, drugs and other sorts of abuses. I've seen it done before, trust me. A couple of months ago, there was a very pretty girl who also defied them. They barbarously bit her, knocked her teeth out, forced her to take drugs and then filmed a savage porn scene where she…Look, it's not my intention to scare you. I just don't want to let them destroy you. Let's plan how to escape instead."

The pain on Nadea's face and the furtive tears in her eyes spoke of genuine suffering and concern. Ksenia was overwhelmed to hear this, yet could not bring herself to say anything.

"Do you not want to get out of here? Is there nothing you'd like to live for?"

The tone of voice and its import made Ksenia's eyes fill silently with tears. She opened her palms, in tight fists till then, and revealed the sign of a cross on her right palm.

"Are you an orphan?" Nadea asked, aware of abandoned children who, in order to establish some kind of family ties in their solitary world, form bonds of blood with other fellow orphans by cutting skin open.

"No, although I have no siblings and I'm not particularly close to my parents either."

Ksenia's throat felt dry and she took a sip of the black tea offered to her before carrying on.

"The dearest people in the world I have, apart from my boyfriend, are my blood sisters – Doina and Larisa. They both have the same cross marked on their hands too."

Nadea held Ksenia's hand compassionately, looking at the symbol etched onto this flimsy, icy palm.

"You will definitely see them again but you have to play by their rules for now. Tell Madame that you agree to work for them. We'll keep a low profile and plan our escape."

Ksenia hesitated.

"You don't have any other choice right now."

Ksenia nodded reluctantly.

"OK, but don't use my real name...Call me...I don't know...Scarlet, from now on...Also get me a pair of scissors."

Donkey-Brown

Old and regular customers usually had their favourites, which they requested time and again. Frequenters of brothels seem to be the faithful type.

The girls had to parade almost naked in front of new clients, so that they could choose their dish. Some made up their minds quickly, others had to touch and squeeze before savouring the delicacy. Most others couldn't care less. All they wanted was *to fuck something*.

The girls stopped being *somebody* the moment they were pushed into that whirlwind of human vice and perversity. It was a world unknown to the freshly shorn Ksenia, but a real and an extremely populated one nonetheless. The demand for it was high, the supply was always matched, willingly or otherwise and the market flourished.

When Ksenia was picked out to offer carnal services for the first time, her body froze and she couldn't speak. The hairy-pawed client, his hair a thinning donkey-brown mane, got on with the business matter of factly. Basic, primal instinct was let loose in all its aggression and force. He handled her like someone handled worthless things: defiling, abusing, scorning.

She closed her eyes in an attempt to shut off and escape as far away from it as possible but her awareness was brought back regularly by his loud, hoggish grunts and stale whiffs of garlic.

Clammy fistfuls of saliva were inserted vigorously and forcefully inside her numb body.

Pink

Ksenia thought of her boyfriend every day. Not knowing what happened to him and where he was made her sick with worry.

"Is he looking for me? Is he alive?"

The thought of her circumstances filled her heart with desperation and she was crumbling from within. Galea – or Madame as she was known in the house – refused to answer any questions Ksenia asked about that fateful night.

"Boris loves me and could not have left willingly. What if Galea is lying? He has plenty of money to pay them off. I'm sure he'd have fought for me. He's strong. What if he's been killed or something? Of course I'm alive because of the commodity I've got to trade. What about Boris? Have they dispatched my boyfriend? I have to find him at all costs."

Ksenia chose to live in the past, banishing the present almost entirely. Her only comfort was to sink into happy memories, which consisted either of her boyfriend or her blood sisters.

She'd never been close to her parents.

Tamara, her mother, was an accountant at the district Courts of Justice, and had never really forgiven her daughter for not following in her footsteps. Petru on the other hand was an alcoholic in denial who praised Communism the more he drank. He advised Ksenia to become a member of the party because he argued, that way she *would want for nothing*.

She never listened to what her father had to say, mainly because he was never sober enough to be aware of his words. Neither did she want to end up like her mother, whom she saw from an early age stuffing bribes and dirty money into a sock under the mattress.

Instead Ksenia followed her heart and studied fine art, a talent she nurtured from her grandfather. He was the best potter in a five village radius and used to hand-make kitchenware for his own use, as well as for thriving sales at weekend markets.

With such an innate gift, Ksenia also worked hard to improve her skills and painted whenever there was time to spare.

She would never forget the moment her mother discovered her choice of degree. The mixture of emotions battling for dominance in Tamara's eyes were all too familiar to Ksenia: guilt, disappointment, despair, sadness, anger and blame. A quick exchange of glances spoke volumes and sealed the nature of their relationship for years to come.

During her final year at university Ksenia met Boris and fell in love with him from their first encounter. She was out at a bar celebrating her twenty-third birthday when a young guy approached and sang *Happy Birthday* to her, almost shyly. Tall – if a little on the gangly side – he wasn't the best looking but Ksenia was swiftly won over by his quiet and unassuming charm. The reluctant admission of his judo accomplishments, which could have sounded boastful from other Moldovan men, was undercut by the confession that he only took up the sport after years of being bullied at school.

They started going out soon after, seeing each other as often as Boris's busy schedule with his family's export business allowed. Always apologetic, he said he helped his father sell crops abroad, hence the frequent travels.

Despite, or perhaps because of, the long absences, Boris treated Ksenia well, taking her to movies and buying her flowers. There was something unpredictable about him and he always managed to surprise Ksenia, like when he handed her a bunch of pink snapdragons.

"They are unusual flowers for a gift." She didn't know what to say.

"Roses are over-rated. Isn't it refreshing to get something else instead? I went for a less popular choice. You know me – I am my own man and do not like to follow the crowds." He smiled humbly.

They got on well, never arguing during their six months together. There was just one occasion that had Ksenia slightly perplexed.

Shortly before they travelled to Italy, he gave her a sparkling silver ring. It wasn't an engagement ring, rather *'a simple present to remind her of his love'*.

"It's not the real thing, I know, but it doesn't need to be when it looks it, right?"

The gesture was adorable, yet the choice of words accompanying it made Ksenia uneasy. Boris's comment didn't sit right with her somehow but she disregarded it, ascribing it to her tendency to over-analyse.

The more Ksenia thought about her boyfriend, the more she missed him, praying day and night to reunite soon.

Her heart was also torn to pieces thinking of Doina and Larisa. They'd been her world since growing up and she had never felt their absence as painfully as she did then, not even when Larisa emigrated to England.

Each night, or more precisely, each morning, after having slaved away till the crack of dawn, Ksenia fell into bed exhausted, in agony and tears.

Cinereous

Despite major reservations and after much agitation, Larisa decided to follow the sunflower-seed-eater's advice and began looking for Ksenia in the red-light districts of the cities she visited.

What initially seemed an unlikely endeavour became part of a strange and painful routine. She trotted those soulless areas scouting faces – empty faces, angry faces, drunk faces, drugged faces, dead faces; nonetheless some were familiar, pale, cinereous faces from prior trips.

Many girls walked away not willing to waste their precious time on something that wasn't going to bring them cash. Others approached, asking with a sad smile: *"Still no news of Ksenia?"* – thus shattering any harboured hopes.

Larisa could only shake her head and ask after their own lives, with all the predictable and unpredictable, heard and unheard of intricacies customary to life in the red-light district of a European city. Some blamed circumstances, others cursed themselves and many were content with their share in this life of subjective realities. A vast array of professions and ages, thrust together indiscriminately by the wicked waves of life.

Emigration is a double-edged sword. Financially it can offer high rewards, providing for a better lifestyle, opportunities and supposedly a rosy future. Psychologically, it can be disastrous. Forcing people to trade identities overnight, it is responsible for much inner turmoil. Doctors become cleaners, teachers become carers and architects become handymen. Those with no skills to trade other than their bodies often take to the street in order to survive. Unable to adjust to the upheaval of displacement – maimed personalities emerge, crippling the potential of entire generations.

This side of migration is rarely, if ever, discussed in the host countries, which tend to dehumanise the whole issue, solely concerning themselves with what the phenomenon does to their economy. The individuals and their lives are, at best, ignored and disregarded, or they are blamed for the adverse socio-economic affairs blighting the countries they emigrate to.

Part Two

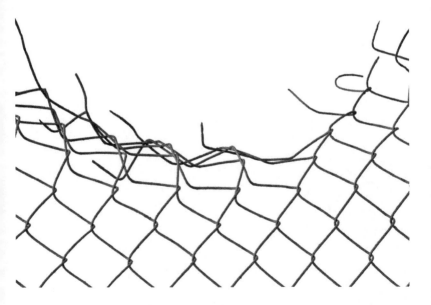

Ivory

Winter had set in and there was still no news of Ksenia. Despite the approaching holidays, Larisa was walking the streets of Milan warmed only by hope and faith. The thin coat she had brought from London was no match for the rapidly deteriorating Lombardy weather. Determined to finish her rounds before flying to Moldova to spend Christmas with Doina, she walked fast, blowing into her hands. The sharp chill bit at her cheeks relentlessly, a constant reminder of the dropping temperatures. Larisa knew how much Ksenia hated the cold and hoped she was at least warm wherever she was.

For as long as she had known her, Ksenia carried baked potatoes in her pockets during winter time. They were her portable and re-chargeable heaters. She laid them by the ridge of the kitchen stove so they absorbed maximum heat without overcooking. The *batteries* lasted a long time, unless she took one tumble too many in which case they became mash that was then immediately shared with Larisa and Doina. It was years before Ksenia realised that was the result Doina and Larisa wanted to achieve all along by pushing and shoving her in the snow constantly.

Unlike Ksenia, Larisa loved winter and its blessings. Since primary school, she had developed the habit of reading shoe-prints in the snow. Walking home after class every day, she had taken to searching for her mother's prints, wanting to know if they pointed home or not and how fresh they were. She could spot them without trouble, recognising their patterns and her mother's small but determined stride. Larisa could also tell how long Silvia had been home. That gave her a clue as to how warm the house would be and if dinner was ready. The snow revealed every move and she could tell if her mother had stopped anywhere on the way, if she had been to Baba Liuba to pick up milk or whether she'd called at Mos Maxim's to give him his daily injection.

The snow turned the road into an open book for Larisa. She could read its tales – and there were many for such a small village. Judging by his prints and their position in relation to the others on the road, Larisa learned when her father visited his mistress.

The ivory, satin canvas of snow sketched people's moves and gossiped about their private lives. Intruding into their innermost secrets, it made them public knowledge for prying eyes. When stories became entangled and difficult to decipher, a new layer of snow gave rise to another chapter, with further twists and revelations.

The snow taught Larisa a great deal. More than anything else it taught her that communication did not always mean words or sound. On the contrary, the basic transmission of knowledge or information could be just as well, if not better, carried out in the absence of those. The snow instilled in her the essence of silent perception.

Thanks to the tell-tale transparency of the snow, Larisa had learned to step into other people's footprints, thus hiding her own. Not that she had any reason to hide them, not at that point in her life anyway. It was just a game she played should anyone be tempted to track down her movements. She had one follower, which Larisa knew about even at that age, courtesy of her Eastern upbringing, but there was no hiding from it. Yet she enjoyed tremendously the bid of confusing and perhaps throwing it off her tracks now and again – oh, the illusion of thinking you are tricking Time!

Larisa thought to use her skills of reading into the snow in the city of Milan too but the sheer number of prints was disorienting and frustrating.

"*The comfortable anonymity of a big city,*" she thought ruefully. The exact thing she'd always sought – now a hindrance.

After another fruitless weekend in Italy, Larisa flew home to celebrate Christmas. Since emigrating to England, she hadn't returned often but on that occasion she felt it was imperative for her and Doina to be together.

Blizzard-Blue

Every winter the Moldovan authorities introduce forced annual electricity savings, switching it off daily between five and ten in the evening. Like burrows, entire villages are left in the dark and hibernation is tacitly encouraged.

Guests and visitors do not venture out during these times – roads are a liability in daytime, let alone at night. The five senses become useless. Only locals can avoid the traps, latching on to memory, habit and intuition.

Night takes on a different meaning in the rural space, away from towns and cities where there is always light from street lamps, shop windows and cars.

In the countryside, the darkness is such as it was meant to be on Earth when it was first created. The primitive night is nothing but a womb. Its essence pertains to the domain of experience, rendering linguistics obsolete.

The only light during the long wintry nights in the village of Marani – like many others across the country – derives from beeswax candles, earthen lamps and the jolly fires in the brick stoves. Outdoors, the bulbless lamp-posts are totally useless and only the snow acts as nature's lantern. When the thick, fine-powdered blankets descend upon the world, their immaculate brightness turns night into day.

In preparation for the Christmas holidays, every household swings into action: cleaning, cooking, baking, mending, drinking.

The landscape too, is in perpetual motion: houses – like small mushrooms half buried in snow – puff with passion from their sooty chimneys, lacing hallucinatory images on the boundless canvas of the blizzard-blue sky.

As soon as Larisa left the main road and turned into the smaller streets leading to her house, she slowed down. The snow was thick and she trod with difficulty. At least she'd arrive to a warm house and hot food: her mother's freshest shoe-prints pointed home. However, they were not the same marks she'd always known.

Larisa felt a pang. Her mother's steps were getting lighter and her stride even shorter. She realised it was not only impossible to trick time – but wishing away the havoc it could wreak upon loved ones was just as futile.

When she reached the neighbourhood, it began snowing and the wind stepped up a few notches, growing into a full-blown blizzard. As she opened the house door it forcibly pushed to enter in with her. They had a tug-of-war for a couple of seconds before Larisa was safely in.

"Close the door quickly, Larisa," Trofim called from the back of the room. "I have kept the fire on the whole day and here you are – inviting the storm into the house."

"Whatever happened to *hello* these days, Father?"

He smiled and gave her a big bear hug.

Even though she had cleaned her boots of all snow, Larisa didn't realise her coat was covered in it too. Silvia took her outside again and with a milo-straw broom swept the white fluff off, carefully enough not to brush her daughter's feet.

As every Bessarabian knows, one never gets married should a broom sweep over your feet.

"Why are you wearing this coat? It might be enough for the British winters but it won't get you far around here. You know what happens if you get sick, don't you?"

Larisa nodded and said nothing.

Bathing in badger's fat, that's what happened when she got sick. The amount Silvia used to smear her daughter with from head to toe made it feel that way.

The traditional cure for colds, asthma, bronchitis and even tuberculosis, the badger's fat is in great demand as an alternative medicine. Thanks to their dietary choices of various medicinal roots, the badgers seal their fate with the like of my people.

The spicy-sour aroma of the *borsch* keeping warm on the stove spread all over the house and Larisa wolfed down a couple of bowls. The rest of the family had already eaten. Her brothers, Oleg and Slavic, played cards on the *lejanca*. Trofim watched a Russian Second World War movie and Silvia was baking *Craciunei* and *kolachi* – ring bread to symbolise eternity – and other traditional pastry-wreaths prepared at Christmas time.

Ensconced by the fireplace after her meal, Larisa watched her mother's dedication in shaping and braiding the dough to her own specifications. Silvia was renowned in the community for her creativity when it came to making the loaves as rich and detailed as possible. She always ended up baking a lot more than her family could ever eat and many were given as presents or alms to relatives and neighbours. Perhaps that was Silvia's intention all along.

As the electricity was switched off, Trofim fumbled to light the earthen lamps and candles. Even though they were never moved from their designated place – on a wooden shelf above the sofa – Trofim still managed to cause pandemonium: tripping on the carpet and hitting the table, breaking plates and swearing like a tractor driver.

When he finally brought about some light, the atmosphere changed instantly. The world suddenly became a fairy tale domain. Each object in the room stirred to life with a fluttering shadow. The candles next to the window betrayed the furious blast of the wind outside, duly passing its energy on to all who witnessed their flicker. Due to the number of candles, Silvia's moving form was distorted erratically and her silhouette acquired a mystical dimension.

Idly caressed by the heat of the stove, Larisa looked out the window. The blizzard was still unleashing its force mercilessly, flurrying the snow in random sweeps and swells. It whistled and howled at the cornices of every house, reminding people of their insignificance. The trees, full of ice, bent furiously from side to side in an attempt to shake it off. Heavily burdened, it seemed they would un-root themselves at any time and run haywire.

So much motion and yet a world so perfectly still!

That was another reason Larisa loved winter. She found it the most generous season in matters of spirituality. It had the power to freeze time and space, blessing people with a glimpse of eternity.

Nothing to do.

Nowhere to hurry.

Time gradually slowed down till it surrendered totally to sleep.

Tick-tock, tick-tock. The comfort of wintry reveries!

"Silviaaaaaa!!!"

The voice calling from the courtyard was unmistakable. Baba Liuba – a half deaf, half blind old woman who lived alone at the edge of their neighbourhood – used to keep them company many a night during the long winters of Larisa's childhood.

Things, it seemed, hadn't changed. As soon as the electricity went off, before Larisa could count to sixty, there was Baba Liuba banging on their gate. Her favourite spot was the inglenook. An old cat warming her bones, she was happiest by the fireplace, spinning out wool into thin thread faster than the eye could keep pace with. Her dexterity and skills were still unmatched by any young woman of the village. Her aged, weak eyes were not much use any more in that type of labour, but her bony hands and crooked fingers followed a well-established pattern of turning wool into perfect fibre, while her loose mouth rattled non-stop putting the world right.

"Why are you wayfaring in foreign lands when there *ith* no *plathe* like home?" the old woman squinted.

"*Funny*," Larisa thought, "*that people who have never left the country should say that.*"

Instead she replied:

"So I can appreciate it more."

"Speak up or come closer."

Larisa chose to keep her distance.

"And why are you *wathting* time with that book now?" Baba Liuba carried on, obviously perturbed by Larisa's impertinence with trivialities like travelling or reading books – something she'd lived her entire life happily without.

Baba Liuba was just heating up.

"*Thilvia*, give your daughter *thome* wool to comb – it'll be more *uthful*."

The heavy lisp was worse than Larisa remembered and she put it down to Baba Liuba's loss of more teeth with age. In fact, she noticed, Baba Liuba's mouth had become totally toothless.

"The young generation is pampered these days. Your daughter *hath* to learn *thome* manual work, you know," she carried on unabated.

"Leave her alone, Baba Liuba." Silvia spoke into the old woman's ear. "Everything in its own time."

"Oh my days, *Thilvia*, what kind of future do you want for your daughter? I bet she can't even cook, can she?" The old woman was steaming. "You should get the dowry ready, teach her *thome* cooking skills and I'll take it upon myself to find her a *nith* husband."

The crone then dashed towards Larisa with the speed of a young maiden. Chanting rapidly under her breath, globules of spit shot through her thin lips stretched back over toothless gums. Larisa's favourite *Gap* top changed from bright orange to a freckled brown, mottled with saliva.

The ritual of incantations involves blowing with a wet mouth. The combination of the air blown and the saliva is considered to be a composition of medicine. The ratio of the mixture has to be right but in the case of Baba Liuba's hollow mouth, the exact quota of precipitation could not be controlled.

The steamy air of the breath includes blessed verses and supplications meant to have a powerful effect. They are sung in a quick beat, similar to what you might call a Rap style but in a low voice or a whisper. The power of the sound is especially strong when coupled with the moisture of breath because it involves emotions, focus and deep engagement with the task at hand. The words themselves do not make much sense – they are not meant to. It is the sound that comes out and the intention from within that's paramount.

Baba Liuba's whispers were devilish and Larisa sprang off the coach as if burnt by acid. There were only two heated rooms in the whole house where she could escape. Outside it was still snowing.

Despite her age, the old woman followed closely as a shadow, chanting and spitting left, right and centre:

"Garden of nine nooks
Bird of nine beaks
of nine flying wings
of nine puffy feet
I stir the lake
Lake stirs the crab
Crab stirs the devil
Devil stirs the luck
So that a good man shall wed her
Sedulous, loquacious
Wherever he'll walk
At Larisa he'll stop
Wherever he'll hike
Larisa he'll find."

"Is she barking mad? Sedulous, loquacious? Who says I want to marry somebody like that? She can keep him to herself, thank you very much," Larisa thought, still jumping around the room.

"Oh my days, *Thilvia* – your precious girl is cursed. She's got the devil inside her. Your child is *pothethed*. You should take her to a monastery, before it's too late."

Silvia grew uncomfortable and decided to change the subject, addressing her daughter sternly:

"Can you make us some tea?"

Pleasantries such as *please* and *thank you* are not common parlance amongst my people.

Larisa filled the kettle with water freshly melted from the snow outside and stuffed it with hibiscus stems and flowers. It was one of the traditional teas alongside linden blossom, mint and other wild herbs dried earlier in the year for that purpose.

She dipped the kettle further into the stove to boil the tea faster.

The design of Bessarabian heater-cookers in rural areas is very old, their origins lost in the mists of time. Each possesses two or three different size holes, one slightly bigger than the other. All of them get covered with three or four sets of Frisbee-type spheres made of iron hoops, until the hole is completely covered. The heat can be controlled pretty well that way. If something requires quick cooking, the hoops are removed and the pot is sunk in up to its handles. If, on the other hand, it needs to be slowed down, simmered or just kept warm, the hoops are replaced until the hole is gradually or completed covered. Practical enough, the method is manual and therefore dangerous should the cook lose control of the piping hot hoops. They travel far and burn deeply whatever comes their way.

The tea boiled in a couple of minutes and as Larisa was serving it to her mother and Baba Liuba, Doina called in.

"Good evening and glad to have found you all well," she greeted them in the traditional manner.

Larisa didn't feel well at all after Baba Liuba's earlier attack but was not in the mood to argue with the presumptuous norm of conventionality.

"You are just in time for a cup of tea."

She rubbed her hands excitedly and came closer to the fireplace.

"Any news from Italy?"

Larisa shook her head.

"It's the Thursday before Christmas tomorrow," Silvia reminded everyone. "Come and join in the ritual sometime before noon."

Larisa knew what that meant – the bloody slaughter of another pig. It was the day of the year Larisa wished was erased from the calendar altogether.

"*Barbaric and sinister*," that's how she described it.

The killing of animals is part of everyday life in a Bessarabian village. Yet the slaying of the pig, even though it carries the same ultimate goal of filling the gut, possesses a ceremonial character bordering on macabre theatre. It is an age long tradition pre-dating Christianity and has nothing to do with Christmas. Yet, no one ever questions it and – Larisa knew – raising any opposition whatsoever in such a carnivorous country was tantamount to social suicide.

Crimson

Larisa woke up early the next day but she was reluctant to get out of bed. Without the fire in the stove, early mornings were almost Siberian. Her thoughts went to Costica, the pig shortly to be stabbed. As a child, she chose to adopt piglets as pets, which unfortunately were always slaughtered the following Christmas, regardless of her feelings.

"Don't cry, you will get another Costica next year," Trofim tried to comfort his daughter each time.

Year in, year out, Larisa went through the same trauma. Despite it, she carried on making pigs her pets and gave them all identical names. Black sense of humour or morbid fascination with life, death and dominion? Perhaps it went deeper – into pain and denial...She never dared to seek the answer.

The blizzard had raged the whole night and by morning drifts of snow had almost buried the entire village.

"Trofim, wake up. I can't open the door because of the snow. Get the shovel and dig some tracks in the yard." Silvia always had difficulty waking her husband up.

Trofim didn't budge.

"Jump out of that bed for God's sake. There is a lot to clear up." She shoved him with the hand-forged stove poker.

By late morning everything was rolling: the stove roared, hosting two dancing pots full of bubbling water; knives were shining bright – Trofim had been sharpening them for the last few days. His two brothers had arrived to help with the slaughter of the animal. It was a big job and it usually required a few people to carry it out.

Everyone was excited.

Larisa was anxious.

They didn't have to wait too long – the shrieks of poor Costica ripped loudly through the frozen air.

He wasn't the only one. The entire day was a continuous echo of pigs' frightful squeals and roosters' cries. These animals were the best contributors to the meat jelly dishes – traditional Moldovan food cooked for special occasions.

The smell of burned meat enveloped the village. Silvia picked the boiling water from the stove and handed it to Larisa.

"Take these buckets to your father and come back for more when they are finished and don't cry like you did in the old days!"

The moment she turned the house corner, the world was bathed in red. The steaming, hot blood had melted last night's snow and the back yard was reduced to a crimson puddle. The contrast with the other world couldn't have been broader and the immaculate snow which had blessed the garden with its impeccable touch only the night before was all but memory now.

"*Perhaps it didn't happen,*" Larisa thought.

What proof does human memory have to satisfy certainty, objectivity or truth? There's a fine line between memory and imagination and who can tell where one ends and the other starts?

"*Am I going crazy?*" She desperately looked around for pegs to support her sanity.

Beyond their garden, an infinity of snow glittered in sunshine and Larisa sighed with relief. The wintry vista offered reassurance.

"Come on closer, join the kids," her father teased her.

The custom is a celebrated family event and everybody is involved in it one way or another. As soon as the pig is butchered, it gets singed all over with clumps of straw used to remove its coarse hair and imbue the meat with a smoky, roasted flavour.

Afterwards the beast is wrapped in old coats and jackets to keep it warm and soften its skin. To foreigners this may not seem a very hygienic procedure, but then very few things can be when living in those rural conditions.

With the dead body securely covered, children rejoice and fight each other to clumber aboard the charred creature. They can sit three, four or more depending on how big the victim is or how old the riding savages are. Chewing on singed tail and ears, they scream in deranged excitement.

"Have you changed your mind? You're never too old to sit on the pig. Go on, it's a lot of fun."

Larisa didn't move.

"Is this your idea of a happy Christmas, Father?"

"What do you mean? It is something we've been doing for generations. I've seen my own father and grandfathers do it."

"It's cruel and unnecessary."

"I tell you what – you've been living in England for too long. I think it's time you returned home for good. Forget about the West – people there have no soul and are only concerned with making money."

145

"Where is your soul, Father, torturing an innocent animal like that?" Larisa raised her voice, gesturing towards the scorched body of Costica."

"What are you talking about? This is part of our culture and heritage. C'mon darling, don't get angry. Here – try this." Trofim held out a chunk of pork ear, like he had done so many times in the past with his daughter's piglet-pets.

Cerise

A couple of days before Christmas, Ksenia's landlady called. Larisa and Doina had kept in touch with Maya regularly.

She was a forty-year-old woman who had been widowed in her early twenties. Leonid was sent to the Transnistrian war four months after their wedding. The military conflict between the Moldovan forces and the separatists in Transnistria – the eastern territory left of Nistru River – started in the aftermath of the USSR disintegration.

Transnistria became a political entity in 1924 with the proclamation of the Moldovan Autonomous Soviet Socialist Republic – Moldovan ASSR – which consisted mostly of today's Transnistria and an area from Ukraine but nothing from Bessarabia, which at the time was part of Romania. One of the reasons for the creation of Moldovan ASSR was that the Soviet Union would eventually incorporate Bessarabia, which it did in 1940, with the aid of a secretive and illegal protocol between Ribbentrop and Molotov. Thus the Moldovan Soviet Socialist Republic (SSR) was created, which lasted until 1991. As a result of the USSR collapse, the

Moldovan SSR *regained* its independence and became the Republic of Moldova.

Out of a fear that Moldova would unite with Romania, the Russian and Ukrainian populations in the eastern region of the country – Transnistria – were manipulated into rebellion. They were soon assisted by the Russian 14th Army – a descendant of the Soviet Army and mercenaries – many of them freshly absolved prisoners from jails all over Russia, who settled in Transnistria for years. In fact the Russian army refuses to leave to this day, under the pretext of peacekeeping. Russia's interest in my territory, their gateway to the Balkans, is as strong as ever.

Since the ceasefire agreement in 1992, Moldova has had no control or influence over Transnistria, which is an unrecognised entity and therefore prohibited from signing any international agreements or conventions. It is a no man's land where crime, corruption and all kinds of racketeering breed and thrive – an issue ignored by the rest of Europe.

Leonid – like many other young Bessarabian lads, whose official numbers have not been revealed by the authorities – never returned from the war. Many who returned did so crippled. The thousands of middle-aged invalids, up and down the country, their limbs blown off in a useless war, are silent testimony to that atrocity.

Maya vowed to not marry again. The forty-year-old woman preserved a cheerful demeanour despite all life had thrown at her. Her chubby cheeks and full figure offered a stark contrast to her bouncy ponytail and her trilling teenage giggle.

Hardly the *femme fatale*, Larisa thought, yet Maya always had a few different boyfriends on the go. They looked after her various needs and provided for a comfortable lifestyle, since the authorities had not helped with anything.

"*He died fighting for this country and yet I have never received a leu, not even at his funeral,*" she told anyone willing to listen. "*I still love my dead husband but a widow has to survive somehow.*"

Not having any siblings or children of her own, Maya had always got on well with Ksenia and viewed her as a younger sister. When her lodger of nearly five years disappeared, the landlady suffered enormously, having lost someone close for a second time. She phoned Doina and Larisa often to see if there were any news about Ksenia.

Silvia had to call out twice to her daughter, who was busy decorating the Christmas tree with Doina.

"Maya's on the phone."

Larisa washed the glitter off her hands.

"Hi Maya. How's it going? Happy Christmas!"

"I've got some news."

Maya's anxious talk made Larisa uneasy.

"Good or bad?"

"I don't know…"

"What is it?"

"Boris was here a few minutes ago."

"What?"

"Yes, he said he missed Ksenia and wanted to have some of her things to remind him of her."

Larisa was baffled and couldn't find her words.

Maya carried on.

"I didn't let him in and said he could come tomorrow instead. I wanted you two to be here. Make sure you are at my flat before ten in the morning."

Next day Larisa and Doina arrived at Maya's flat as instructed. The three of them speculated about Boris's visit.

"He seemed sad and dejected," Maya was filing her nails.

"I just don't understand why he hasn't got in touch with us earlier."

"I hope he's not the bearer of bad news."

"I asked him through the door if he knew where Ksenia was. He said he didn't…"

"This is all very strange, don't you think?" Larisa frowned.

"Let's not jump to conclusions. You never really liked him anyway. The guy might have something to say for himself."

There was a knock on the door. The three of them jumped and went to open it. Boris stood in the hallway, leaning on the peeling wall, his head drooping.

"Come in."

Still standing in the middle of the room, he eyed Doina and Larisa with red, watery eyes.

"I am sorry. I'm so, so sorry!"

"Take a seat." Doina had just enough time for a touch of hospitality before Larisa began grilling him.

"Where is Ksenia?"

"I think of her day and night…It's all my fault…"

"What happened, Boris?"

"I'm sorry I couldn't save her."

"What do you mean? She's not dead, is she?"

"No…I don't know…she wasn't…"

"This doesn't make any sense. Start from the beginning."

"They've destroyed my life…"

"Who are *they*?"

"A Moldovan gang, trafficking women in Italy…I don't remember much – I think our drinks had been spiked. They beat me up and threatened to kill Ksiusha if I went to the police. I didn't want to put her life in danger…"

Even though Larisa had been looking for Ksenia in the red-light districts of the Italian cities, from Milan to Naples, nothing could prepare her or Doina for the feared confirmation of such awful news: their beloved friend was indeed being exploited as a sex slave abroad.

"Why didn't you contact us earlier?"

Boris paused and took a deep sigh.

"I couldn't face you or her family. I feel guilty and ashamed. All that judo training and I couldn't protect my princess…"

"We need to let the police know about it. This is new evidence, the authorities will have to reopen the file now."

"Did you not hear me? If they catch wind that I've gone to the police, Ksiusha will suffer. I won't live with myself if they kill her. Anyway, like I told you, I don't remember much so there's nothing I could say that would help the case…"

"Are you kidding? We've got to get the police involved."

"The gang said they wouldn't keep Ksiusha for long."

"And do you trust them? It's already been over six months." Even Doina was loosing her cool. "When will they let her go? What if Ksenia doesn't make it through to the time she's freed?"

"Only God knows how much I suffer. Not one day passes without me thinking of things I could have or should have done differently. It drives me crazy. Trust me, I want to help but I'm too scared it may harm my Ksiusha."

"Listen, Boris, with your help or without, we'll keep on searching for our friend. I can't believe you've given up like that."

"Please don't be so cruel. I love my princess more than anything in the world…"

"Why are you here now?" Larisa cut him short.

"I came to fetch some of her things to remind me of her, a scarf or a dress or anything with her scent on it."

Maya brought one of the bags in which she had stored Ksenia's things. Boris picked out a cerise scarf and a little black dress.

"Can I also have those peacock earrings? They were a special present from me and are her favourites. I'd like to keep them as a token of love and give them to her again when I see her next. Nothing will make her more happy."

Boris placed the things carefully in his bag and turned to leave.

"Let us know if you change your mind. I'm sure Ksenia would appreciate it." Larisa had not taken her drilling eyes off Boris since the minute he entered the flat.

"I wish you understood…"

"Give us your number in case there is any news." Doina handed him a piece of paper. "You have ours, right?"

Boris nodded.

He walked out looking doleful as a drenched hen.

The door had hardly closed when Larisa flared up.

"I can't believe this is an ex-judo wrestler."

"It's not easy for him either. He is crushed by guilt."

"Doina, he is a man and should behave like one. Feeling sorry for himself is not going to bring Ksenia back."

"The trouble with our men, I tell you, is that they lack in spirit," Maya said with the confident air that can only spring from experience. "Our men are weak. They are only at their best when there is a woman behind them. Otherwise they are empty. Trust me, I know what I'm saying."

"Boris is no different from the majority of Moldovans who let their wives go abroad for work and they themselves stay behind, drinking and whimpering."

"That's not really the case, Larisa."

"It is. He knows Ksenia is suffering, wherever she is, yet does nothing to try and save her. He could at least be more proactive, that's all I'm saying."

"You sound so foreign talking like that."

"What does it even mean, this *practive* word?" Maya wanted to know.

"That Boris could move his arse and help us find Ksenia," Larisa obliged. "I wouldn't want to generalise…actually no, I am happy to generalise, and I am sorry if it upsets you, but he does seem to represent the psyche of the Moldovan male."

"You are exaggerating," Doina stood up and got ready to go.

"I don't think she is," Maya offered in support. "I've been saying this for years. Our men fall into two categories – alcoholics or criminals."

"C'mon now, there are plenty of honest men around. Well, apart from my father of course, who ticks both those boxes…"

Larisa and Maya exchanged glances, smiling.

"Look at all the well-to-do men in this country: the police, those in the security sector, customs, government. What do they all have in common? They are all notorious for taking bribes and breaking the law. I should know – I've had plenty of them in my bed." Maya winked. "The rest of our men turn to drinking and their wives are forced to look abroad for means to survive."

"Men go abroad too," Doina said, even though she knew she had lost the argument.

"There are twice as many women as men working in foreign countries."

"I just think that you two are disproportionately and excessively critical. We've got to give them the benefit of the doubt."

"No need when the facts speak for themselves, Doina. Let's go."

The girls left the city with a mixture of emotions. Their happiness that Ksenia was still alive had been overshadowed by the stark thought of what she must be going through.

Ghost-White

The clock had long struck noon and Ksenia was still in bed – not asleep and not quite awake either. She must have cried in her sleep for her face was wet and her throat felt dry. The bitter taste of cheap make-up crept into her mouth and the reality of the dark days hit her with the power of a tidal wave. Her bruised lilac skin and aching body instantly brought back the whole awareness of where she was, as much as she despised and resisted it.

A strong urge to close her eyes again overwhelmed Ksenia but something more primal kicked in – fear. She had learned it the hard way. If not gilded up before the first client arrived, she would be punished and there wasn't much more her feeble body could take. Neither was she curious to find out.

Getting dressed was a long ritual, not because of the dressing part – there was hardly anything to put on – but the bruises and bashes were taking longer to conceal. Her weak body easily betrayed any abuse inflicted on it and a lengthy process was required each day to cover a painful reality.

"Still in bed? It's Christmas today! Get up now or I will send in the boys to give you a hand," Madame warned as she entered the dormitory.

It could hardly be called a dormitory. Many of the girls slept on the floor due to lack of space – the rest of the rooms in the house were reserved for business purposes. They got used to taking turns sleeping on the floor. Ksenia didn't mind that and would have happily kept that corner of the ground to herself. Unfortunately, though, privacy was amongst the very first things she was stripped of when falling into their tight claws, alongside honour, pride, choice and pretty much everything else, including consciousness the first few times she resisted their will.

Before leaving the room, Madame felt the need to prompt her again:

"I expect you to be in reception as soon as possible. It's a special day today – Jesus was born, if you don't mind me reminding you. We are expecting some important guests later on and they'll need to be specially taken care of. Get ready now."

Ksenia knew she had to shake off the comfort of sleep straight away. Madame wasn't the joking type and another confrontation with her watchdogs wasn't at all appealing, to say the very least. Both Ghena and Igor were on standby like a pair of vicious, if not psychotic, watchdogs straining at the leash to sort out any issues.

Digging deep, Ksenia plucked whatever mental and physical strength she could muster in order to start another day.

She shuffled to the bathroom. It was never empty and its door lock had been removed as a security measure, preventing anyone from grabbing any privacy. It took her a while to become comfortable with other people being around.

A few girls were chatting, busy arranging their skimpy Christmas outfits in preparation for the work shift to start soon. Others were taking care of various bodily needs, totally oblivious to their intrusive noises. Cheap, red lingerie for Miss Santas were handed out: bustiers with ruffles, buckle or feather marabou G-strings, lace-ups, stockings and garters.

Ksenia stopped in the bathroom doorway and looked in the mirror. An emotionless, dishevelled face and scrawny figure stared defiantly back at her. No longer did she want, or have the ability, to identify herself with the alien image reflected in the glass.

"It's not me," she whispered, *"it's just a temporary mask that will eventually come off. It has to come off because I am suffocating in it."*

"Check you out, Miss, standing there admiring yourself," one of the girls sneered. "There is nothing to admire, apart from the various shades of blue on your skeletal body."

"Like a stick of mouldy cheese," somebody else jeered.

Their laughter came as an echo from another world, a world Ksenia did not want to be part of, yet could not escape. She was between the hammer and the anvil, a place which could only be called – limbo. A painful limbo.

"Leave her alone," another one replied in the same distant voice.

Ksenia ignored them and carried on gazing at the ghost-white figure cast in the mirror. She studied it closely as if meeting someone for the first time. It was a habitual undertaking each morning – the only time when she could see her real face, before it was hid under the vulgar masque heavy with make-up.

After splashing her face at length with cold water, forcing herself back into life, she walked to the window of the lounge to get a glimpse of the world outside. It was snowing peacefully, covering the ugliness of the world. The street below wasn't too busy. None of the people to-ing and fro-ing ever looked up, either to admire the beautiful snowflakes or at the girl's face squashed against the silent glass. Ksenia couldn't open the window without Madame's permission and she didn't feel like asking for it.

"It's time to make you beautiful," a voice called from behind.

It was the make-up girl.

All the other girls did it on their own but Ksenia said she wasn't good at it, hoping she'd be spared the whole charade. Madame would have none of it and ordered Angela to help out.

In fact Ksenia was very good at applying make-up. She learned to use her mother's vintage cake mascara from an early age. Spitting into the narrow, plastic box to moisten the hard-pressed powder, she painted each of her eyelashes individually with a match dipped in the black dye. The small brush had long been lost and Tamara was accustomed to using matches instead. Even though mother poked herself in the eye many times, Ksenia was far more accurate and successful practising that dangerous technique.

Being an artist, Ksenia was fond of colours and liked playing with them to express, alter or hide reality at her whim. However, she was not going to use those skills for something as degrading as decorating misery.

Without turning around, Ksenia pleaded:

"Start with the bruising on my back before you can do my face."

"*That*," she thought to herself, "*will give me more time to enjoy the view. Maybe I should ask permission to open the window and then just dive down. Maybe that's the only way out of here.*"

Instinctively she lifted her arm and looked at the small cross, etched deep into the flesh of her right

158

palm, the one that connected her to the two people most precious to her and remained the only ray of light in her ordeal. It dawned – death was not an option. She wanted to live.

Dun

The Moldovan authorities are loyal to the Russian Orthodox Church, which runs by the Julian Calendar – thirteen days behind the Gregorian one. Christmas therefore is observed on January 7th even though the New Year's fireworks are displayed on December 31st. Marking the birth of Christ according to one calendar and the New Year according to another defies common sense yet seems perfectly logical to those in power.

Torn between wanting to keep up with the rest of the world and staying true to their own traditions, many Bessarabians end up celebrating Christmas and New Year twice.

The old New Year – on January 14th, is defined by many traditions and rituals pre-dating Christianity. They go back to a time when pagan Romans celebrated *Saturnalia* – a winter festival dedicated to Saturn, the God of Agriculture.

Those early celebrations were loose and debauched, laced with masquerades, partying, drinking, naked singing and dancing, pagan rites and worshipping idolatrous deities. Due to the nature of the festival, early Christian leaders tried to overlap *Saturnalia* with the celebration of Christmas and convert the pagan holidays into Christian ones. They named its last day, December 25th, to be the day when Jesus was born. Even though many *Saturnalia* festivities had been absorbed into the celebration of Christmas with the passing of years, many practices or variations of them survived to the present day.

The Christian and pre-Christian elements of the holidays have lasted unhampered for thousands of years and reached such a natural fusion that there is a great deal of confusion between the two, much to the dismay of the Church and historians.

Bessarabians still practise variations of them. On the eve of the old New Year, cohorts of well-wishers go from house to house to wish a prosperous and abundant year ahead. The tradition is called the carol of the *Little Plough* and it is an agrarian folk custom, par excellence. The ballads recited vary in length and describe the sequence of agrarian work – from ploughing the land to baking the bread. At the end the hosts are wished a prosperous and abundant new year, for which the cohorts are thanked with sweets, biscuits, *kolachi*, some coins and even wine, if they are old enough.

The well-wishers are accompanied by cattle bells, whips and a traditional instrument called *Buhai*, in translation *'the bull'* or *'the ox'*, due to its bellowing. Their noise can go through the roof, often drowning all words.

The *Buhai* is an open-ended small barrel. Similar to a one-sided drum, it is fixed with a piece of goat or sheep skin. Through a hole made in the centre of the skin, a rope or a tuft of horsehair is passed. Two performers are usually needed to operate this instrument, one to hold it and the other to pull the horsehair in a milking motion. For a better grip and stronger sound, boys and young men dip their fingers in pickle juice or fermented wheat barn water.

Often the only audible words in all ballads and performances come at the beginning or at the end, when the well-wisher urges the rest to join him in a chorus with a loud "*Hai, Hai!*" exclamation.

Old people allow for this commotion, claiming the noise made with all these appurtenances chases away any malefic forces from the coming year: draught, hail, pests and animals inimical to crops.

Adults also form groups of well-wishers, scouring the villages later on at night. They are much more organised, performing with flutes, accordions and trumpets. Others perform humorous short skits involving the goat. One or two young lads equip themselves with horns, animal skin, multicoloured ribbons, beads, embroidered carpets, bright-coloured towels and all sorts of other celebratory materials. The goat is a pagan element representing the god of fertility. The skits show the goat dying and then being brought back to life, symbolising the death of winter and the birth of spring. Many of these traditions carry beliefs in the magic powers of the most important elements of life: the sun, fire, water, bread and plants.

The festivities continue till early the following morning on January 14th, when another peculiar custom is performed: people '*sow*' each other with whatever seeds they can lay their hands on: corn, wheat, rice – exchanging wishes of abundance, health and happiness.

Larisa always made a point of waking up early on January 14th because friends and relatives tended to come straight into her bedroom and scatter seeds all over the place.

After *sowing* Trofim and Silvia in the living room, Doina entered Larisa's bedroom, hurling grains at her:

"May you live and blossom
Like the apple-trees, like the pear-trees
In the middle of summer
Like the abundant autumn
of this year and of many more to come!"

"I can't believe you too are doing this to me," Larisa grumbled.

"Not good to react like that. The way you start the new year is the way you will end up spending it," she teased. "I am only wishing you well."

"It's not you who has to sleep in a bed full of cereal tonight. Where is the fun in that? I'll be thinking of you when I'm picking seeds out of my hair and sheets."

Sweeping the grains out is not to be done until the following day. Otherwise it means chasing away abundance and wealth.

"You sound like Ksenia now. Don't worry, you can throw them to the floor – just don't take them out of the house, Miss Grumpy."

"Thanks for enlightening me. I feel a lot better now."

Doina nudged.

"Come on, forget about that. Let's go see Florica, the cow."

The suggestion made Larisa smile. It was something the three of them used to do as young teens.

One of the many customs on this particular day is that young girls can find out when they'll marry by asking a cow. Doina, Ksenia and Larisa visited the mangy, dun animal in the barn first thing in the morning to update the information they had got from the yesteryear.

"Florica darling, tell me – when am I going to get married? This year? Next year?" – all the while kicking the resting cow every time a year was added.

At whatever number the animal stood up, the custom said, that would be the year the girl gets married. Doina and Ksenia took turns every other year. Unwilling to entrust her future to a dumb creature, Larisa was always out of the game. Out of all three of them, Ksenia was the one to take it most seriously and got upset if by the time they got to the barn, the cow was standing.

Taking Doina's suggestion as a joke, Larisa teased:

"Why? Do you want to find out if the year of your marriage has changed?"

"Actually, I was thinking about Ksenia. Maybe the cow can tell us when we'll find her."

"Not funny at all, Doina."

"I wasn't joking."

"That's even worse. Don't tell me you are willing to take the cow's *advice* on such a serious matter."

"It can't hurt."

"This is not exactly the right time to be superstitious, you know?"

"I'm desperate and willing to try anything, to be honest."

"We can't rely on consulting a dumb animal. We've got to find Ksenia as soon as possible no matter what the cow says."

Doina nodded reluctantly, thinking that if it was up to her, she'd still drop by the barn.

Unlike Ksenia, Doina was less superstitious yet much more tolerant of traditional lore than Larisa.

Wild Carmine

By March, Larisa had been to Italy four more times. Though the visits hadn't been fruitful, she kept serene and optimistic. The advance of spring certainly had something to do with it. Despite her love of winter, Larisa welcomed the change in seasons. Animals, plants and humans alike rejoiced and life redeemed what was its due. The sun chased away the old season, which, soft and flabby, scuttled away gradually, compliantly. Longer, warmer days came through, burning winter and tearing her to patches of dirty snow.

The New is always merciless towards the Old. That perhaps is a superficial observation, one of impression and not of substance. Intrinsic to the nature of cycle, the New becomes Old and the Old becomes New. Expelling the perception of Time from this complex equation reveals a double-faced reality. Akin to absorbing the symbolism of Janus, the Roman God of beginnings and endings, the apparent duality dissipates like dew upon the first rays of the sun: New and Old emerge as One. To grasp the totality of implications resulting from such a paradoxical assertion goes beyond the mind's dominion. Logic and reason are deemed inadequate and incomplete.

Fathoming the unfathomable connects with other faculties.

Months flew by and before long it was time for Easter. Pigs were spared on that occasion. Instead it was the lamb's turn.

"Why do we sacrifice the lamb?" Larisa asked the question many times.

"Because it's in the Bible."

That was all the explanation she ever got from her folks, as to why they performed a ritual pertaining to the Jewish Passover, which commemorated the liberation of Israelites from the Egyptian slavery in order to celebrate Christian resurrection.

The day before Easter, women prepare food, paint eggs and bake special cheese and sponge cakes – ideally made with a cow's beestings instead of milk, due to its superior dietary and health benefits.

Some of these goodies are taken to the church at midnight, when villagers listen to the Resurrection liturgy till dawn, have their produce sprinkled with holy water and return home to celebrate Easter.

Like Christmas, Easter has its own pagan origins. Throughout the night, *vigil fires* are lit on hills and high grounds all over the country. Night turns into day and the world becomes a beehive.

When she was younger, Larisa used to go to the foothills and watch the Easter fires with Ksenia and Doina. Groups of guys gathered to spin burning rubber, tying pieces of tyres with strings of wire and whirling them round like madmen. The stronger would spin whole burning tyres, displaying an incredible visual show. In their circular motion, they hit the ground regularly, expelling thousands of sparks. The more the tyre burned, the more arrows of melted caoutchouc pierced the forest, damaging nature and people's health alike.

That way of celebrating distorted a tradition, which initially involved people making fires out of wood, straw and vegetable remnants. Transforming darkness into light, they were lit for 'purgatory' purposes where stories were told, songs were sung, and prayers were whispered. But over the years, the purification process turned into pollution, profanation and contamination.

Older now, Larisa and Doina watched the wild, carmine fire show in silence and from a safe distance. It was almost a year since Ksenia disappeared. Despite all their efforts and hope, they were not any closer to finding their friend than they were the previous spring.

The loud noise of the circus on the hill drowned their heavy sighs.

Faded-Fern

The whole village knew of Ksenia's plight the minute the local gossipmongers got wind of it. But like any news, it was of concern for a short period. The inevitable, fine dust of time obscured the event and apart from her parents and blood sisters, the rest of the village gradually moved on.

Although there was one more person who worried about Ksenia's fate.

Many nights her parents were woken by soft whimpers in the yard but when Tamara went to investigate, bearing her heaviest rolling pin, she could see no one. Only once, on the night of a full moon, was she able to catch a quick glimpse of Zuzu's fleeting shadow vanishing around the corner of their house.

Larisa's own family was supportive at first, but after a year suggested she too let go and carry on with her life. Her mother seized the opportunity during Larisa's next visit.

"There is nothing you can do about it. We just have to trust that she is OK and comes back home one day," Silvia said one afternoon, as she and her daughter were plucking a freshly killed goose on the porch.

It was a job Larisa hadn't done for years and she struggled with it. The meat she was now used to buying from London supermarkets didn't need any plucking and she was out of tune with the job. She carried on picking at the feathers of the bodyless head slumped on her lap while her mother was taking care of the goose's headless body. All the big feathers had been cleared but there were a multitude of short stubs, which Larisa was determined to pull out – all of them, one by one. Her short nails made it a difficult task. The eyebrow pincers were the only answer.

Plucking in silence, the tension mounted.

Passers-by walking up and down the street, greeted them in traditional way:

"Good-day."

"Good-day," Silvia nodded each time, checking out who was wearing what, how it fitted them and how they carried themselves: was the young girl's outfit too short? Was the young man smoking? Did the neighbour swing her hips too much? Did the mayor trip? Was he drunk? Was the priest wearing his cross? Were the teacher's heels too high?

A small community where national or international news was slow to permeate, the village people needed their own gossip to keep them entertained. It gave a purpose to their lives.

The thin plank fence did not only allow Silvia a clear sight line of the road but it also meant that passers-by were able see what was happening in her yard and judge the household by it: was the courtyard neat and clean or full of rubbish and misplaced pots? Was the host seen keeping herself busy or lazing about? Did they seem like homemakers or drinkers and squanderers?

Thus, a simple bidding of *good-day* could speak volumes to those engaged in the exchange, giving rise to all manner of village gossip.

Larisa did not recognise all the well-wishers and let her mother respond to them. Instead, she kept her head down and carried on with the job in hand, all the while thinking of Ksenia.

Silvia sensed her daughter's troubled thoughts.

"What if Ksenia doesn't want to be found? Have you thought about that? We don't know what she had to go through. Perhaps she is too ashamed to come back home."

"Mother, you forget we are best friends. More than that – we are blood sisters. However distressed and embarrassed Ksenia would be, she'd still get in touch with me and Doina."

"Don't be so sure. These things can't be easy to deal with. You can't predict how someone would react to something like that."

Not getting another reaction from her daughter, Silvia pressed on with her agenda.

"It's time you focused on your own life, Larisa. You graduated last year but haven't got a full-time job yet. I know you are doing bits and pieces here and there but it's time to do it properly and start thinking about settling down."

Larisa knew that was her mother's way of saying: *"Get married, and do it soon."*

Silvia was testing her daughter's mood beyond the wall of her silence. Still not getting a response, she ran out of patience.

"I am getting old and I'd like to have some grand-children, you know."

It wasn't the direct approach that startled Larisa, but the casual tone of the request, as if her mother was merely asking for some potatoes to be fetched from the garden.

"I know your bellyache, Mum, yet I'm not Mary, able to get impregnated by thin air."

Larisa was about to say *Virgin Mary* but she stopped just in time not to involuntarily confess to her sin. Her hymen, along with her long hair, were the first things she had hastily got rid of after moving abroad. She had always seen it as a cobweb, and now it was blown away, life seemed so much sharper.

The subject of marriage and procreation bored and annoyed Larisa. Ever since turning eighteen, they were the two topics that bookended all mother–daughter conversations.

"Don't be cheeky with me now."

"I have already told you many times before that I will get married when I find *the one*."

"But what's stopping you from finding him?"

"I'm pretty happy by myself right now," Larisa answered, wanting to add "*with my toys*," but decided that was another facet of foreign life to keep from her mother.

"Maybe you should go to see a priest at the monastery."

"Why, to see if the priest would be *the one*?"

Silvia startled and the headless goose jumped out of her lap. Leaning to pick it up, she shook her head disapprovingly.

"God forbid, you silly girl. How do all these foolish thoughts even cross your mind? Shocking. There was me thinking I schooled you decently and you talk like Satan himself. You know exactly why I have mentioned the priest and the monastery. It will cleanse your soul and help you find a good husband."

A short version of what a Bessarabian mother means when she wishes a *good* husband for her daughter is: all the beauties, riches and intelligence of this world and all the others that might exist in the entire universe and all the parallel ones, embodied in a single person.

Silvia would not compromise on this matter in the slightest by, say, allowing Larisa to have a spouse and plenty of lovers, as local men did. Compromise was not Silvia's strongest point and her dream of seeing Larisa married soon was doomed.

"The priest is like a doctor, except that he deals with spiritual matters. How about Father Dumitru from Toanca Monastery? He can sort you out."

Larisa couldn't tell her mother the kind of sorting out she'd have liked from Father Dumitru – the tall, slim, dark-bearded priest on the sunny side of his thirties.

"You will see results straight away and find your man in no time. Otherwise, you'll remain a spinster," Silvia continued, not in the least aware of her daughter's thoughts.

"Mother, I am only in my twenties. What are you talking about?"

"I got married at eighteen, darling."

"Give me a break. There is nothing wrong with me. There is something wrong with the guys. Take *them* to the monastery."

Silvia's faded-fern eyes dimmed briskly.

"Listen to me. I will arrange for my brother to drive us to Toanca Monastery on Sunday. We'll just go there for the morning sermon then come straight home. No funny business, I promise."

"The whole thing you are suggesting is a funny business, Mum. Look, I am not cursed and I don't have the Devil inside me. Why don't you test me right here? Bring the broom to see if it takes off. Do you think I haven't tried it before? I have, Mother, but the damn thing wouldn't budge an inch, let alone fly. Why don't you believe me? I'm perfectly fine."

"I'm afraid it's gotta be done."

Ever since the experience at Baba Vera's house, which Silvia believed to be a place infested with spells

172

and spirits, she feared some unearthly presence had latched on to Larisa, as one might catch a cold. There could be no other explanation for her daughter's enduring spinsterhood and something had to be done about it.

Larisa decided that surrender might help close the chapter on this matter and agreed to visit the Toanca Monastery.

Warm Vermillion

Moldovans believe that any sacred piece of land has to have a well and a church.

In such a spirit they've built plenty of both, up and down the country. Many of them go back centuries, when their foundation stones were laid by famous voivodes.

One such figure was Stephen the Great and Holy, who ruled medieval Moldova. Like his cousin Vlad the Impaler – more famous in the West as Dracula and who was reigning in Wallachia at the time – Stephen the Great was a warlord fighting to keep the Muslim Ottomans out of the country. For his outstanding operations, Pope Sixtus IV regarded him as a true champion of the Christendom. Chronicles noted he won forty-four or forty-six battles out of forty-eight and that he allegedly founded a church or a monastery after each important military victory.

Many of those monumental buildings are considered valuable cultural and historical jewels and some are still standing to this day.

Toanca Monastery, where Silvia was planning on taking her daughter, had a more recent history. Built in the seventeenth century by a local boyar, it was burned down by the tartars and re-built in the eighteenth century. Over two hundred years later in the aftermath of the Second World War, the Communists transformed it into a sanatorium. When Moldova regained its independence in 1991 after the Soviet collapse, the monastery recommenced its activity and was now flourishing. Silvia told Larisa it had become a very popular place and that flocks of people gathered there every Sunday.

With the fall of Communism, ideology had been replaced by blind religion. The former cosmologic system, which explained the world, was no longer and people felt disoriented again. The propaganda they were used to had been substituted with advertising and marketing. Because these concepts were alien and viewed suspiciously as dangerous western tricks, not many people rushed to embrace them. A void was left behind which the Church moved swiftly to fill, seeking to reverse the national focus back to religion. Community pressure speeded up the process and people flooded the churches across the country.

Even though Toanca wasn't the closest monastery to where they lived, Silvia had her own reasons for taking Larisa to that famous and infamous place.

Eager to get going lest her daughter changed her mind, she woke up bright and early on Sunday morning.

The smell of freshly baked bread and biscuits was abundantly floating in the air. Silvia put some of it in a basket along with one bottle of red wine and one of sunflower oil.

Larisa watched her mother with eyes half asleep and couldn't help thinking that it didn't look like they were going to God's halidom – more likely to a *La Grande Bouffe* party, which would have certainly suited her much better.

In her fluster to get everything ready, Silvia didn't notice she was being watched. A woman on a mission, she made sure everything was ready. With a big sigh as if a massive rock was lifted from her chest, she closed the bag finally and handed her daughter a black batik dyed with bold red peonies.

"This is to cover your head with when we enter the monastery."

Spotting Larisa's attire, her mother carried on with arms akimbo.

"We are going to a monastery, darling, not a nightclub. Those jeans will have to come right off. I've prepared a long frock for you, over there on that chair."

Catching sight of the ancient apparel, Larisa almost choked and started to argue but Silvia had no time for dissension.

"It's got to be done. Let's not waste time on all this fuss. You are a woman and so you should dress like one, especially on this occasion."

"But it doesn't make sense. God knows who I am regardless of what I am or not wearing. He certainly knows what I've got underneath those jeans and spelling it out by wearing a skirt or a dress or whatever that horrible looking thing may be, is insulting his omniscient powers."

Larisa loved her London Bershka whitewashed jeans and because of the mocking height she'd been endowed with, long dresses had never been flattering. She was prone to tripping over the hem at the most inopportune moments and she hated them for that.

"There's no time to enter a debate and certainly not on a Sunday. Also, it's a long way to the monastery and we don't want to be late for the sermon."

"I am sorry but what you are asking me to wear is an absolute affront to all of my fashion and aesthetic values, Mother." Larisa continued to object even though she knew she'd lost the battle.

"We are not going to a fashion pageant, you know? C'mon now, Miss Moldova! Chop-chop!"

Silvia left the room.

Larisa had no choice but do what she was told.

Ready for breakfast, she called to her mother that the kettle was on but before the words left her mouth, Silvia rushed back in.

"We can't eat anything before taking the Holy Communion. No drop of water or crumb of bread whatsoever before noon," and she disappeared into *Casa Mare* again.

Casa Mare is a sort of living room in country homes, kept closed most of the times and only intended for the use of honoured guests, similar to a Western parlour.

Silvia took great care to decorate it with hand-made pieces from the family treasure trunk. They displayed the exquisite needlework skills which her mother and grandmother were renowned for. A scattering of embroidered pillows adorned the sofa, a white crocheted spread measured the table and colourful drapes fell in gracious pleats. An icon depicting Mary holding baby Jesus was fixed on the eastern corner with a wisp of dry basil and an earthen lamp underneath. Traditional, hand-woven carpets lined the walls on all sides. Most of the tapestry and upholstery pieces were part of the dowry Silvia received from her parents when she got married and which she intended to pass on to her daughter.

Larisa readied herself and carried all the provisions to the car, yet her mother was held up by something in *Casa Mare*. She went to check, not because she was eager or excited about the monastery but because Larisa wanted to get the ridiculous business over and done with as soon as possible.

She found her mother engrossed in sorting out a heap of belts scattered all over the floor. For a brief moment, Larisa imagined she was to be taken to a more

177

exciting place than a monastery but Silvia wasn't the type to even joke about such things – she would most certainly have branded them as sinful, damned and disgraceful.

"What are they for, mother? I thought the priests were only interested in food and wine," Larisa couldn't abstain from dropping a hint.

"Oh…nothing, nothing at all," Silvia stumbled over her words. "Go to the car and I will follow shortly."

Confused and at a loss as to what she'd seen, Larisa was worried.

Nikolai, her uncle, was busy with last minute checks under the bonnet of his *Sputnik* car – brand new in 1984 – all the while smoking like a chimney. He saw her sulking and shrugged his shoulders.

"That's your mother – you know her."

"She is your younger sister, Uncle. You could try and talk some sense into her."

He laughed.

"Do you think that has never occurred to me?"

Larisa let out a long sigh of despair and got into the car.

"What if mother doesn't love me as much I think she does? After all, what good am I to her if I don't produce the offspring she's after?"

Silvia came out of the house eventually, as flustered as a fish on the dry.

"OK, Nikolai, let's get going."

Larisa felt restless all the way to the monastery. Ridiculous thoughts kept nagging at her like gadflies on hot summer days. She was worried she could share the fate of useless dogs in Moldova: to be abandoned or hanged in the woods. In the eyes of the community Larisa thought she was definitely seen as useless, for not conforming to its values of prioritising breeding before anything else.

Like many other monasteries, Toanca was hidden away, tucked into the greenery of high woods. What was an hour and a half of travelling felt to Larisa more like a century. She jumped out of the car as soon as the engine stopped rattling. They parked on top of the hill and walked all the way down to the bottom. The whole valley was full of cars, carts and coaches.

Through the long and thin ears of the fir wood, the gleaming towering dome of the monastery peered through boldly. Nesting up there comfortably in its solitude, it looked down nonchalantly and with heavenly pride at the poor mortals bustling about like ants – and in Larisa's case, concerned she could die the death of worthless dogs.

Before entering the monastery Silvia asked her daughter to wait outside and whispered something to her brother. Despite Larisa's best efforts to catch the murmur, it was instantly lost to the hum of the crowds. Silvia turned to go and was at once swallowed by the heavy flow of all those jostling to get into the abbey. Nikolai and Larisa swiftly stepped aside, to avoid being trampled underfoot. He lit another cigarette and puffed at it heartily.

Larisa admired the colourful frescoes adorning the outer walls. Leaving aside their religious messages, they were a harmonious and mesmerising combination of gold, sapphire and warm vermillion.

Outside the monastery to the left of the entrance a nun was selling crosses, holy medals, candles and other church appurtenances – all carefully placed on a shaky wooden table. She kept bending down in futile attempts to fix the wobble but none of the stones she tried under the table legs were good in size.

Larisa studied the nun with interest and thought her short-tempered for someone in the service of God. The inner peace and unconditional love those people were believed to have attained were nowhere to be sensed in her aura. She was hasty and impatient with all her customers.

"What's the price of this small wooden cross?" someone asked her.

"The tag is right there, can't you see?" she snapped back in one breath.

"Well, I don't think the tag I see is for the cross I'm asking about..."

"If you don't feel like buying, don't buy. Leave me alone and don't waste my time..."

"It doesn't look like anyone can waste your time, dear nun," Larisa thought. *"You seem to have plenty to spare judging by your air of boredom."*

Silvia appeared from nowhere, holding a bucket full of holy water. Without putting it down she elbowed Larisa, causing her to startle.

"Oh, for God's sake, Mother – you scared the hell out of me." She quickly spat into her bosom.

It's a common practice for Bessarabians to spit into their bosom when someone or something takes them by surprise. Larisa had always thought that only a pervert could've started such a tradition, nevertheless it was a habit that took her a long time to shake. Like many of her countrymen, it was hard wired into her system and only an effort of conscious thinking plus the blessing of time helped her overcome it.

"What's with the bucket of water?"

The morning had taken its toll on Larisa and by the looks of it the rest of the day wasn't going to get any better. Larisa felt she had been dragged out of her comfort zone and tossed miles away from the normality she had got used to in the West over the last five years. Each and every time Larisa went home, she was pitched back and forth between two opposite cultures with the precision and the unfailing certainty of a cosmic law.

"It's not just any water, darling, but holy water. C'mon, we haven't got time for questions. Let's go in now." Silvia started to walk ahead not leaving her daughter any option than to silently and obediently follow her lead.

The interior of the monastery was the usual Orthodox church décor – a huge hall with a high ceiling topped by a dome. Every wall was covered in stylised scenes from the Bible. Myriad candles sprinkled and sparkled everywhere, exploring and exposing every dark corner of the massive hall. Despite its vast size, the room felt crowded and claustrophobic to Larisa.

Scores of swarming sinners blocked their way but the strong, sonorous voice of the priest permeated the entire space effortlessly. Eventually Larisa managed to get a glimpse of him when the most pious devotees kneeled in deep prayer. Singing his sermon, he meticulously spread incense right, left and centre from his golden, smoking censer. The priest-monk descended the stairs and drew closer to the crowds. He blessed all those queuing up by painting the sign of the cross with thick oil on their foreheads.

Plucked from her reverie, Larisa suddenly had the unmistakable feeling of being watched. Silvia was staring at her intently as if she was seeing her daughter for the first time.

"Are you OK, darling?"

"Funny you ask because I was going to ask you the same question, Mum. You look anxious."

Silvia nodded she was fine but carried on staring at her daughter. It was unnerving for Larisa to see how expectant her mother was for something transformative to happen to her right there and then.

As the monk approached the congregation formed rows so that he could walk though the middle and bless them all with his oily brush.

Suddenly a young girl began shrieking and pulling away from the man and woman – presumably her parents – who were holding her tight.

"Poor thing – so young and beautiful and already possessed. God help her!" a wizened woman next to Larisa whispered to another and they both crossed themselves profusely.

"Oh God, may your powers rid her of the evil spirit," people whispered from all sides.

Seconds later, a different girl followed suit, bucking on the floor like a condemned convict in the electric chair. She too was crying her lungs out.

Then a third one.

Larisa stood there puzzled, not knowing what to make of it all.

"Why is it that just the young girls seem to be possessed, when the old ladies are tranquil and proper? Can it be that Satan too is only fond of young girls? Or is it that the young ones are more likely to have the energy to go on screaming like that?"

Larisa couldn't tell.

She observed the nearest girl.

The two people holding her did not seem particularly affected by what was happening. They held her down looking bored and dull, like people who had been doing a menial job for far too long. It was amazing how speedy and efficient they were in tying her down with a mixture of belts and ropes.

Then the penny dropped: the belt mystery was no longer a mystery and the image of Silvia in the middle of *Casa Mare* pondering upon which ones to bring to the monastery made Larisa smile for the first time that day.

She couldn't help but think what that place would be like if all the young girls, including herself, decided to act insane and played the victims of possession as one. If only she had been a better actress, Larisa would have definitely given it a go and joined in. Her imagination surged wayward and she could picture it: the monastic marble floors covered by beautiful, young, writhing female bodies, securely tied in all manner of different bonds and cords.

Realising that Silvia looked ready to throw that bucket of holy water at her slightest misbehaviour or alarming gesture, Larisa had to be aware of her body language.

"Holy or not, the water will ruin my mascara and make my clothes cling tightly to my skin. Unfortunately, this is neither the right place nor the right time for a wet t-shirt competition."

The oppressive candle and incense smoke made her dizzy and she craved fresh air. Larisa told her mother she had had enough and headed swiftly for the exit.

Silvia followed at her heels.

"But, sweetheart, you can't leave so soon. You have to stay longer if you want the monk's sermon to have any effect on you. The evil spirits can be stubborn and it may take a while...C'mon now, let's stay a little longer."

"It didn't take much for those three girls to be cured, Mother. On the contrary, they looked like a group of choristers cued up by a conductor."

"What are you trying to say, Larisa? How dare you insult God's powers, and on his own territory too? I won't tolerate such audacity."

Silvia threw her hands towards the sky.

"Oh God, please forgive my child for she knows not what she is talking about..."

"I'm done with this. Let's just go home. I feel cleansed now. Honest."

Without waiting for a reply, Larisa started to walk away from the monastery.

People were swarming all over the holy grounds, which were probably the size of five football pitches and shared the ambience of a bazaar. It would have been a very peaceful place to come and rest were it not for the noisy pandemonium, for all those people trashing and spoiling it with their meaningless hustle and bustle.

The huge gardens breathed with a rainbow of flowers arranged in geometric shapes and patterns – an abundance of light, colour, vibrancy and beauty.

Apart from the main church where sermons and *exorcisms* took place, there were two other buildings nearby. All sorts of knick-knacks were on sale there, catering for all tastes and tasteless pockets – UK, US and European: crosses, icons and statues of Jesus and a full gamut of saints in all sizes.

Larisa went to the edge of the garden and lay down on the refreshing grass. This to her was Paradise – lying on the ground, watching the sky and absorbing all the energies Earth and universe had to offer.

The familiar scent of freshly dug earth brought back comforting memories of childhood and freedom. It plumbed into her emotions to a greater extent than the smell of baking bread. Even though she woke up to the latter many times when growing up, the fragrance of their garden and raw earth was more powerful in retaining and recalling past experiences. Larisa was perpetually amazed at the wonder of how different smells get filed away into the human software only to be available for instant retrieval when encountered again.

"What's up? Are you feeling sick? You look pale."

"I'm perfectly fine, Mother, now that I am far away from the crowds and enjoying some peace and quiet."

Larisa smiled at the irony of the situation. There she was searching for her idea of Paradise, an attempt which was prevented and hindered by other people searching for their own.

"Don't be silly. This whole world would be a far better place to live in, if only more people came to God instead of turning away from him."

"As far as I am concerned, I've found my God right here – in this beautiful space amongst flowers, trees and fresh soil. Perhaps if there was a God in that hall of the monastery, he would have fled to the gardens too or maybe somewhere even further."

"Oh good Lord," Silvia prayed again, "how have I sinned before you that you are making me suffer so?"

Her tone of voice made Silvia sound more vexed with God rather than asking for penitence.

"C'mon, darling, let's go back inside the monastery. The monk will work wonders, you'll see."

"Why go back inside? Do you prefer the work of man over that of God?" Larisa decided to tease her mother, for she was getting nowhere by any other means.

"Stop that nonsense."

"I really don't get it, Mum. Why are you so hot and bothered about this now when you've never been the religious type before? What has got into you all of a sudden?"

It was true, Silvia had never been much of a church-goer, except on special occasions, like christenings or weddings. Every other time she excused herself, implying that she was on that time of the month when a woman was not allowed to enter the House of God. Growing up, Larisa thought her mother was cursed with eternal bleeding.

"It's never too late to come back to God, you know. The kingdom of light renders everlasting peace to those who seek it."

"How can that be when light itself is transient? It comes on and goes out all the time. It springs out of darkness and when the fire is gone – darkness resumes.

I prefer the silence and wisdom of complete blackout – the womb of all life."

Silvia crossed herself in extravagant manner.

"Where did you learn such profanities? Heaven is all about light and hell is sunk into darkness…"

"Who says that, mother? You want me to believe something illogical just because it obeys convention."

"What are you talking about, my child? Light is life. Without it everything dies."

"I'm not disputing that. All I am saying is that darkness doesn't have to mean hell and that the kingdom of light, by its own temporary nature, can't provide everlasting peace as you insist. This is just ridiculous mumbo-jumbo. Sorry, Mother, but I am not willing to take somebody's word if it goes against logic and my own experience."

"It serves me right for letting you go to the West. Look what it's done to you! I've always said they have no values or morals over there and you are falling into their sin. I've had enough of your silly talk today. We are going in." Silvia helped Larisa off the ground.

When she realised her daughter had walked away from the entrance and headed towards the other side of the monastery, Silvia dropped her hands with a mixture of desperation and resignation.

More flower and vegetable plots stretched along the path, all the way to the tinkling spring, which like a sparkly jewel adorned one of the last gardens close to the woods.

"That's not such a bad idea," Silvia called.

Larisa didn't understand the comment and kept walking.

"This is a sacred spring," her mother carried on. "The monk sprinkles it with holy water every morning. Some people come a long way to get a dip in here. It's a magical place, said to have healing powers."

The small crowd around it was surging gradually. Larisa couldn't get too close to the water because of a wide mud cordon, spreading a few feet around the whole spring. The shape of it was similar to Diana's fountain in Hyde Park but on a much larger scale.

Once blessed with an oil cross on their foreheads, church-goers came out of the monastery and queued up – barefoot, shoes in hand – for a chance to get into the spring. The word went that walking three times in its holy water cast illnesses and evil spirits away.

Larisa decided to give it a go but not for any purging reasons – she was too fond of all her past experiences for that.

"Experiences are memory and memory is essential to one's identity," she thought, *"especially where enough damage to it had already been caused."*

She took her shoes off hastily and joined the queue. The afternoon air had cooled and by the time Larisa made it to the spring, she almost changed her mind but went ahead, if only to wash the clay off her feet. Had she known how cold the water was, she would have opted to clean them any other way than stepping into the icy stream.

"Ouch, oooouch! This is bloody cold," she cried out loud.

It felt like stepping onto a thousand sharp needles.

People from all sides looked at her disapprovingly, yet Larisa couldn't stop jumping. She swept the crowd with a quick glance and found her mother chuckling with amusement.

"Thank God she's retained her sense of humour."

Shaking like a leaf, Larisa got out as quickly as she went in and asked her mother through chattering teeth:

"Did you say people came here to heal themselves? One is more likely to get ill. Go try it for yourself."

Silvia shook her head and they headed towards the exit.

The monastic experience didn't prove to be the exorcism her mother had hoped for and Larisa sensed this was a chapter that would never close. Yet she didn't have time, nor the inclination, to dwell on it long. Finding Ksenia was a priority. All her energy and efforts were focused on that and she couldn't wait to go back to Italy again.

Bleached Blonde

"Prostitution is an art and requires talent and skill," preached Madame during morning exercises.

She was a well groomed woman in her late thirties or early forties – no one knew her true age – who left Moldova when she was sixteen. She could not speak any one language fluently any longer. Her conversations were always a fractured mixture of Romanian, Italian and Russian.

Her name, Galea, was a Russian feminine form of *Galen* – the great Greek physician, or perhaps it originated from *Galene* – the goddess of calm seas. Regardless of the origin of the name, Ksenia and many other girls at the brothel resorted to calling her Madame.

Of short stature, Galea always wore heels be there guests or not. She liked to clank around the house and give orders. Heavily made up and provocatively dressed with low cut tops and short skirts, she swayed her hips and pushed out her chest. In fact, she never stepped out of her domineering doll role. Even when dressed down, her outfits consisted of five inch

Marabou satin slippers accessorised with silk or chiffon robes and gowns.

Her bleached blonde hair offered a stark comparison to her dark complexion and glossy black eyebrows exaggerated the contrast, no matter how hard she tried to cover them with a long fringe.

An air of harshness sprang from her thin lips and wide nostrils, despite the soft touch of the dimple in her chin. The glare of her big brown eyes combined cruelty and greed, seeming to disguise everything else which might have been going on at a deeper level, provided there was one.

"And who can tell me, what's the basic tool of our ancient trade?" Madame asked the girls who were exercising on the floor in order to strengthen their pelvic muscles or the '*love muscles*' as she used to say.

Madame had implemented a daily routine of exercise, which the girls were forced to practise without exemption. Lying horizontally with knees bent, they had to lift their bottoms up in quick movements, simulating the sexual act. There were also long-shaped vegetables and toys to practise on and overcome the gagging reflex.

Panting away, none of the girls answered the question and she repeated it:

"Does no one know the basic tool we work with, then?"

"I do," Tania – a lanky girl who always took her time to do anything – replied nonchalantly. "It's the prick and the pussy."

Stifled chuckles. "How vulgar!" Madame shook her head disapprovingly. "Anyone else?"

"The cock and the cunt," Nina called bitterly from the other side of the room.

"I am extremely shocked by your inability to see beyond appearances." Madame stared with bulging eyes as big as the hair rollers sticking out of her leopard print bandanna. "Let me open your eyes and minds and tell you what the noble tool of this age-old craft is. No, it's not the dick nor the dime slot but a thing called: love! That's what the tool is – love! It's all about love!"

Some girls laughed, others chose to ignore her disbelievingly.

"Don't get me wrong," she carried on. "You can still get by without it, if you can act well, but that's just complicating your life for no reason and denying yourselves its fleeting pleasures. What you experience here is poetry of the senses and peaks of sensual delights…"

"Get fucked!" Nina hissed through her teeth and turned the other way. She never concealed her contempt and frequently swore and cursed Madame to her face. Nina's usual gaunt and gothic appearance with her shiny black dyed hair and smoky eye make-up reinforced her acidic attitude.

Choosing to ignore her, Madame carried on:

"This is *Life* but I see many of you miss it by getting trapped in tattles and moaning. Practice is the real test not theory. Body, not mind is the primary connection to life. Pleasures of the mind are nothing but dry thoughts and not even old farts would choose them over the juicy rewards of carnal bliss. Go ask 'em all. They may not admit it but I tell you it is so. Here we offer you freedom – freedom to experience real life."

"What a crock of shit. Never heard anything more absurd," Elena, the only married female in the house, scoffed.

"Really? Isn't it the limited ways of looking at and understanding your lives that's gone tits up? Let's take you as an example, Elena. Your husband has beaten you up from the day of your wedding. Yet you stayed with him for more than five years and served his demands. And all for free too. Or look at Ana's history: she's been banged by her father since she was ten. Or

191

take any of you for that matter – all of you have been abused one way or another, yet you dealt with it without any fuss. Here you are remunerated for your generosity. It's a win–win situation for all. You could unwind, enjoy and make money but you prefer to go against the flow and sit there bitching and moaning."

"What remuneration are you talking about?" Nina asked, looking from under her sooty eyebrows. "I haven's seen a penny."

"That's because many of you are still paying your debts. Once that's been cleared, you can start saving. Of course, we'll still keep the money for you for when you are free to go but I can tell you it'll be a lump sum in the end if you work hard."

"Bullshit."

"Broaden your horizons if you want to make it through."

"We are pretty *broad* as it is – thanks to your business," Nina jeered over her shoulder.

"Listen to me, smartarse, I've been in your situation many years ago and I know what I'm talking about. What doesn't break you makes you stronger."

"Or it strips you of all humanity," Ksenia spoke up for the first time.

"Oh, you've woken up, have you? Look – it's all a matter of choice in this life and your fucking problem is that you refuse to see it, you stubborn mules. Go on and suffer then, but for my sake, shut the fuck up and stop whining."

Madame chewed fiercely on her favourite spearmint gum and eyed the girls haughtily.

When Ksenia first noticed the fully blown bubbles discarded generously into rubbish bins around the house, she thought Madame did it for cleansing purposes. But Ksenia learned soon after that Galea was not an OCD sufferer and then assumed that Galea's addiction was more of an oral fixation.

Madame carried on noisily sculpting different sized bubbles.

"Tell me something – when did your husbands last appreciate you, financially or otherwise? Huh? Oh, you've all gone quiet now. Have the mice eaten your tongues? See, the thing is, you are not used to being valued and choose to feel sorry for yourselves rather than be happy. I guess you deserve your fate if you don't ask for more in this life. Here we give you more but that's not good enough for you either, is it? What is it that you want? Do you, yourselves, even know it?"

"It's different with our husbands. At least we are free to leave them," Elena spoke defiantly.

"And how many women actually leave their violent husbands?"

"More these days than ever before. The point is that at least we've got the option to leave an abusive husband. Here, on the other hand, we have no choice and are forced to do things out of fear."

"Of course you have a choice but you choose fear by default because you refuse to employ the feeling of love I am talking about. It's your own doing, thanks to your own inflexibility and close-mindedness." The shrew was relentless.

"It's kind of hard to feel love when your nose is broken," Tania pre-empted Elena's response.

"If it's the preventative measures you are referring to, then case closed – they have to be carried out or you will all get out of line. If it's something else you are hinting at, then perhaps try and change your attitude."

Silence.

More popping bubbles.

"Anyway, what surprises me is your vehement reaction towards our job, as if it's something new to you. Is there any difference between a well-paid strumpet and someone who sells herself for life to her husband? Many women look for rich husbands these days, innit? The only difference between the two is that the former admits freely to her trade while the latter hides behind 'love', goes to church regularly and preaches piety to all the rest. Those women conveniently forget that they've sold themselves out before everyone else.At least here we are not hypocrites – that's what you should keep in mind."

"What about the single girls like me and Ksenia?" Angela, a twenty-one year old redhead, asked. "We never married rich men, nor did we get abused by anyone. On the contrary, we are independent women and have got jobs back home. Why keep us locked in here?"

Madame laughed raucously:

"What good jobs? Ksenia is a doodler and you are a back-street seamstress in Chisinau. Is that worthwhile? Besides, we all know how meagre the salaries are in that shitty country."

"I was planning to open my own business," Angela said defensively.

"How? By what means? Don't make me laugh."

"At least at home we can decide if it's worthwhile or not," Ksenia stared unflinchingly. "We'll be doing what we love doing, talking of love."

Not liking to be contradicted, Madame decided to end her lecture.

"Enough with this idle talk. Get back to the floor and focus on your exercises. No, Angela – you can't eat those cucumbers. They are for training purposes."

Khaki

With the sun going down, the girls were painted and gilded like gaudy, caged parakeets. Awaiting clients, they played cards on the lounge floor. Through a curtain of heavy smoke, Ksenia watched their lazy silhouettes twine into each other in slow motion, to a rhythm all of their own. She closed her eyes trying to banish reality but it invaded her awareness by other means.

The smell and sound were strong and intrusive. The cheap perfume blended in with cigarette smoke provoked a whirling of emotions and mixed reactions. Ksenia was surprised to find that she liked it, perhaps because it was fused with so much candidness and common bond. Puffing and chatting away, the girls talked freely about their experiences.

"I'd been sold three times before I got to this place. I don't think I will ever be able to trust anyone again – I know too much. They burned me with cigarettes and hot oil in Kosovo, threatened to use acid on me if I tried to run away."

"I've been sold more than once, in Turkey, Albania, Macedonia, Italy. It was hard at home. Both my parents were drinkers and we survived on grandma's pension. I was promised a waitressing job in the West. My best friend sold me out for two hundred dollars."

"My mother died of cancer and we had to pay for her funeral somehow. Father's salary as a keeper at the local petrol station was not enough to pay it all back. A family friend told me she could help me get a well-paid job abroad, working in a boutique shop. She arranged all my paperwork. I went to Ukraine and then flew to Turkey."

"My father went to Russia as a labourer. Him and twelve others were given work straight away but their payment kept getting postponed. When they threatened to leave, the boss hired guards to watch over them. They were fed bread and vodka and kept in a cold and damp basement after an eighteen-hour shift. After six months my father managed to escape and return home weak and sick with tuberculosis. Mother's concoctions of herbs and honey did not help much and without any other means to treat him properly, he coughed himself to death three months later. I was the oldest in the family and it fell on my shoulders to provide for the rest of us. My best friend said she could help me get a job in Berlin and she paid for me to get there. I got as far as Bosnia and was informed I'd been sold as a prostitute. I refused but they beat the crap out of me and here I am today."

"You know what I am most scared of? Dying in a foreign land. Everything else – everything that we are going through in this damn house – is secondary."

"I am here because of my two kids. I couldn't provide for them, so I came abroad in search for work. They need food, clothes, education."

"To be honest, it's not so bad here compared with how I had it at home. My father raped me when I was ten...did it for years to come. My mother knew all about it but she was just as frightened of him as I was and we both just took the abuse till I managed to run away. And you know what? I will do this for as long as necessary to buy a house and not see his evil mug ever again or I will chop his head off with an axe, like he used to threaten me."

"There were five of us at the start of the journey, five girls from all over the country, all of us promised domestic jobs as nannies or carers in Athens. Our group travelled on one of the best established routes, as the guide bragged. From Bucharest we went to Sofia, then Skopje in Macedonia and finally we reached Greece by crossing the Voras mountains. Two girls who couldn't keep up the pace were left behind. God knows what happened to them.

"*'Not many make it in this life'* the guide said. *'Never mind, the blizzard will take care of them.'* Further up, we saw a frozen corpse by the side of the road.

"*'...previous journeys'* the same guide laughed. I remember like it was yesterday. He was standing there in his crappy khaki trousers, grinning like an idiot. Anyway, we kept quiet and trod on, eating snow and praying to God for our lives."

The casual tone of the girls' voices describing the horrific experiences which had brought them together made Ksenia realise they had long been used to hardships, traumas and abuse. Dire poverty and domestic violence had blistered their life experience when they were still at home. Despite stepping into the world on the left foot, they were hopeful to make a life for themselves and be happy.

The monstrosity of human and organ trafficking is an issue that permeates all strata of Moldovan society. Its far-reaching tentacles are strangling my nation.

Milky-Twilight

It was more than a year since Larisa began searching for her friend and all attempts had proved fruitless, knocking back her hopes time and again.

Though her trips abroad did not help find Ksenia, each one of them took Larisa deeper into the existence of her people in exile. She was a witness to their struggle to cope in a foreign country and adapt to alien, painful, humiliating situations in order to survive. Highly qualified migrants sacrificed their dignity, peace of mind and health in order to keep their stomachs silent and provide for their families. They ploughed through their new existences unquestioningly, performing menial and degrading jobs far away from home.

Each time Larisa left Italy, her heart was a little heavier, weighed down not only with her own grief but also that of the people she met.

She was pondering such issues while looking out the window on a late evening train to Verona. The countless faces she'd met for the past year rushed through her mind.

All those images belonged to real people with real stories, by turns interesting, sad, inspirational, painful, shocking, humiliating, devastating, encouraging – all of them timeless. Yet, they would disappear into time, traceless – like dew upon the kiss of the sun – unless they were noticed, helped, celebrated, learned from, appreciated, documented and accepted before a new dawn.

Larisa's reflection in the carriage window acquired a sharper focus as the milky twilight retracted over the brow of the hill and night rapidly descended. She studied her figure as if it was somebody else's. The relentless probing loosened the conviction that her face defined her being. It seemed an alien image looking back from the other side of the world.

In that suspended dream state, an idea was born and – with it – a new reality: those people scattered all over Europe and beyond in search of a better life needed a voice – a space where they could come out, connect and help each other. The concept of an international magazine for the Bessarabian diaspora, which would help transform their current circumstances, began germinating in Larisa's mind.

Contrary to Larisa's personal views, the message of the magazine was not going to be one of revolution but of a social, informative, practical and humanitarian nature.

Eager to impart her vision, she called Doina the following day and told her of her plan.

"Are you kidding?" Doina asked disbelievingly. "I didn't think you'd ever want to have anything to do with our people. I know even the fact that you have to rub shoulders with our diaspora abroad is already an effort, let alone a long-term involvement with it…C'mon now, what's the real reason behind your change of attitude? You can't fool me, you know…"

Larisa smiled sheepishly.

"I don't know what you mean…"

"You certainly do, Miss."

"OK – you got me. I was just thinking that the idea of a magazine will aid our search for Ksenia. We could feature a special page for all the missing people – we both know very well Ksenia isn't the only one." Larisa reminded Doina of all those files they had seen piled up at the police office in Chisinau when the authorities were first investigating their friend's disappearance.

Doina fell silent.

"I guess you are right…"

"By the way, any news from Boris?" Larisa asked before hanging up.

"He hasn't got in touch, no. Last time I spoke to him, which was over a month ago, he said he didn't have any news. Haven't been able to contact him since."

"I don't think he's that bothered, to be honest."

"Have some faith in humanity, you cynical woman. I don't think it's any easier for him than it is for us. Give him a break."

"He could move his arse and search for his sweetheart, that's all I am saying."

"Don't measure the world by your standards, Larisa. Allow for other species to roam around. There's space for everyone under the sun, you know?"

"Unfortunately…"

"Chill Adolph, will you. Go for one of your bike rides – that will relax you," Doina's merry laughter rang in Larisa's head long after her friend hung up.

Since coming to London, Larisa had taken up cycling. It was a unique way of exploring the city. Besides, it offered freedom of moving around and saved time by avoiding the traffic. She especially loved the long weekend morning rides, which took her sometimes as far as Windsor, refreshing and invigorating her like nothing else.

Murky-Claret

Larisa designed a business plan for the *Diaspora* magazine and began contacting sponsors and organisations for possible funding. In her mind, the sooner she got the project working, the sooner she'd find Ksenia. The idea was that most of the Moldovan community abroad would see the *Missing* page and that it would speed up the process of finding her dear friend.

A year after Ksenia's disappearance, at the beginning of summer Doina called again with other life changing news.

"I'm coming to the UK."

"You know you are more than welcome to visit me any time you want. Just give me some warning next time." Larisa was excited.

"Not like that. I mean – for work."

"Why? You haven't lost your job, have you?"

"My brother…" Doina's voice cracked over the phone. "…Valentin had a motorbike accident and got paralysed from the waist down."

The news struck Larisa dumb.

"Oh Jesus…how terrible…"

Valentin had been helping his friend Andrei cut up logs for firewood. As they worked, they drank their way through a five-litre container of homemade wine and half a bottle of moonshine. Even though both were still just about standing by the time they finished the job, neither of them could work out how to open the gate when it was time to leave, nor were they able to jump over it. Before long, Valentin knocked the plank barrier down to pieces with the chainsaw he'd been using earlier.

Despite his drunkenness, he managed to clamber onto the *Yava* but lost control of it at the end of the road and hit the minibus carrying supplies to the village's only bar. The bus was hardly damaged, other than a smashed window and a bent door. However its furious driver refused to take the bleeding Valentin to the hospital. Unable to find any alternative means of transport, his friend Andrei had no choice but to rush Valentin to A&E – by hitching a ride. Nobody was willing to pick up a bloody and howling passenger until two hours later when a kindly truck driver with an arched red wine moustache across his top lip stopped and took pity on him.

***

Valentin had built his *Yava* from scratch, using pieces of scrap he had found and bought at various markets. The ones he could not find or did not have the money for, he simply helped himself to from other people's bikes and properties. A smooth shade himself, he moved skilfully in the midst of many shady nights, when neither the aloof gaze of the moon nor the twinkling eye of a single star could witness his misdemeanours.

He laboured on the *Yava* project for two whole years and was ecstatic when the bike was fully assembled.

Upon hearing its powerful and husky rattle, Valentin laughed like a madman. The thing that he was most proud of was the fact that he managed to get hold of a *Yava* engine – the logo of the engine defined the brand of the motorbike. In the Balkans, *Yava* was the fastest and therefore most desirable bike around, proof of which were the numerous accidents involving one.

Valentin was utterly protective of his bike and would not let anyone ride it, except for two people: his father and sister, albeit for very different reasons. Valentin feared Simion and secretly hoped that the steel horse would throw off his blockhead of a father and unburden their family from his alcoholic rages once and for all.

Like many other families in the village and throughout the small country of Moldova, the Plateevs' home was under the spell of Lord Bacchus and the upkeep of the household was carried out by the paternal grandmother, who was old and feeble.

Simion was not only a boozer but also a despotic tyrant. Violence was commonplace in their family, materialising at any hour of day or night. Valentin hated his father and wished him dead but Simion was usually too drunk to mount the bike or not quite drunk enough to crash it. Eventually Valentin gave up on the idea of contriving his father's death. Instead he addressed the good Lord to take the task upon himself.

Doina, on the other hand, he let drive the bike out of love. They had a close bond and he loved her dearly, despite the five year age gap and against the Eastern European gender divide. Even so, that was not the reason why Doina was allowed on the motorcycle in the first place.

Valentin had challenged his father over his violent behaviour one evening over half a year ago. Simion was an ex USSR marine and though he was well past his prime – the mermaid and anchor tattoos hanging loosely on his flabby arms – he managed to overpower his young son and broke his left arm.

That was not the only time Valentin suffered at the hands of his father. He also had a deep scar on his right thigh from when Simion chased and attacked him with a hayfork a couple of years before. Valentin had tried to protect his mother from being abused thereby bringing his father's wrath upon himself.

With a broken arm, Valentin was unable to drive and see his sweetheart. He urged his friend Andrei to teach Doina how to ride the *Yava*. Doina picked it up quickly and was soon chauffeuring her brother around. Before long, she was acting as a taxi service to fetch or drop off his girlfriend, who lived in the neighbouring village.

During the long summer months while Valentin recovered from his broken arm, Doina was left in charge of the bike. She was always to be seen wheezing around at full speed. Her love of velocity was upheld since childhood when she liked to swing from tree-tops and use oil on the sleigh to race it down the hills. It was illegal to have three people on a bike but squeezed between her two Amazon friends, Larisa was hardly visible. Other than that Doina was a responsible driver.

The three of them got so used to having the motorbike at their disposal that when Valentin recovered and took the *Yava* back, they felt like their wings had been clipped. That's when their savvy negotiations with him began.

Though the girls lived in a close-knit community where people helped each other in dire need, when it came to getting something from someone, it was always a smoother run if you had something else to offer in return.

It's not a new or alien concept. In fact, it's a universal truth – this constant exchange of energies keeps the world in balance and makes it go round.

As an inducement to borrow his bike, the girls gave Valentin a jar of milk, which he in turn bartered for a jar of wine. It was a beneficial trade all around and everyone was happy, other than Larisa's parents, who were puzzled as to why Florica – their cow – suddenly began coming home from the meadow empty-uddered.

When Valentin took back his bike, Doina's first idea to win his favour was to collect cigarette butts. That unfortunately wasn't very productive because generous butts were a rare commodity.

Without trains or buses to catch or any other distractions to make them discard half-smoked cigarettes, the village smokers are in the habit of smoking right up to the filter. Many of them go even further and measure time itself by the life of their cigarette, smoking until it burns to nothingness.

Valentin was a fussy smoker and never swapped his bike for butts less than two fingers wide. He still accepted those that didn't measure up but they didn't count against the quota the girls had to raise in order to secure the *Yava*.

It was Doina, renowned for her lateral thinking and keen eye for an opportunity, who suggested they played to his other vice and try to quench his thirst.

There was only one place where they could obtain wine – Larisa's household. Doina's was out of question for obvious reasons – the cellar was always empty – and Ksenia's was perpetually locked to keep her father away from the barrels.

Larisa, on the other hand, could easily access their vault, where the magic liquor was kept all year round. The Cerberus her mother was, who would allow no male specimen to pass when she was on guard, had no suspicions in the case of her daughter and trusted Larisa enough to share the lock-key's secret hiding place.

Wine is high currency in Bessarabia and, like petrol in other countries, can secure much power and grant many favours.

However, as soon as they had identified and implemented the solution, the girls were met with another challenge.

Wine is stored in wooden barrels, which have bungholes in the head ends as well as in the staves at their sides. Because they are positioned horizontally, it is usually quicker to get the wine out by removing the head-end bung. Unfortunately, that's only the case if you know what you are doing or strong enough to push it back, especially if the barrel is full.

Unaware of this small, practical detail, the girls were soon to learn it the hard way.

One day, with no-one at home, Larisa removed the keys from their stash and went to the cellar with Doina, while Ksenia acted as lookout. The clock was ticking and the operation had to be swift.

As soon as they descended the four metres underground, a frowsty waft of air filled their nostrils. A mixture of scents invaded their senses with the musty odour of mould being most pungent. If it weren't for the sweet-citrusy fragrance of the three shelves of quince and the tangy whiff of pickled vegetables – the dim space would seem a tomb.

Larisa walked ahead of Doina and moved the wooden boxes her father used as table and chairs for when he played *Seca* with his friends.

Once their eyes and lungs grew accustomed to the subterranean world, the girls proceeded with their task. They both took turns and pulled at the bung in the barrel. Unable to get it out, they decided to join forces. Larisa grasped the wooden plug firmly while Doina grabbed her by the waist and tugged with all her power. The stopper gave and they fell on top of each other with the murky-claret wine gushing out like blood from a burst vein. It wasn't easy to find the hole and stop the outpouring jet – their eyes were stinging as if hosting ten thousand bees. The bung once out, seemed way too big to go back into the tiny aperture.

Eventually they managed to squeeze it back in, but not after losing a few good buckets of wine. Thankfully the earthen floor effortlessly absorbed the spillage, keeping silent about the crime.

Although the first attempt was an abject failure, they refused to give up and mustered another plan – to obtain the wine via the side hole instead.

This is technically a more difficult procedure, since it involves dipping a hose into the barrel and sucking out the wine.

Two days later, they were back in the vault. This time Ksenia offered to accompany Larisa and Doina replaced her as the lookout.

Once in the cellar, Larisa brought the hose down from the wall where her father kept it at all times and drew on it with ardour. Her attempts, however, resulted only in mouthfuls of wine, which she choked on and swallowed one after the other.

The expected flow did not happen.

Ksenia scolded Larisa for her inadequacy.

"I'm trying my best here, you know. Why don't you do it then?"

"Shhh! Not so loud. C'mon, give me the pipe."

It didn't take long before Ksenia realised her efforts were just as futile.

The young girls kept taking turns, becoming more and more courageous and determined to get the booze flowing. Yet all they managed were swigs which both kept downing happily.

Their anxiety and nerves evaporated and the mood noticeably changed. Everything was suddenly hilarious and their earlier cautious whispers turned into unrestrained, strident laughter. A warm wave, alien to their senses till then, enveloped the girls and they welcomed its light-headedness. Persisting with the task until completely smashed, the duo toppled into a heap at the bottom of a wicker basket.

Worried there might have been another flood, Doina came to investigate and found the pair fast asleep. The dark, vinous moustaches round their lips explained everything.

She tried to wake them by cajoling and shoving but not even a canon could have done the job. Desperate and alone to solve the crisis, Doina decided to lock the cellar and come back early next morning. Knowing that temperatures underground fell significantly at night, Doina insulated her friends with a blanket of straw.

Unfortunately Ksenia and Larisa woke up well before dawn. The cold had crawled to their backbones and they'd been shaking for two hours by the time Doina came to unlock the doors.

Safe and warm in Ksenia's home around the corner, it took a couple more hours to get rid of the shivers. She prepared hot tea for everyone.

"There's got to be another way."

"I'm afraid that wine is the only thing which can get us the bike from my brother."

"I no longer care. There is no way I am going down that cellar to steal wine ever again," Larisa's refusal was unconditional.

"Perhaps we need another accomplice to help us out," Ksenia suggested.

"As if the three of us were not enough. Any more and we are bust. I don't trust anyone else enough to give them the key to our cellar; Mother will find out and I am dead. Do you want to see me flayed alive?"

Doina agreed:

"We should try and keep it between ourselves. Besides, they'll only want a share as well and we can only fit three of us on that bike. How about we try and get eggs instead?"

"But will your brother accept them as payment?"

"He doesn't need to," a cheeky glint lurked in her eyes.

"What do you mean?"

"He could use them for barter in exchange for wine," Doina said and leaned backwards, convinced that she'd found the way out.

However, Larisa quickly spotted the flaw in her reasoning.

"If you think getting wine was difficult – finding eggs is ten times more arduous. Our dotty hens hide their eggs in the entrails of earth as if they are made of gold."

"How about getting milk instead? Doina carried on undeterred. "You know how to milk Florica, right?"

The girls began paying visits to the cow on the meadow. They milked it twice a week at midday, when it was very hot and there weren't too many people around to witness it. Valentin got a three-litre jar of milk every time and used it to get bootleg wine from those who were after milk. Many times he bartered the wine further to gain other favours from other people.

Sadly, alcohol is often a viable substitute for money amongst my people.

***

Following the motorbike accident, Valentin needed money to pay for his treatment and medical care. The poverty the Plateevs grappled with meant no one could help except Doina, who was the only one earning a decent wage in their clan. In fact, she was the only member of the family to pursue higher education. Fascinated by the human psyche, she had graduated in psychology.

Not many of my people choose this path because they confuse it with psychiatry. The general consensus coming from authorities is that there aren't any psychological or behavioural issues in the country, until someone is clearly off the rails. In that case, they are simply branded *crazy* and banged up at the famous psychiatric clinic of *Cuculeni* – far away from *normal* people.

Normal people are denied any feelings of depression or anxiety – they are expected to act like robots, to stop imagining things and mind their own business: work hard, procreate prolifically and ask no question.

After five arduous years at the Moldovan State University, Doina had graduated successfully and was employed as a therapist at a private clinic, yet her earnings were not enough to help Valentin. Rent and living expenses in the capital city were prohibitive and there was hardly any money left at the end of the month. To cope with her mounting debts and help her brother, Doina decided to look for a better-paid job abroad.

Doina wasn't fond of the idea but she saw no other way.

"I am prepared to bite the bullet for a while and do whatever jobs are available so that I can help Valentin recover," she told Larisa during another telephone conversation. "Then I'll come back home."

Larisa knew it was not going to be as simple as that. Doina could end up like the many people Larisa had encountered in her travels – far away from home and further away from whom they were, trying to earn a living on the margins of foreign societies. She wanted to spare Doina such a fate.

"I can help out with Valentin's expenses if that saves you the life of a trade migrant."

"Thank you but you've got your own family to look after. Hopefully it won't take too long."

Doina felt a brief spell abroad could not do her any harm but Larisa worried her friend would lose herself for years on end, like so many other Bessarabians did.

"Sounds like you've made up our mind. Perhaps it's not that bad if it's just short-term. You know I will try to help as much as I can."

"I'm not happy about it but I can see no other option right now. You know my views on emigration. I am not as rigidly against it as Ksenia but not totally for it either. In any case, it makes a huge difference the fact that you are already there."

"I really look forward to having you here. It won't be easy but we'll have each other and we'll get through, come rain or sunshine. Can't wait to see you."

Larisa hang up swiftly. The lump in her throat was stifling the words and she didn't want Doina to suspect anything. Happy to re-unite with one of her blood sisters, she abhorred the circumstances and conditions of that re-union.

Electric-Teal

Doina arrived in London a month later and contacted a large number of recruitment agencies. With poor English and a Moldovan degree holding her back, all she was able to acquire was a cleaning job, which she took without grudge – knowing it was the only way to help her brother. The doctors had said there was a chance he would walk again and she needed all the money she could earn to facilitate the manifestation of such a miracle. Neither sister nor brother lacked faith and they went along praying for it.

Doina actually did more than that – she worked from dawn to dusk to make it happen, cleaning offices early in the morning and family homes for the rest of the day. It was back-breaking labour but she'd been born into hardship and never complained. Her spirits were high and her glass was always half full.

It was just three months before Doina was able to put her business acumen into full effect and set up her own cleaning company. Flying solo annoyed many of her former colleagues who, envious of the bold move, accused her of wanting to run before she could walk, as if scrubbing was some sort of rocket science. They had no idea about Doina's entrepreneurial track record.

Turning a deaf ear to these gossiping mouths, she carried on purposefully. Doina treated each client as family and let all her personal values find expression in the job wholeheartedly.

Punctual at all times, fast and efficient, she tidied and freshened up homes with care and attention. Intrinsic to her nature to go the extra mile, she always made sure to leave colourful flowers in the living rooms after each visit. People appreciated the kind gesture and were quick to recommend her services. Word of mouth helped the enterprise grow quickly and successfully. In the space of six months she registered as a limited company and employed over a dozen Eastern European girls.

Doina's business flair had long been obvious, ever since her childhood days when she delighted in coming up with numerous money-making ideas, from stealing fruit and milk, to selling lice on the highway.

***

It was towards the end of summer.

Time was timeless yet life was never lifeless.

Money was scarce but joy was boundless.

Familiar with the hardships their parents struggled with, especially in Doina's household, the girls had often to fend for themselves. Not out of a sense of responsibility – far from it. It was more a case of an ingrained survival instinct kicking in. With no direct pressure falling on their small shoulders, they were able to dream, be bold and dare.

Selling fruit and vegetables by the side of the road was a common way of earning money but also competitive and unrewarding. Doina decided this ancient racket could do with a revamp.

213

"This is crap. We end up sitting by the side of the road for a whole day or two just to sell one bucket of apples or pears. Everybody else has the same idea and there's only so much demand for it."

Those who had lots of produce to sell delivered it to the markets but for those who only had a smallholding or stole bits and pieces from gardens and orchards, such as Ksenia, Doina and Larisa, the roadside was the only viable sales outlet.

Cars drove by, one after the other, yet not one stopped. The two full buckets of juicy pears, which the girls brought in the morning, were by late afternoon reduced to one: as, without customers and hungry themselves, they kept reaching for the ripe fruit.

"We've got to start selling other stuff besides fruit," Doina suggested.

"That wouldn't be a problem if we had anything else," Larisa replied.

"It's not our fruit, yet we are selling it," Ksenia argued.

"You have a point but we can't just go stealing right, left and centre now...or we'll end up at *Rusca*."

Rusca is Hincesti district's female prison.

"That's not what I was thinking." Doina suddenly got defensive.

"What were you thinking then?"

"I wasn't – I was only trying to."

"And I thought you had some ideas..."

They felt silent, racking their brains as to how best to bring in some money.

"Isn't it absurd that we are selling what's not ours and what we have ourselves, we cannot sell?" Doina spoke with conviction.

The heat of the scorching sun deflecting back to its primordial source bent everything out of focus and made the world lose its shape. The young vendors gazed in vain along the road, whose curves swept graciously towards the dancing horizon – there were still no cars in sight.

"What do you mean? We can't read your mind, you know," Ksenia said after exchanging glances with Larisa.

Doina hesitated, scratching her head, not sure how the other two would take it.

"We've got lice, plenty of them – might as well start a business, you know…"

"I thought about that too," Larisa smiled.

"Are you serious? Not in a million years," Ksenia shook her head. "We are not gypsies, what's wrong with you two?"

Gypsies were notorious for selling lice and nit-combs at five lei a piece at Sunday markets. They usually hung around the gates, a prime location, where rivers of people poured in and out. Urging people to buy one or the other, they called out loud:

"Plump and healthy looking lice for sale, five lei a piece. But if you have your own, come get the nit-comb to get rid of them," their husky, singing voices raised well above the market hum.

Folklore has it that lice can cure jaundice and hepatitis, especially type A, which is the most common in Moldova. The recipe involves swallowing forty individuals in two doses, usually served as fillings in candy. These parasitic insects are said to contain a distinct type of protein, foreign to the human body, which can prevent the reproduction of hepatic viruses.

"We may not be gypsies," Doina turned towards Ksenia, "but we've got lice right now. It wouldn't hurt if while trying to get rid of them, we also made some money."

"I can't believe it. You've both gone completely nuts."

"It's worth a shot – we've got nothing to lose."

Doina and Larisa were excited with the new idea, while Ksenia was annoyed she was in the minority. The trinity they were locked in meant things were easy to decide. As long as two of them agreed or disagreed on something, the dilemma was sorted.

"When do we start on it?" Larisa rubbed her hands enthusiastically.

"We've got to breed some more, to begin with. As of tonight, we start collecting them until we have forty between us."

Doina was touched with genius when it came to details like that. She had a head full of ideas, as well as lice.

"Why do we have to breed more? Can we not start with just a few and see what the demand for this creepy business is first?" Ksenia tried to reason.

"We've got to offer a full treatment, forty lice in one go. Nobody will bother otherwise. It makes no sense to buy any less if only forty of these hungry bastards cures jaundice."

Eager to start this new venture, they were impatient to know what inventory they possessed and how much more was needed. Once at home, the girls hid in the chicken-coop and spread a white sheet on their laps to comb the lice out onto. Between them they counted fifteen bugs.

"Not bad," Larisa was delighted.

Doina made some premature calculations:

"I reckon we'll be able to put our first crop on the market in two days."

"Where do we keep these in the meantime?" Ksenia was eager to know. "Shall I get a jar or something?"

"What do you mean, a jar?" Doina frowned. "They might die and I am not willing to take that risk."

"You are not suggesting…"

Without answering, Doina picked her seven bugs and put them back in her hair.

"Larisa, here are your five and the other three are Ksenia's."

Larisa dutifully picked her lot off the white sheet. The tiny, black dots had to be collected meticulously one by one.

"Can we not mix them with fleas?" Ksenia was desperate for a way around it. "I'm pretty sure we can gather the remaining twenty-five insects from our chickens and dogs."

"That's cheating and we can't play with people's health like that. Only lice can do the job. Besides, what about our reputation in case people come back for more? Don't be silly."

"They are all the same."

"No, they are not."

"Go on, clever-clogs. What's a louse and what's a flea?"

"The fleas are jumpy buggers and we'll get bust if they start leaping in front of the buyers," Doina remained unyielding.

"Just think what we can buy with all that money – notebooks, pens, a new school uniform and a load of lace cuffs and collars to match," Larisa tried to tempt her friend.

"Or perhaps we'd make so much money that we wouldn't even have to go to school any longer. Think about that. Wouldn't that be great?" Doina took it further.

These were not the kind of motivations Ksenia surrendered for. She glanced at the cross in her palm – their sisterhood marked in blood was meant to be for life.

The gestation period took longer than expected and the two days they hoped for stretched into more than a week. Daily, the girls combed out the lice and counted them. It wasn't until the tenth day that they reached the target, by which time the itch had got out of control. In

217

fact, the merchandise combed out was more than needed. Doina shoved forty lice in a jar and split the other twelve evenly between them to be released back into their hair.

"Why don't we kill the remaining ones?" Ksenia wanted to know.

"We can't afford to do that, now that we've started the ball rolling," Doina explained the business concept. "We sell this lot today and if we keep it going, we'll squeeze in a couple more sales by the start of the school year."

"That's only two weeks away," fretted Ksenia.

"Well then, the sooner we start, the better."

At the highway, they placed the jar next to a basket of apples they had stolen from the neighbours. Doina used it as a support for her signpost.

"Natural remedy to treat Jaundice sold here!"

An hour passed and not one car stopped.

With the sun burning mercilessly, the girls withdrew to the cool shade of the walnut trees on the side of the road. The thick brush of the branches reduced the heat, but was not enough to protect them from the annoying dust of the country road. The indiscriminate touch of that flying debris covered all earthly things. Swirling and twirling, the minute particles were totally absorbed in the dancing grace, blissfully unaware of their own transience.

The screeching brakes of a stopping car made them jump. Doina and Larisa were by the jar in a trice.

Three people got out. Two young men in electric-teal Fila tracksuits lit up cigarettes by the car and a young lady approached the girls with swaying hips. Wearing a cropped top and tight jeans, she flaunted her city attitude.

"Since when are apples a cure for jaundice?" she asked mockingly.

"Oh, the apples are not," Doina chirped "but these are," as she opened the jar.

"Jesus! What are they? Yuck!"

"Lice. Forty individuals exactly. The treatment is to swallow them in two rounds and you are rid of jaundice once and for all. As simple as that."

The young lady burst out laughing.

"Are you kidding me?"

"No, I am not. Ask your grandmother – this is an age-old cure for jaundice, passed down from our ancestors." Doina spoke with such conviction as if she herself had been cured of it.

"Never heard such nonsense."

"The gypsies sell them all over the markets but they charge a lot more than we do."

"Is that so?" the city girl asked wryly.

"You can have them for one leu a piece instead of five, like the gypsies charge. Isn't that a great deal?"

"It certainly is. How much are the apples?"

"Ten lei for the whole basket," Doina's voice dropped.

The woman inspected some of them.

"They've got worm holes."

"Of course they have – they are organic."

"You bumpkins really do have an answer for everything, don't you?" the city lady turned and headed towards the car.

"If you don't want to buy any, here – have one for free," Doina called after her. "You will taste the difference of organic apples."

"Are you sure?"

"Absolutely."

As soon as the car pulled away, Larisa broke loose:

"Are you mad? If you give apples away for free, we'll end up with an empty basket and empty pockets."

"They are not our apples anyway. Besides, she really pissed me off by thinking wormless apples were better. That'll teach her to call us bumpkins."

They returned to the soothing shade.

More curious people stopped to enquire about the natural treatment advertised but most of them ridiculed the idea and drove off laughing.

The sun was quickly descending and the girls were just about to give up for the day. At that moment, a blue *Zhiguli* – brand new in 1970 – pulled over and a gap-toothed, middle-aged woman alighted from the passenger's side.

She squinted at the jar.

"Is that milk-thistle seeds you got in there?"

"Pardon?" Doina gaped in astonishment at the unexpected query.

The woman repeated the question but because of her strong lisp and speed of talk, the girls didn't catch on straight away.

"Oh no, we've finished them already,"Doina replied shamelessly. "But this remedy is just as efficient."

"What is it? I can't see very well without my glasses but it doesn't look like celandine either. Besides, their season is well past." The woman inspected the jar.

"They are lice, forty of them, the exact dosage to treat jaundice."

"Ah…lice! Well you see, I've been trying to convince my son to swallow them for the last six months but he won't do it."

Larisa secretly rejoiced – finally somebody was on their wave-length. Even if the middle-aged woman was not going to be a customer, it was better than the open mockery they'd suffered till then.

"It's milk-thistle seeds or nothing else with him," she carried on. "Anyway, what else have you got here? Only apples?"

"We've sold everything else, I'm afraid," Doina lied brazenly.

"Look, girls, your village is surrounded by woods. You'd be better off selling forest fruit and berries – they are all full of good stuff of one kind or another and would be in great demand, I tell you. I'd buy some right now if you had any."

"You mean like sloes and rose hips?"

"Yes, those too," the woman nodded. "Also try to find cornelian cherries, hawthorn and especially buckthorn berries. They have great curative powers and are in season now."

As soon as the woman left, Larisa and Doina ran to Ksenia, who was still under the walnut trees, to tell her the good news.

"Thank God we are done with the lice business," she sighed with relief.

"That's not what we meant." A slight frown took shape on Doina's forehead.

"I thought we'd moved on to a new idea."

"We certainly have but we're not quitting on the lice yet. While we've got them, we might as well try and make a sale. Otherwise all our efforts and pain of the last ten days will have been in vain."

"I am not putting them back into my hair," Doina stated categorically. "They are half-starved by now and I'll be eaten alive. There won't be a drop of blood left in my brain after they dine tonight."

"You are not suggesting we give it all up, are you?" Doina was genuinely worried.

"We can carry on trying to sell this lot, as long as they survive in the jar, but I am not releasing them back into my hair today or ever again. Actually, I'm planning to get rid of all the other ones I've got. I don't want to go to school bald again."

A couple of years previously, the girls had experimented with producing homemade chewing gum out of tree sap and melted sugar. Needless to say, the experiment didn't go smoothly and most of the paste ended up in their hair, tangling it irrevocably. No amount of vinegar could save their precious manes and on the first of September all three returned to school bald as freshly plucked geese.

The mere memory of this event caused Larisa to switch sides. The thought of losing her hair again was not at all appealing.

"I agree. We should focus on trading this bunch first before we breed any more. They are definitely not selling like hot cakes and we can't afford to keep any stocks."

Aware that she was in the minority, Doina caved in.

As soon as evening descended on the village, the girls assembled at Ksenia's house. They closed themselves into the farthest room and started combing their hair. Plump lice, engorged with blood, rained down on the white cotton sheet.

"There are more now than there were yesterday," Ksenia said with trepidation.

"That's because many were fresh out of their eggs and too small for our comb to catch."

Doina's explanation did not reassure Ksenia.

"But you know what that means. New deliveries every day for God knows how long."

She inspected some of the fallen hair on the sheet – it was gilded with tassels of nits, many of them still active.

The depth of the trouble they were in finally hit home. There was no way to get clean in time for the pre-school check-up, which was in less than a week. Something urgent had to be done. Some sort of method had to be found and they were ready to try anything as long as there was a slight chance of avoiding the impending disaster.

"How about creolin?" Doina suggested.

Creolin is a chemical made out of coal tar which farmers use to rid livestock of fleas and other parasites.

"No way. Its stench will stay with us for ever," opposed Larisa.

"Worse than that – it could easily burn our hair," Ksenia pointed out.

"You are right, it's not worth the risk. How about using ash?" Doina asked.

"It certainly won't hurt to give it a go. It's not like we are spoilt for choice really and it works on chickens most of the time," Ksenia's face lit up. "I'll go get some."

There are no refuse collectors in that part of the world. Each household in the village takes care of its own waste disposal, usually by burning it in a specially made hole in the ground somewhere at the back of the garden.

Ksenia returned with a bowl full of ash and the cleansing ceremony started. They rubbed it in thoroughly, scrubbing every inch of their scalps.

Content with their efforts, the girls went to bed hopeful to have killed all the lice and looking forward to a clean morning.

They woke up soon after with their heads stinging as if ablaze. Their ash rubbing must have been too eager. Such was the pain and haste to cool off their heads that they couldn't find a basin and water quick enough. Scurrying, they tripped on carpets and stumbled over furniture, causing bedlam in the house. Soon, Ksenia's mother appeared in the doorway, like a raging bull at a gate. Tamara didn't scratch the ground but digging both hands deep in her bounteous hips, she seemed just as foreboding.

"What on earth is happening here?"

Unfortunately for Tamara, it wasn't the right time to ask the girls questions. They carried on arduously washing their hair. Tamara stood still in the doorway watching closely. Witnessing such distress, the penny eventually dropped and she took pity on their plight.

Compressing fresh cabbage leaves with sunflower oil, Ksenia's mother staunched all three heads with a thick padding of the soothing vegetables and the girls' howling gradually stopped.

Now was the time for interrogation.

"Good God, your heads are crammed with lice. I've never seen anything like this in my entire life. How did it get to this point? Why didn't you tell me about this earlier, Ksenia?"

A gulping silence.

"Why did you not tell me you had lice?" Tamara pressed on, staring at her daughter, who was inspecting the walls and ceiling meticulously as if they held the answer to the world's mysteries.

Tamara was a wise woman and elected not to press the matter any further. She knew it was easier to draw water from a dry well than drag the truth out of the girls. However, she fixed her daughter with an icy stare.

"There is no choice but to shave your hair off. You start school soon and we have no time to deal with it otherwise."

The certainty of that statement caused them all to flinch. Even though the verdict was aimed primarily at Ksenia, it had direct repercussions on Doina and Larisa. They were all in it together and if one was rendered bald, the other two would have to follow suit. The worst of it was that Tamara decided to shave Ksenia there and then, at that ungodly hour.

"I am getting rid of these parasites right now and will start with her," she pointed at her daughter. "If you two want to stay here the night, I'm afraid you'll have to join the trend. Otherwise I won't be able to keep you inside."

Larisa and Doina didn't mind sleeping in the shed outside – it wouldn't be the first time anyway. But they couldn't leave Ksenia the only one to be sheared. The unwavering reality was that they would also have to do it sooner or later and there was no point in delaying the fateful hour.

Miserable and disgruntled, they silently nodded their assent.

Thus all three started the year bald-headed for the second time in three years. It wasn't long before everyone caught wind of what happened. Yet, the reason behind their drama remained a secret, which two of them carried to the grave.

Heavy Mahogany

Ksenia's daily grind was sad and repulsive. She looked at clients as mere ciphers but it was not always easy to disengage from the physical encounter, which cankered deeper at her core.

"They're peeling layers and layers off me, one after the other – dignity, identity, privacy, humanity. What does that leave? Anything at all? What I thought was me – this bruised body – proved to be a lie. It is just a shell hosting Me, a place which others can use and abuse at their whim. My body is just a treacherous fleshy form that pleases many but to me it only brings pain and degradation. At least I now know I'm also something else which they can't touch and never will. They'll never lay their dirty hands on Me."

The bald client grinned and grabbed her like a savage.

"Come here, my doll. Come here you little, filthy whore. Let Daddy lick your pretty pussy. Spread your legs…"

Coming from a culture where – at least in rural areas – oral sex is looked upon as a filthy and degrading endeavour, Ksenia knew what it entailed but had never been subjected to it previously, willingly or otherwise. She had her own flamboyant theory on the potential cause for such restraint, about which she used to laugh with Doina and Larisa many times:

"After working the land all day, our rustic orifices are too full of soil for these kind of pursuits."

The bald client carried on with his queasy cunnilingus.

Ksenia shot her eyes up to the ceiling, counting the cracks.

She felt her soul climb out of her body in a bid to detach itself from the raw biology battering beneath. The carnal dimension did not belong to her any longer. In order to make it through, it was necessary to evade that side of reality, which she – in any case – could not control.

Clients came in day and night: married, single, young, old, clean, dirty, happy, unhappy. Their naked bodies – some hairy, others wrinkly, most clammy and all of them smelly, reminded her of Zuzu's bloated frogs at the waterside.

"There isn't much more to these men than there was to those toads. How can there ever be? The one involved in many vulvas, does not evolve," she thought in a daze and like a chant, the words echoed ceaselessly in her head.

"The one involved in many vulvas, does not evolve! The one involved in many vulvas…"

She grabbed a pencil and half an hour later ended up with a sheet of elaborate, oversized vaginas teeming with small male figures wearing identical white masks – hidden, obscured or trapped by the commanding, bare flesh.

"God, please make their wives and girlfriends take care of these men. I've had enough of being used, misused and abused. Take them back to their homes and make them find there what they are looking for here."

Ksenia thought daily about different ways to escape. Together with Nadea, they conspired and ran through their options. It seemed hopeless, given that the front door was always locked and shifts of two guards and a dog kept an eye on the girls. They threatened to kill anyone who tried to run away.

"I've been thinking of writing letters to appeal for help," she told Nadea one afternoon.

"And do what? Give them to the guards to post?"

"Drop them out the kitchen window."

"What are you going to say? We don't even know where we are."

"I'll write that we are sex-slaves living on the third floor of the house directly opposite number forty-four of this street. Dropped out the kitchen window, the letters won't land too far away."

"What if they find them?"

"Don't jinx. Anyway, if you are worried, I'll write them left-handed as a precaution."

"I guess it's worth trying."

Letters, tied with high hopes, were released to the outside world once every week and they waited patiently.

Surely enough, the karmic boomerang did return but – alas – not with the outcome they had so hoped for.

A couple of weeks later, Ghena, the one eyed guard entered the house surly as a bear. He lined the girls up in the lounge, handed them each a pen and paper and told them to write something.

"What do you want us to write?" Tania asked the question which all the girls were thinking.

"Something, anything…that you are fucking whores trying to escape…" he shouted and looked at them with his only seeing eye.

The girls exchanged glances with each other, all of them confused.

Ksenia knew what she'd write. The voice of memory whispered a well-known poem, which reached her often during many sleepless nights. She put down the mystic's words:

"Such a deep silence surrounds me,
that I think I hear
moonbeams striking on the windows.
In my chest,
a strange voice is awoken
and a song plays inside me
a longing that is not mine..."

"Bring over your papers when you finish," Ghena barked.

Ksenia was done and looked around. Other girls were still writing. To the left Tania was drafting a letter to her family, telling them how much she missed them. Elena cropped a message to her daughter, reminding her how much she loved her. Everyone was laboriously writing away, so much so that when Ghena told them to stop, many girls asked for more time.

"We are not done yet."

"This is not a fucking composition class," the One-Eyed Monster snapped. "Can all of you bring the papers to me – right now!"

Reluctantly, they handed him the records of their innermost woes. It was obvious the task had perturbed the girls and induced a melancholic mood of longing. What was a test had become a therapy exercise, giving voice to thoughts which they had previously tried to stifle or ignore in order to avoid unbearable pain. Given the opportunity to turn inwards, however briefly, the girls were able to reconnect with themselves and remember who they were. Externalising their feelings by putting thoughts to paper and attaching a narrative to their plight, made them all feel lighter and less guilty – almost reconciled with Fate.

"Can we have them back after you read them?" Angela asked meekly.

"Maybe…after I wipe my arse with them." He sketched a cruel smile while studying each letter against a piece of paper that he had retrieved from his trousers pocket.

Ghena didn't seem to be reading the content of what was written but merely comparing it with something else he held in his hands. When he got to Ksenia's, the neat column of the poem must have caught his one eye and tickled his funny bone. He started laughing like a lunatic.

"Who's the crazy one to write a poem? You whores are losing it…" he said and carried on inspecting the handwriting on the rest of the sheets.

When done, he squinted at them and hissed:

"So this is how it is, huh? One of you is a shrewd bitch and I swear to God I will find her out, I swear to God."

Ghena looked each girl in the face.

"One of you managed to drop this letter out the window somehow but I found it," and he flung a creased piece of paper to their faces. "Heaven forbid I find another one. You do it again and you are all fucked. I won't waste any more time but chop a finger off each one of you. Understood?"

He scattered the papers across the heavy mahogany, filthy floor and slammed the lounge door behind him.

The girls immediately fell to their hands and knees. As each found their letter, they clutched it dearly to their chests like a piece of treasure.

The failed plan and resulting threats left Ksenia shaking but the inner cry beseeching freedom could not be silenced. While she allowed her body to be used for the perverted pleasures of many, she tried to numb the pain by devising more schemes to escape.

"One of us has to befriend the guards," she told Nadea one morning.

"Which one?"

"Which one of us or which one of them to befriend?"

"Both."

Ksenia hesitated – not because she wanted to protect herself. Strictly speaking, Nadea was in a better position to attempt it because she'd been there longer and didn't cause as much trouble for them as Ksenia did.

"You want me to do the dirty work, don't you?" Nadea asked reluctantly.

"Only because I think you stand a better chance to get under his skin. If you think you can't do it, I will. Either way we've got to try."

Nadea lit a cigarette, watching Ksenia with a remote and silent look.

The clock struck twelve. Some of the girls were getting ready, others chatted on the lounge floor, drinking coffee or smoking while waiting their turn to use the only shower in the house.

"Which guard do you have in mind?" she puffed.

"The One-Eyed Monster."

"Why does it have to be him? Can't I go for someone less hideous?"

"I think that's in our favour. He is only used to taking girls by force and plays the tough guy. If you could get over his disfigurement and be nice, he'd be putty in your hands."

"That's if he's got any humanity left, which I doubt. Where do I start anyway?"

"By being the best actress ever. Your attitude has to seem genuine."

"That's not gonna be easy. I find him absolutely repulsive," Nadea spat with disgust into the rubbish bin. "I guess he still has his way with me against my will regardless, just like he does with everyone else around here. If anything, it will probably feel better if I'm the one making the first move – that way at least I'll have some control of the situation."

"That's not a bad way of looking at it."

Fulvous

A week into the new plan and Nadea reported back that Ghena started actively avoiding her.

"It's not working. He goes out of his way to not cross my path."

"That's because he's not used to people liking him. Who knows when it last happened, if ever. Keep at it a little longer and we'll see."

Nadea carried on pretending to like Ghena. Every morning on his shift, she offered to make him coffee, spent more time chatting to him and often cooked his favourite pancakes with honey and walnuts. He was abrupt, rude and kept her at arm's length. However, Nadea faked her affection and interest with the zeal of one whose freedom and life depended on it.

Gradually, the One-Eyed Monster let his guard down. He stopped abusing her and didn't allow the other guards to do it either. The plan seemed to work well, so much so that Ksenia worried Nadea might have fallen for real.

"Have you heard of Stockholm syndrome?"

"No and it doesn't matter. We are not in Stockholm, are we?"

"It's when the victim becomes attached to her captor…"

"Don't be ridiculous," Nadea didn't let her finish.

"Just saying. It might take a long time before a chance to escape comes up and a lot can happen in the meantime. Life can be unpredictable like that."

"Shut up, Ksenia…I mean – Scarlet. I hate him. I hate all of them. I'd kill them all given half the chance. Don't worry about your Swedish syndromes – we'll both get out of here very soon. I promise."

The opportunity to escape came unexpectedly. Even though she didn't know what it would look like, Nadea recognised the chance when it had presented itself.

She had found out about Ghena's sweet tooth.

"Can you cook our traditional semolina pudding?" he asked her one day.

"Of course. My mother bakes the best cakes in the village. She taught me a recipe with apples, cinnamon and a drop of walnut brandy. Absolutely divine."

"Can you do one?"

"Sure, I just need the right ingredients."

"Write them down and I'll get them for you."

Nadea did so and handed him the list.

"Make sure the semolina isn't too coarse or too thin. It has to be just right otherwise the tart won't taste the same."

"What do you mean? Isn't semolina just semolina?"

"No, it comes in different types. Check out the picture on the package and get the medium one."

"This is all too complicated. Get ready – you are coming shopping with me. We'll leave in an hour."

Nadea's heart raced. The plan was working. Afraid that her voice would betray her emotions, she only nodded and left the kitchen.

Ksenia was by the window, whispering under her breath.

"The one involved in many vulvas does not evolve, the one involved in many vulvas does not evolve..."

Nadea could not hear the words but this was not the first time she had caught Ksenia mumbling to herself recently and it worried her.

"What's the weather like?" She asked the question trying to get her friend's attention.

"It looks sunny but people aren't wearing short sleeves any longer. Mustn't be that warm," Ksenia answered impassively and turned around.

Nadea winked and anxiously motioned her head for Ksenia to follow her into the bathroom.

The news was whispered.

A strategy had to be put together quickly but it wasn't easy. They had no idea what the outside world looked like in that foreign city.

"If the worst comes to the worst, I'll just hide in a toilet and won't come out until the police arrive," Nadea said.

"Please be careful. I don't want you to get hurt."

"It can't be any worse than where I am right now. It's better to be dead than walking dead."

"Don't be silly. Remember to check the name of this street so you know what to tell the police."

The door opened abruptly and Madame burst into the bathroom without the loud clacking of stilettos that usually preceded her arrival. Nadea and Ksenia were forced to change the subject hastily.

The house was busy and the girls couldn't talk anywhere else. Moreover, they had to keep cool so as not to arouse any suspicions.

Nadea chain-smoked while getting ready to go shopping. It was too early for clients and Ksenia pretended to casually doodle in her notebook, while she racked her brains how Nadea could run away.

Madame strutted past noiselessly in a pair of turquoise shoes Ksenia had not seen before. Her attention was drawn to their uncharacteristically discreet kitten heel and a memory from long ago popped into her head. The shoe incident in Brighton filled her mind.

Ksenia urgently needed to somehow tell Nadea about this sudden brainwave but could not get a moment alone with her. Just as Ghena and Nadea were about to leave, Ksenia decided to throw caution to the wind and drop the hint:

"Hey Nadea, remember this isn't Moldova. They tag products electronically here. Make sure you don't make a fool of yourself, especially if you want to surprise us with champagne."

Nadea looked puzzled and Ksenia couldn't tell if her suggestion had gone over her friend's head or not.

"You'll drink champagne when you deserve it," Ghena snapped and locked the fulvous door from the other side.

After thirteen months of biting her nails, Ksenia had practically none left. Despite her bald fingertips, she kept biting them more and more.

A couple of hours after Ghena and Nadea left, her fingers started bleeding and she had to dress them. Unable to deal with the mounting tension otherwise, Ksenia turned to biting her hands and arms, leaving deep teeth marks in her flesh.

"How slowly time can pass sometimes! Crawling or sprinting, it does one or the other but always in defiance and contrary to expectations. The bastard!"

Ksenia's heart jumped the moment the entrance door slammed shut.

Ghena burst into the hallway, shouting and swearing like a lunatic.

236

Colourless

Despite sharing a flat, Doina and Larisa hardly saw each other. One was busy with the magazine project and the other with her cleaning business. Over a year after Ksenia's disappearance, neither of them ever forgot about their friend – Ksenia was always at the back of their minds and she played a crucial role in all their decision-making.

Before she could make the magazine project a reality, Larisa needed a network of people she could trust and financial backing. Weeks and months were spent bringing her plan to fruition. Night after night she put pen furiously to paper. All the ins and outs of the grand scheme were detailed in a business proposal which was then mailed round various national and international organisations, appealing for support.

After months of silence, Larisa had almost given up. Then a reply – and not just from anyone – but from the United Nations Development Programme offering financial help for projects intended for the betterment of Third World countries. Larisa smiled at the thought of how Ksenia would have reacted to such a demeaning tag for Moldova.

All of a sudden, the *Diaspora* magazine was no longer a dream. It finally entered the realm of existence, offering a place of connection for all the Bessarabian migrants who had inspired the idea.

Even with the funding in place, it was still a couple more months before the project was off the ground. In the meantime, Larisa formed a team of Moldovan ex-journalists who were scattered across all four corners of Europe, scraping a living. Happy and willing to do something they loved, the contributors took the work to their hearts and, like Larisa, made the magazine's success their mission. Unlike previous jobs, when they were bound to an editorial agenda imposed by the dictatorial regime in their country of origin, they were free to write whatever they wanted in order to inform and improve their peers' lives and experiences in Western Europe.

Although Larisa chose to publish it in Moldova for cost reasons, the magazine was distributed in five EU countries – UK, France, Italy, Spain and Portugal.

It provided a forum of knowledge and information not only about integration and survival – employment, training, qualification, legal framework, skill upgrading, accessing services – but also encouraging and facilitating an eventual return to Moldova and re-connecting therein.

Larisa likened the *Diaspora* magazine to a village square where people met on Sundays and holy days, providing an opportunity to meet and mingle.

Experiences were shared, tips were swapped, information was exchanged, pleas were made and calls of help were heard.

The magazine proved popular but, despite its success, Larisa couldn't help feeling sad and powerless. All her efforts and appeals to find Ksenia went unanswered, as if the earth had swallowed her friend.

Doina and Larisa reflected on the irony of life. For all Ksenia's rabid views on migration and her total contempt of people who readily surfed its waves, she too was affected by this ruthless social phenomenon.

Even Ksenia – my most loyal daughter – couldn't escape being dragged away by the powerful, colourless currents sweeping mercilessly through my land.

Bored-Beige

A raging Ghena told Madame that Nadea had bolted while at the supermarket. Hardly able to hide her excitement, Ksenia sneaked to the bathroom and sunk to the floor crying.

"We're saved," was all she could think. *"The police will be here any minute and we'll all be saved."*

"I looked for her everywhere. I searched the entire fuckin' shop, aisle by aisle, and drove around every street in the neighbourhood. I don't know where she hid or how she ran away but she did it pretty quickly, the filthy whore. I swear I will kill her with my own hands when I find her, as God's my witness."

Madame and the guards disappeared to the kitchen. They closed the door behind them but the thin, bored-beige walls betrayed their secret crisis talks. The plan was to move to a new location straight away.

On hearing this, Ksenia panicked and prayed more desperately than at any other time in her life, begging God for the police to arrive before the gang had time to move them away.

"*Please save me, Lord. Please save me! The one involved in many vulvas does not evolve. Please save me. The one involved in many vulvas...*"

Alas, it wasn't to be.

Her words weren't heeded.

That night the girls were taken to a different, bigger, house where they joined other similar service providers. Strutting around wearing next to nothing, the work force of the host abode eyed the newcomers with arrogance and suspicion.

Before the night set in, clients swiftly followed and by midnight life in the brothel was back into its perverse routine, as if the other house had only been a dream.

Ksenia knelt in a corner and sobbed with abandon.

"*Why are you so cruel, God? Why did you let Nadea betray me? You know what? I've got something to tell you. You are a masochist! Don't be surprised to hear that. Well, you shouldn't be – in your over-rated, over-praised, shitty omniscience. You seem to be enjoying my distress and keeping me here, despite all my pain and suffering. You think you are the big shot, don't ya? The Big Creator? Constantly busy yet busy with what? With destroying people's lives, like you do with mine. Is that what your grand design is all about? When will you have had enough? When I am dead? Is that where it's going? I want to get out of here, do you understand? Listen to my heart's throbbing desire: I want to live! Please set me free!*"

Ruby-Blue

To celebrate the first issue of the magazine, Larisa treated Doina to dinner at her favourite place in Dalston – the Ruby-Blue Tapas Bar.

A girl around their age, whom they hadn't seen before, greeted them at the door. The cold and distant look of her grey eyes was strangely discomfiting. A potato-shaped birthmark on the left cheek somehow foreshadowed that side of the face and made her seem even more solitary.

"Must be new," Larisa said as the waitress went to fetch their drinks.

"I bet she comes from the same part of the world as us."

"You think she is Moldovan?"

"Wouldn't be surprised," Doina said it nonchalantly.

"You reckon?"

"Why don't you ask her?"

"I think I will now."

The beautiful, if slightly wistful, young lady returned with two glasses of New Zealand Sauvignon Blanc – Larisa's favourite. Moldovan wine had yet to find its way to the tables of London restaurants and even if it had, she'd have probably avoided it on principle.

"Here are the food menus and these are our specials today."

As Larisa reached out for them, the waitress caught a glimpse of a dark coloured mark on Larisa's right palm. The gesture was very quick and it didn't offer enough time to make out exactly what it was. Yet the waitress seemed to shudder at the possibility of what she thought it could be.

"Oh, don't be silly," she told herself. *"People have all sorts of things drawn on their hands these days. Especially in East London. I'll see if I can get a better look at it when I come back for their order."*

As she turned away, Larisa asked:

"Excuse me, Miss, we are debating as to where you come from. My friend thinks you are from Eastern Europe but I am not so sure."

"Good guess."

"What country?"

"One you probably haven't heard of."

"It can't be more obscure than our country…"

"Are you from Moldova?" Doina lost her patience and asked the question so abruptly, it sounded more like a statement.

"Are you Moldovan too?" she replied in true Bessarabian fashion, asking another question in return.

The tone of the waitress's voice betrayed a slight disquiet, as if she knew or feared the answer.

"Yes, we are."

"Can it really be them? Or am I just imagining things?"

"What part of the country are you from?"

"Are you OK?"

The questions of the two girls reached her as distant echoes.

"Oh sorry, yes – I am fine."

243

"It's probably been a long day, hasn't it?"

"Not too bad, actually," the waitress managed to smile. "Are you ready to order?"

Doina read out from the menu and the waitress wrote the name of the dishes robotically, as if on autopilot. Her mind was swarming with a thousand and one thoughts.

"This is too much of a coincidence not to be them. Shall I just openly ask to see their palms? But then what?"

"Thank you," the girls handed her back the menus. "By the way, I am Larisa and this is Doina."

"Oh my God, it IS them," the waitress swallowed hard and nodded her head.

"I'm Nadea. Nice to meet you. Your food won't be long." And she left their table hurriedly.

"She's a bit weird, isn't she?" Larisa observed.

"Probably tired. You know how spaced out I am at the end of a working day. Working in a restaurant can't be any easier than cleaning, I am sure."

The waitress watched the two girls discreetly from the back of the room.

"Shall I tell them? But they will hate me if I do. They won't forgive me for not saving Ksenia. I think it's wiser to keep quiet. It's already been three months since I last saw her and surely it's too late to stir things up now anyway."

Sheer-Platinum

Following Nadea's bolt for freedom, another girl tried to escape but wasn't so lucky. Victoria – one of the tallest girls in the house, and pretty despite the uneven shapes of her thread-thin eyebrows, which she plucked at every day – had her neck snapped. Her fine, sheer-platinum hair was usually straightened till it looked wispy and damaged. To offset that, Victoria regularly made an effort to dry it naturally, over-gelling it for a wet look and pinning it up into an impeccable Audrey Hepburn style French bun. Notwithstanding the forty minutes it took to fix her hair in place, Victoria took immense pride in parading it at weekends.

"It makes me feel more of a lady – you see – not much else around here does…"

Not that her clients cared for or paid any attention to her perfectly perched bun. Her main asset in the house of vice was her bounteous, perky bust and tight waist, for which she was in high demand.

Like the two different hairstyles she sported, Victoria usually ran on two speeds: she was either subdued and lethargic from having smoked too much weed, or mad and unpredictable from consuming harder substances. In her mellow mood, you wouldn't know she was around, but when ruffled, she was as tempestuous as a late summer storm. Plenty of times she abused and on several occasions even slapped other girls who dared help themselves to her cigarettes. Once she broke a glass over her client's head when he had refused to buy her more wine and drew blood from another after biting him wildly during a rough sex session.

On that fateful day, only Ghena was left on watch. The other guard didn't await his replacement and went home earlier than usual. Victoria decided this was her chance to strike. She volunteered to clean the kitchen, armed herself with a serrated bread knife and viciously attacked the One-Eyed Monster from his blind side as he munched on roasted chicken.

Ghena clattered to the floor, clutching his head and roaring with pain. Victoria snatched the key ring from his belt and rushed towards the door. With sweaty hands, she frantically tried each of the seven keys in turn but none seemed to match. In her panic, she dropped the key ring to the floor and had to start all over. The keyhole, however, kept spitting them out until the last but one, which finally turned in the lock.

By then, Ghena had recovered enough to hold his split and bleeding ear and stagger after Victoria. She was half way out the door when he managed to grab her by her tight French bun. She was just about able to scream for help before he dragged her back in the house, stifling any further cries by cracking her neck between his crimson, ursine hands.

By end of the day, all traces of the dead girl had been removed and her name was not mentioned again. The only things left of Victoria were her lingerie – her *working outfits* – which came with the job and stayed with it.

Madame had distributed her pieces to the rest of the girls who matched her size. Unfortunately for Ksenia, she was one of them. She was ordered to wear a pink, see-through nightie with black lace and matching thong that same night.

Ksenia did so but made sure it wouldn't happen again.

Ingeniously, she manipulated one of her clients, whom she knew to be a primary school teacher, into tearing it off her in the midst of a sexual scene she had staged to that effect. The teacher was of course charged for the damage but he more than readily and happily paid for it.

Despite Victoria's temperament alienating her from the other girls, her murder affected them all. Shock and fear lodged in their hearts. The house was quieter than usual and only whispers teemed in all corners.

Ksenia felt sick and for the next month could hardly asleep. Despite the exhaustion of pleasing over two dozen men every night, each dawn found her wide eyed and restless. Horror and desperation kept peace at bay. Any short spell of rest she managed was spun with nightmares, snapping her awake breathlessly and in a cold sweat.

In the soft light of the early morning, when everyone was asleep recovering and preparing for the hard day's labour ahead, Ksenia wandered the house like a ghost. By the time the other girls woke up at noon, she was ready to slumber but all too late. Coffee and Red Bull were shoved down the throat to numb fatigue and sorrow. Ksenia was wilting.

Ghastly, bloody flashbacks strobed her mind.

She could not forget Victoria's battered body, unceremoniously stuffed into blue, plastic bin bags and dragged out of the house like rubbish. The twenty-four year old was killed for attempting what they all dreamed about and prayed for every day – freedom.

Life at the brothel carried on *business as usual* and cheap, heavy make-up covered all signs of deep misery. Drugs, cigarettes and alcohol stifled spirits and kept the work force dosed-up and docile.

Week followed week, each day mirroring the previous one. Whether it was a trick of circumstances or of the mind – it no longer mattered. The girls were caught in the crushing wheel of the cycle and with shallow breathing they bore the yoke of slavery.

Ripe-Tomato

The waitress emerged from the kitchen, carrying a tray full of Spanish tapas – simmered squid, *patatas bravas*, plump Padron peppers, two bean salads, goats cheese with honey on toast, sautéed mushrooms and two generous portions of black rice.

She quietly placed the dishes on the table and was turning to leave when Larisa spoke:

"We are celebrating the publication of the first issue of the Moldovan *Diaspora* magazine. Wanna have a look?"

Without waiting for the waitress's answer, Larisa retrieved a copy from her bag.

"It's got some good articles and useful information for those of us living abroad. You can keep it."

Nadea started flipping through the magazine but after only a few pages, suddenly dropped it to the floor. She picked it back up with shaking hands.

"I'm sorry," Nadea mumbled and scurried towards the back of the restaurant.

The magazine lay open at the *Missing Persons* page.

Ksenia's face stared out at them.

Doina just about managed to retain her composure, while Larisa felt a string of cold shivers running down her spine. No shred of breath or thought – just an overall stillness arresting all her bodily and mental functions. She felt simultaneously dead and more alive than ever before. Then a gush of energy surged rapidly and spiralled off towards her head, switching on a million bulbs. However, her body felt like it was crumbling, suddenly aware of the tremendous force of gravity.

"Do you feel what I am feeling?"

"Do you think what I am thinking?"

The age-old Moldovan ritual of answering a question with another question.

Larisa nodded. They were on the same page. Looking over her shoulder, she sought out Nadea.

"Excuse me," Larisa called to another waiter. "Is Nadea OK? Can we talk to her for a minute?"

"She's not feeling very well and went outside to get some fresh air. I will send her over as soon as she is back in."

Half an hour passed. Neither Doina nor Larisa could eat and the food had grown cold. Their appetite had disappeared.

Larisa called to the waiter a second time – patience had never been one of her virtues and now was not the time for any experimentation with new patterns of behaviour.

"Are you sure Nadea is OK? She has not come back in yet, has she?"

"She's got a headache and she's going home."

"No, she can't." Before she was able to stop herself, Larisa sprang up.

Ever rational, Doina intervened and took control.

"Could you please let her know that we'd like to talk to her? We think she may be able to help us with something very important and we'd really appreciate if she gave us a few minutes."

"Jeez, such a long and unnecessary shower of words at this critical time," Larisa thought.

Sensing her friend's apprehension, Doina squeezed her arm. But as soon as the waiter went away, Larisa erupted:

"Why the hell is she avoiding us? Does she have bad news? What is she hiding, Doina, what?"

"What's got into you? Chill, woman. I am sure Nadea will speak to us as soon as she is ready."

Larisa hated Doina's dispassionate cool sometimes and this was definitely one of those times.

"Does she not know how important this is? How can she be so calm right now?"

"You can chill if you want, hun, but I have no intention of doing so until I've spoken to that girl."

As Larisa was about to leave the table, Nadea emerged from the kitchen and approached them with heavy feet. She had decided to open up to Ksenia's friends, hoping that the burden of guilt weighing her down since her bolt would get lighter.

"I need to talk to you, but not here," she almost whispered.

"Why not here?"

"Give me your telephone number and we can arrange a better time and place." Nadea ignored Larisa's question.

"What has this woman got to hide? If she really thinks she's going to get away from us tonight – from me at any rate – then she must be properly mad or plain stupid," Larisa fretted but before she could grab Nadea's hand, Doina spoke in a calm voice.

"We are done with our dinner and are ready to listen," and she stood up. "We'll settle the bill and go somewhere else to have a chat."

"But you haven't even touched your food," Nadea tried to object; but as she spoke, her voice trailed off.

Perhaps Doina's attitude and demeanour stirred memories of someone else she had met in another place at another time.

They left the restaurant with stomachs empty but hearts full of hope and, in Larisa's case, with eyes full of tears, which she was desperately fighting. Silently and fervently she prayed for some news, any news, just some kind of news.

An irrational fear that Nadea might run out on them was growing stronger and Larisa had to make a conscious effort not to grab the stranger's hand. Nadea looked scared enough as it was. Sensing the tension, Doina rescued the situation.

"Let's go in here. It's a bar where the DJ is not deaf like all the rest of his profession seem to be. We should be able to have a proper conversation, without getting drowned in noise."

"*...for we've got a situation where body language alone won't do...*" Larisa wanted to add but her thoughts were running haywire, like scared cattle on an endless steppe.

As with these herds, when each beast is lost in the rising dust and deafening noise of their hooves, so was Larisa unable to distinguish her thoughts individually. Due to the increasing tension and inner turbulence steaming up her perceptions, all she was aware of was just a heavy flow ransacking her being.

As soon as they entered the bar and sat down, the three of them put the drinks on the table almost instantaneously. The rattling noise of the ice in the glasses readily betrayed their nerves but Nadea spoke soon enough to take the edge away.

"You must be Scarlet's blood sisters..."

252

"*Scarlet...? What Scarlet? I don't know any Scarlet...*" Larisa's mind raced. "*All I care about right now is Ksenia and only her...*"

Nadea carried on before either Doina or Larisa could utter a word in their bewilderment.

"I meant to say Ksenia," Nadea corrected herself, unaware that she could have been guilty of manslaughter had the two girls been of a weaker heart. "Ksenia used another name in the brothel in order to protect her real self from all that went on in that cursed house. I am sorry to tell you but that's where I know her from."

"Is she alive?" Larisa interrupted bluntly.

Nadea looked taken aback. She paused and seemed concerned while pondering the question.

"She was when I escaped."

"When was that?"

"Three months ago."

Larisa couldn't hold the piercing tears back any longer and they shamelessly filled her eyes.

"*Ksenia is alive,*" was all she could think. "*Thank you, God. Thank you! Thank you!*"

Larisa fervently kissed her right palm, which hosted the sacred mark.

"I liked Ksenia from the beginning. I admired her spirit," Nadea carried on. "When she was brought to the house, Ksenia was in shock and refused to sell her body. The guards had beaten her repeatedly and Madame kept her starving and battered in the basement for days on end. She reminded me of myself when I first arrived and I wanted to protect her from any further pain but Ksenia trusted no one."

Nadea's story was painful to listen to but neither Larisa nor Doina interrupted. Having escaped from hell, her voice was talking from another world.

"*What does it take to get through this kind of distress and torment? How can somebody overcome such ordeals?*"

Larisa wondered. An all enveloping desire to sweep the Earth inside out to find Ksenia burnt through her like a wild fire.

"We have to find her before it's too late," she thought.

"Ksenia couldn't bring herself to be a sex-slave and more punishment followed. I didn't want her to end up addicted to drugs like so many other girls did in that place or wake up with a mysterious scar on her back, like I did or even worse – disappear forever. The bastards who controlled our lives stopped at nothing. We were just livestock to them, to be bought and sold at their whim. Eventually Ksenia realised it was best to keep a low profile. She gave in and we started to think of ways to escape."

Nadea paused to take a sip of water. There were so many things flooding her mind which she was tempted to reveal – the rapes, the beatings, the drugs, the German Shepherd and all the other humiliations the mere memory of which made her sweat and panic. However, she realised they would be too painful and shocking for Doina and Larisa. Nadea chose to spare them these details.

"We thought about running away all the time but they kept a close eye on us constantly and there was no chance to do it until one day luck smiled upon us…upon me anyway. Ghena, one of the guards at the brothel, asked me to go out food-shopping with him and I took my chance."

Nadea paused again, her face twisted by the pain of confronting her memories.

"Just as Ghena and I were about to leave the house, Ksenia said something which didn't make any sense to me at the time. I mean, things were getting to her and she sounded a bit…odd at times. Anyway, she mentioned something about products being electronically tagged. It didn't make any sense until I got to the store and saw the security guards at the entrance. After we'd finished shopping and started heading to the checkout, I decided to take my chance. I was too full of adrenaline to feel nervous. I had asked Ghena if I could go back and get my favourite chocolate biscuits. He told me to be quick. I ran towards the alcohol section, grabbed four bottles of the most expensive champagne I could find and legged it to the nearest exit. I searched for the shop security and started walking out, right under his nose. The alarm went off and the security guard grabbed me and took me to a back room. As soon as the door closed behind me, I started kissing his hands like a psycho, thanking him for saving my life. Not understanding a word I was babbling in, he looked at me as though I was mad. Especially when he heard me asking for the police.

"*Police, politzia, militia,*" I tried all versions I knew, hoping he'd understand one of them.

The guard started laughing, perhaps amused that a thief was asking for the police. But I just kept repeating to him: "*Police please, politzia...*"

I was desperate to tell the police about Ksenia and the rest of the girls before it was too late. I had to speak to authorities urgently. There was no time to waste.

The police did arrive soon after and I was taken to the station. I tried to tell them all along what the issue was by employing a mixture of English, Russian and Romanian. When that didn't work, I began flailing my hands and gesturing wildly – yet to no avail. They did not get the message. Eventually they called an interpreter. I almost fainted when they showed me on their fingers the time the interpreter was going to arrive: nine in the evening. It was only five o'clock.

"*In four hours the criminals will flee and wipe all traces a hundred times over,*" I told them in a mix of languages. My screams and desperation did nothing but get me in a cell, behind a heavy, iron door."

255

Tears glistened in Nadea's eyes and she wiped them with the back of her hand before they could roll down her cheeks.

"I was at the end of my wits when the interpreter finally arrived and I wasn't making much sense. The final blow came when the police officers, after interviewing me for another few hours and wasting more precious, vital time, told me they would not be able to do anything that night because they had to run it past their sergeant or inspector or something like that.

"'It might already be too late now after all this fluffing but if we leave it till tomorrow, it will definitely be too late.' I begged and begged and begged, pulling my hair out, but it was decided.

"That was the longest night of my life. I could not save Ksenia as I'd promised. The anxiety of what might happen to her and the rest of the girls as a consequence of my bolting crept to the marrow of my bones and with my eyes wide awake and my heart bleeding, I paced the tiny cell all night.

"The next day, the police took me to Via Dolorosa – the street where the brothel was but I couldn't tell them the number of the door. In my anxiety, I had forgotten to look for it when I left the house the previous day. I asked them to drive slowly down the street so I could spot the house. When I did, the police were sceptical about my account because I pointed out a building on the left hand-side of the road when I had been looking out on the right side all along. Of course, they had no idea that the houses opposite were my only view for nearly three years while I was held captive and I could recognise them out of a million.

"The police went in to raid the flat but of course all too late – it was empty. The case was closed and I got repatriated soon after."

"How come you are in England now?"

"To scared to stay home. They knew where I was from and I thought they'd come after me. Not long after the Italian authorities sent me back to Moldova, I got out and came to stay with friends in England for a while."

Nadea downed another glass of water. Her glance crept back from far away places, full of remorse, as she slowly focused it on the girls in front of her.

"I am so sorry," she whispered.

Doina and Larisa did not reply straight away, but not because they held her responsible for failing to save Ksenia. The realisation that they were not any closer in finding their beloved friend hit them hard, crushing all hopes to smithereens once more.

"Please do not worry. You tried your best," Doina assured Nadea half-heartedly.

Deflated, Larisa silently cursed fate:

"Merciless mockery of lowest line! Shameless sham! Cheep charade! A con! A hoax!"

Nadea looked dejected. Tears brimmed her eyes and this time she gave up on wiping them. Doina closed in and tried to console her with a long, warm hug.

Larisa didn't know what to do. Doina was already doing her best to comfort Nadea. Never having been the emotional type, five years of living in England had made Larisa even more out of touch with her inner guiding system.

She stood up fidgeting.

"What shall I do? What shall I do?"

Tempted to offer Nadea a cup of tea, Larisa remembered she was dealing with a Moldovan. Although she suspected Nadea could have done with a glass of wine, she opted for a jug of water and brought over some more napkins.

Nadea excused herself and went to the bathroom.

"Why did she take her bag?" Larisa asked anxiously.

"You talk like a guy. Why do you think girls need their bags in the bathroom? Especially in this case. The poor girl is distraught, can't you see?" Doina snapped.

"I'm just afraid she might do a runner on us, that's all."

"Stop it, will you? Nadea is talking to us of her own will. Isn't that obvious? Besides, she has no reason to run away. She doesn't know where Ksenia is any more, do you understand?"

Larisa did but she was still on edge.

Nadea returned looking more composed.

An uncomfortable pause followed.

"I am sorry if I gave you false hope."

"Never mind, we will carry on searching." Larisa didn't know what else to say.

"Have you been looking for her, I mean apart from the *Missing People* poster in the *Diaspora* magazine?"

"I've been to every major city in Italy with a Moldovan community. I went to the local churches our people attend and the places they meet. I've been to the back streets of Milan and Rome – Via Vantaggio, Via Ardore, Via Peccati, Via Punizione – you name it, I've been there, but nobody could help. I now understand why – Ksenia's been kept under lock and key all this time."

"Did you say Via Vantaggio?" Nadea asked.

"Yes, I did."

"A girl used to sometimes replace us when we were on our period. There were always weirdos who wanted to fuck menstruating women but if the demand for *clean* fun was greater, they brought her in. Monica was a Via Vantaggio street girl, had been for years and she was willingly up for it. In the brothel she was at least guaranteed customers and a hot shower afterwards."

"Monica?" Larisa raced through her memory bank of endless faces. "Ripe-tomato kind of hair colour?"

"That's right. Do you know her?"

"I met her a couple of times on the backstreets of Milan but she never said she knew anything about Ksenia," Larisa remembered the girl because of the obviously false details she'd given her – Monica is not a Bessarabian name.

"She might have only known Ksenia by the name of Scarlet."

"I showed her a photo too."

"The one you've published in the magazine?"

"Yes."

"She looks nothing like that any more. Ksenia cut her hair with a pair of scissors I slipped her soon after she got there. She kept it chopped like that from then on. Also, her face is thinner these days and always heavily made-up."

Another uncomfortable pause followed.

"There's still a chance you can help us find Ksenia." Larisa leant over the low table.

"How?"

"You know Monica. I can recognise her too but I don't know the rest of the people involved. I won't know who's picking her up, if they are clients or people related to the gang or even Ghena himself."

"Oh, you'll be able to recognise him – he's only got one eye."

"How would you feel about coming to Milan with me?" Larisa asked bluntly.

A plan was hatching in her mind. Perhaps there could have been a subtler way to put it but Larisa was feverish.

"To do what?"

"To get Ksenia."

"How? Monica will never tell us where they've moved to. She's a hard-faced bitch and she would not shoot herself in the foot like that. She knows what will happen if she blows the whistle on them."

Larisa hadn't thought all the details through but started improvising.

"She doesn't need to know. We don't have to ask her directly."

"What do you have in mind?"

"I'm thinking that we locate Monica and keep an eye on her. If she is still in contact with people from the house, she's bound to meet one of them at some point. That's where we need your help. You will be able to recognise them and they will lead us to where Ksenia is. I know it's a long shot but it's the only one we've got right now."

"You are asking me to go back there? I don't think I can face that," Nadea started squeezing her hands. "I am too scared to even think about it, let alone face them once more."

She was clearly in distress and even Larisa knew not to push her any further.

"I understand your fear and I'm not going to insist. All I'll promise is that they won't see you. Here is my number and if you change your mind, please get in touch. I will pray that you do."

Nadea grabbed her bag and left in a hurry.

Doina and Larisa remained quiet for a few minutes before the latter spoke:

"At least we've got a new lead."

"Monica."

Taupe

The following week Larisa returned to Milan but couldn't find Monica. During previous visits there were times when that mop of red curls seemed to pop up constantly but three whole days of searching for it this time resulted in nothing. Larisa started to worry that she may have left the city, given up, or maybe worse.

In Milan, the street girls worked in shifts according to nationality: African girls during the day, replaced by South Americans early evening and Eastern Europeans later at night. This order was reversed in different locations, thus offering both the suppliers and recipients of carnal services the chance to move around and make their selection.

Battling her instincts, Larisa played it cautiously and didn't ask any of the street girls about Monica, observing instead from her taupe hired car, scanning the array of *workers* and waiting patiently.

It was on the fourth day that she finally spotted the redhead who was bewitching beholders in the timeless manner of all skilled courtesans.

Larisa watched and followed Monica for a few days, until it was clear that three men in particular seemed to be more than just clients, due to their frequent proximity. One of them, Larisa noticed, turned his head rather clumsily.

"*Is he the One-Eyed Monster?*" she thought. "*He could just happen to turn his head that way. I need Nadea to identify him.*"

Larisa thought of travelling back to London as soon as possible to fetch Nadea.

Thanks to the budget airlines and the necessity of an interpreter in London's delivery rooms, increasingly busy with Eastern European mothers, Larisa was able to afford the luxury of frequent flying.

Before asking Nadea to travel to Italy, Larisa needed to find out more about the man she believed to be the One-Eyed Monster. She abandoned Monica and began following him instead.

After a couple more days, Larisa had noted two addresses which he visited regularly. She parked daily outside both houses in turn and studied the windows of each one, hoping to spot Ksenia. But they were always shut tight and seemingly sworn to everlasting secrecy. Very quickly Larisa started to panic.

"*What if I've got the wrong guy and I'm just wasting my time on him? I need to get Nadea to see him one way or another.*"

She Skyped Doina later that night. Ever since her friend had come to London, communication had been a lot easier. Doina had a mobile phone for the first time in her life and Larisa also taught her how to use Skype.

"I believe I've found the One-Eyed Monster but I could be wrong. I am only going by instinct and by the fact that he turns his head in a strange way. We desperately need Nadea to come to Italy and identify him."

"What about sending us pictures?"

"Thanks for the advice, Sherlock! I already tried snapping away but because I am keeping a safe distance from him, I can't get a clear shot."

"OK, I will speak to Nadea and let you know. Keep your Skype on."

Larisa decided to carry on watching the two houses until she heard back from Doina. She parked for hours on end outside both properties until it was clear to her that one of them was a brothel. Judging by the number of people going in and out, mostly men – all sorts of men – it could only be a brothel. She decided to keep an eye on the house.

On Thursday lunchtime, just as she was getting ready to drive to the other address, Larisa cast her eyes upwards one more time and…there she was – Ksenia looking out, her eyes vacantly sweeping the street from side to side.

Thinking she might be hallucinating, Larisa turned away and felt her heart beating furiously, pressing to escape the suddenly tight cage of her ribs. She looked up again and validated the vision: Ksenia was standing by the window staring at the street below.

Larisa broke down blubbering. Worries that her loud sobs and the beating throbs of the heart would travel outside the car and soar to the window forced her to drive a safe distance away. Ksenia didn't have to see her. It would be too much of a shock and she could be being watched.

Larisa parked the car at the end of the street and collapsed in a heap. Her weight on the steering wheel caused the horn to sound loud and sharp. Ksenia however, was too far behind to hear or see anything and the noise barely registered with Larisa.

When she was able to speak again, Larisa called Doina.

"I've found her."

More sobs followed, despite Larisa biting her lip to make it stop.

"How? Where?"

"At the window. I've just seen her at the window of the flat looking out into the street."

A long pause ensued. Overwhelmed and speechless, the girls digested the news. Their superstitious manner, wrought over the centuries, precluded any celebrations. Ksenia was not rescued yet and things could still go wrong. Premature rejoicing was in neither their culture nor their character.

"Have you called the police?"

"Not yet. I'm trying to work out how best to go about it."

"Are you crazy? You need to call the police and get her out of there as soon as possible."

"I'm scared of messing it up. It may be our last chance to save her."

"Let the police do their job."

"How do we know they will? What if they don't take me seriously? I don't want to spoil the whole thing."

"Larisa, I share your pain, remember? Listen to me – don't do anything stupid. You can't get Ksenia out of there by yourself. This is a criminal gang we are talking about. Don't you dare think you can handle them on your own."

"Doina, I've got Ksenia's life in my hands right now and all I can do is shake. If she doesn't make it out, I will kill myself."

"Stop this nonsense and listen to me. If you are worried the police may not take you seriously, how about we ask Nadea to go to Italy and report it? The police will certainly react if she says she can expose her traffickers."

"I'm not leaving this country without Ksenia."

"I'm not saying you should. You can stay there and I'll see if I can persuade Nadea to join you. I'll go to the restaurant tonight and speak to her."

"Call me when you do it."

It was well past midnight when Doina called. She waited for Nadea to finish her shift before she could see her and break the news about Ksenia. She had invited Nadea to one of the quieter Turkish restaurants in Dalston which stayed open till late. They had ordered baklava and strong black tea. Doina phoned Larisa.

"I've got Nadea with me."

Doina put Nadea on the phone.

"Are you sure it was Ksenia?" she asked. "I mean I know she liked to stare out the window but was it her?"

Was Larisa sure? She could have taken hours, explaining in verbose detail to that stranger what Ksenia meant to her…"

"Yes, I am sure."

Larisa didn't know how to broach the subject of Nadea's indispensable importance to the rescue operation, which meant asking her to return to a place she hated and only wanted to forget.

"What are you going to do now?" Nadea asked.

"I am frightened cold about handling this opportunity and do not want to mess it up for Ksenia. I won't live with myself if I screw this up."

"Do you have a plan?" she asked again.

Larisa sighed.

"We need your help."

"Why? What do you mean? You know where Ksenia is now…I don't understand…" Nadea stumbled over her words.

"I do, but it won't be the same if I contact the police. They won't listen to me. They've already got your details and based on your case we might get a more prompt reaction this time."

"Look, Larisa, these aren't the sort of people you mess with. I was lucky to get away from them once and I do not want to tempt fate again, do you understand? I'm scared for my life. Actually, I am paralysed with fear. Do you know what that means? I don't think you do, otherwise you wouldn't push me like this, forcing me back to a time of my life which I want to forget."

Nadea passed the phone back to Doina.

"Larisa, I'll ring back." And she hung up.

It was close to midnight. The long, stressful days were getting to Larisa and she passed out fully dressed on top of the bed. The night chill caused her to wake up at five in the morning. Larisa tried to get back to sleep but cold on top of the duvet, a million thoughts poked her mind. Still hopeful to escape into the dream world, she slipped under the sheets. Sleep was the only time she could break away from the nightmare she'd been caught in for over a year and a half. She checked the clock again and it was already six.

Her mobile phone beeped with a Skype message.

"It can only be Doina," she thought. *"What is she doing up at this hour, five a.m. London time? Perhaps she is just as restless."*

Larisa searched for her phone, which she kept under the pillow every night, in case of any news.

She rubbed her eyes and looked at the screen.

Larisa didn't recognise the number with an Italian prefix but the message made her jump out of bed.

Dark-Navy

The brothel was never entirely quiet, except for a few, brief hours in the morning when the last client had left and the girls collapsed to rest and recover, as if back from war. At all other times, the house was abustle. Heavy steps, high heels clacking, squeaky beds and bestial groans were sounds so familiar that they had long stopped being audible.

Whiffs of cheap feminine perfume mingled with the sex odour of both genders floated abundantly in the air. Ksenia thought it was a unique, intense and permanent kind of scent, not to be forgotten or mistaken for anything else – "*the scent of the fallen world*" as she called it.

"*Surely if the police trained dogs to recognise it, every whorehouse in the world would get busted.*"

"Where is Scarlet? Scarlet!" Ksenia heard Madame looking for her but she didn't move.

Contemplating the rain outside and the droplets trickling down the dirty window somehow soothed her inner ache.

"There you are. I hope you haven't forgotten you are on webcam duty this afternoon. The request is for a prison scene – right up your street, isn't it, with your hair cut short like that?" she laughed. "Look, you better get ready – make yourself look beautiful. You are lucky – we've got a hunk coming soon. He'll play the guard who fucks you and Angela. C'mon, chop-chop now."

There was a special room – the *studio* – fitted with a wide screen computer and a webcam for the purpose of providing a virtual thrill for customers who couldn't make it to the brothel. The girls took turns to perform shows as requested by those prepared to pay a lot of money. It involved anything from single to double, triple or multiple acts of same or mixed genders. The guys were usually recruited from the outside for this purpose.

A quarter of an hour before three o'clock, they had to go into the *studio* and get ready for the thirty minute show. Ksenia and Angela were both perched on *skyscraper* high heels.

The girls at the brothel referred to their footwear in three ways: *stilts* – heels of seven inches, *scaffolds* – platform shoes with chunky heels, and *skyscrapers* – eight inch stiletto heels.

As costumes, Madame gave the two *inmates* short see-through skirts matched with black and white stripy low-cut tops. The *prison guard* was suited in a light grey shirt and dark-navy trousers. He held two pairs of shiny, metal handcuffs, which he used to tether Angela to one side of the bed frame by her ankle and Ksenia's right wrist to the other.

The show started.

Ksenia closed her eyes.

"Look into the camera, bitch," he slapped her in the face. "Right there…yes keep your eyes open…" he took his belt off and lashed her repeatedly across her back.

He delightedly abused the two girls, combining different elements of position, action and mood, forcing them to entwine in all possible ways involving three people.

After twenty minutes, he untied Ksenia and shoved her closer to the camera to lick the screen with the intention to engage more intimately the client on the other side. Unwittingly she pressed the power button and the computer shut down.

Madame was called in to reboot the system. She was in such a hurry to get it back up and running so as not to lose business that she did not realise Ksenia was standing right behind her.

In five minutes the show resumed but it took all of Ksenia's effort not to betray her emotions. It was something she was progressively getting worse at. Her heart hammered away and her facial muscles twitched involuntarily. She had found out what the password was.

The whole of the next day and all through the night, Ksenia was in a daze. Men mounted and dismounted her with Ksenia hardly noticing what was going on. She had evaded the present, concerned only with what the future was to bring – the near future – as near as the coming morning.

Shortly before sunrise, the house fell quiet. Ksenia heard the door slam behind the last customer. Once the guards checked all the rooms to make sure everything was in order, they gathered in the kitchen for their usual shots of vodka. Gradually the voices and clinking of glass died down too. Ksenia waited for another half hour, listening carefully but there were no other sounds coming from the house apart from snoring.

Cars could already be heard in the street and the early birds started chirping, announcing the start of a new day.

Ksenia rolled off the mattress on the ground in the corner where she slept and tiptoed out of the room. Despite the absence of light, she avoided all the squeaky boards of the old wooden floor. Moving across carefully as if navigating a chessboard, she had successfully reached the *studio* without making any noise. However, Ksenia struggled to open the door, which broke the silence of the night with a high pitched creak.

The monotonous snoring of the guards stopped briefly.

Ksenia's breath also stopped.

The snuffles resumed.

She sighed.

Not wanting to risk it again, she thought of using oil on the door but that would involve going to the kitchen, and besides, the cupboard where it was kept was just as noisy to open.

She considered using a soap bar or candlesticks but it meant wandering around the house looking for them. Instead Ksenia opted for something less effective but at least readily available – KY jelly. She always had a tube tied on a piece of string round her neck.

In fact, most girls in the house had lubricant close at hand. That and cigarette lighters were the only items used over and over again regardless of the time of day or night.

Ksenia squeezed out a fistful of lotion and nervously rubbed it onto the hinges of the door, more so where the metal knuckles overlapped. Then she tried again. Her efforts hadn't silenced the door completely but allowed her to open it just enough for her to slip into the *studio*. With shaky hands and fluttering breath, she switched on the computer and followed Madame's process from the day before. Skype opened automatically and Ksenia typed in Larisa's mobile number, which she knew by heart.

"*Forever grateful to you, Alex.*" She thought back to the days in Brighton when she learned what Skype was.

Not wanting to risk making any noise by calling, Ksenia urgently tapped out a brief SMS.

"It's Ksenia...are you there...? Don't call...Text only..."

No reply.

Ksenia fretted.

"Larisa, read your messages for God's sake..."

No reply.

"Oh, c'mon Larisa, check your bloody phone. I can't be on Skype for ever..."

Notwithstanding the early hour, Ksenia hoped her blood sister would be there for her.

"What if they've forgotten all about me? It's been more than a year and a half now...They probably think I am dead anyway..."

Ksenia stared blankly at the silent screen aware for the first time how strenuous a process simple breathing was.

Thinking her messages were vanishing into the void, she typed a final one:

"Et tu, Brutus...?"

A shade after six in the morning, Larisa, who had been tossing and turning for the past hour, jumped out of bed.

She gaped at her phone screen, reading and re-reading the first message. Her brain refused to take in what her eyes were seeing and she stood there vacantly, with her mouth agape. Her hands started shaking and Larisa couldn't type back quick enough.

"Oh my God...Ksiusha...How are you?"

"What do you mean, Skype? It shows a mobile number on my phone."

It was only as she read the final message that Larisa was seized by the horror that her friend was never going to get her replies. Larisa suddenly realised that if Ksenia wasn't reading her messages, somebody else must have been.

271

"The curse of modern technology…" she thought and prayed fervently that Ksenia would stop texting.

Larisa's phone, however, buzzed again. The same number flashed up on the screen.

"Fuck you both – you dirty, filthy whores. I will show you."

Larisa felt sick and numb. Her palms began sweating and the phone slid to the floor.

Madame was in deep slumber when her phone started beeping. That usually meant *business* and regardless of the hour, Galea always answered it. She had to read the messages a few times before they made sense. She sprang to her feet when they did. Without a moment to waste after threatening Larisa, Madame went to wake up the guards.

Swearing and shouting at the top of his lungs, Ghena hoofed straight to the studio. Madame strutted along. The raging One-Eyed Monster grabbed Ksenia and dragged her out by her neck, along the corridor and into the kitchen. He always said it was easier to clean up the mess from the linoleum floor there, rather than deal with spurted blood in the carpeted parts of the house.

Ksenia curled up trying to protect her head, abandoning everything else to the bludgeoning kicks and blows showering her from all sides.

Vanilla

It wasn't until a few days after the attack that Ksenia was able to stand and walk again. And then, only just. If it hadn't been for the garish *maquillage*, her ghostly translucence would've lifted her off the ground.

She floated about the house, searching ardently in the rubbish bins. For the past couple of months Ksenia had grown obsessed with bursting the gum bubbles which Madame discarded all over the house. Ksenia saw each different sized globule of air as a mini copy of Madame.

"Every one of these contains a piece of the shrew's breath. I'll put them all out, one by one. The time will come when I'll extinguish the final one and then she'll be dead."

Ksenia took obvious pleasure in popping each bubble repeatedly with a needle.

Having carried out this ritual of vengeance, Ksenia withdrew to her favourite spot by the lounge window.

She was quiet – snowed under with thoughts.

"Why am I being punished to be a prisoner of life? What was Madame on about saying that we lived life to the full here? Whose life? I am not living mine but someone else's.

Used as a tool to help others live their depraved and distorted lives, I'm being sacrificed and rendered down to the value of a toy, a mechanic doll to satisfy debauchery, perverted lust and rotten urges."

Madame stormed in.

"There are clients waiting downstairs. What are you doing kneeling like that? Praying? This is a brothel, darling, not a bethel. And you don't look like no church-goer either, flaunting your tits like that," Galea almost choked on her vanilla gum, laughing at her own joke. "Move your arse."

Ksenia headed to the bathroom. She couldn't splash her face as she so wished. Doing her makeup once had taken long enough. Instead she sprinkled cold water on her crown. It always helped with hushing the mind and the little voices she had started hearing recently, which kept telling her how worthless and filthy she was. Ksenia studied her reflection.

"The one involved in many vulvas does not evolve! The one involved in many…"

Ksenia couldn't figure out whether the chant came from her own head or from the ghastly reflection in the mirror. Her eyes filled with fright and she turned away. The chant, however, carried on, matching the rhythmic throbbing of the vein in her temple.

"The one involved in many vulvas…"

In her efforts to block out the repetitive phrase, Ksenia became aware of another sound – a familiar male voice.

She startled and pricked up her ears.

"Where shall we drop her?" somebody asked.

"On that sofa over there."

Convinced that these were coming from somewhere outside her head, she cracked the bathroom door to peek into the open-plan lounge.

Ksenia instantly drew back.

Now she knew her brain was playing tricks on her – first the odd noises and whispers driving her mad for the past few weeks and on top of that, it seemed, she had started hallucinating too.

"Leave her here and I'll speak to Galea," a man she didn't recognise told another with his back towards her, holding a sleeping girl in his arms.

"The client in the Hawaiian shirt you saw waiting in the reception area – he likes his bitches in this state. He'll pay good money for her," the first man gestured towards the slumped woman.

"No problem – I can get them by the dozen," the other laughed.

"Isn't she fuckable, spread out like that and with her legs wide open, huh? She's not wearing any knickers either, is she?"

"Nah, I took care of that, man – had to try the merchandise before passing it on, you know the going …"

Ksenia still couldn't see his face. His voice, however, ruffled her. She flung the bathroom door open, slamming it against the wall. The two men turned and stared back at her.

Ksenia's gaze remained fixed on the taller one and her jaw dropped.

Smoky-Citrine

Doina was determined to talk Nadea into travelling to Italy and filing a police report. The latter, however, was just as keen to avoid it at all costs. After she had spoken to Larisa and handed the phone back to Doina, Nadea didn't know how to leave quickly enough.

"I'm sorry but I have to go. It's getting late. I wish you and Larisa understood my circumstances."

"At least you are alive…" Doina didn't move.

"So is Ksenia."

"…but only you are free."

"Please don't make me feel guilty. I tried my best to get Ksenia out too, you know…"

"You say you did but how do I know it's true?"

Nadea was taken aback.

"Are you for real? I told you how things happened. I did all I could. Don't look at me like that. I honestly did."

"If that's the case, why don't you want to help this time? It may be our last chance to save Ksenia, who knows?" Doina held Nadea's stare. "I couldn't live

276

with myself if she doesn't make it out of there." She paused and drew Nadea in, "Could you?"

It was close to midnight and the restaurant was almost empty. Smoky-citrine glass lamps, hung all over the ceiling, were dimmed and their hues mellowed the space.

Doina watched Nadea patiently, waiting for her reaction. She had deliberately adopted an insinuating tone, hoping it would rile Nadea into acquiescing to her wish.

"What exactly do you want me to do, for God's sake?"

"Nothing that would put you under any risk. You join Larisa in Milan and contact the Italian authorities to inform them that you've managed to hunt down your former traffickers. Once you file the report and the police have taken all the details, you can come back to London and I promise we'll leave you in peace for ever after."

The realisation that she might have to return to the city she swore to never visit again caused Nadea to shake. She looked at Doina but her gaze went beyond – perhaps she was already back at the brothel. She looked frightened. Doina felt a strong urge to hug Nadea but she waited.

Silence. Sticky, choky silence.

Finally Nadea nodded, if only imperceptibly.

"Everything will be OK, I promise." Doina went around the table and hugged Nadea.

With the heavy weight of expectation lifted off her shoulders, Doina let out a long sigh. Genuine care and compassion filled her heart for this stranger who was helping them to find Ksenia.

"Don't promise me anything. I don't need your empty assurances. All you care for is your friend and don't give a damn about me. Do you think I am stupid and don't understand what's happening here?"

"Please don't talk like that, Nadiusha…"

"Don't you *Nadiusha* me!"

"Look, I have a lot of respect for you and all the other girls who have gone through that hell. I know what you are thinking, but trust me – I mean what I say. You are all strong women who know about life and humanity, or shall I say inhumanity, more than anyone else. In many ways, you know more about life than the rest of us ever will or ever want to. You are someone who's travelled to the darker side and come back alive – that's not a simple thing."

"Spare me your lecture. We are wounded souls but you can't see that, can you? You know damn well how scared I am yet you have no remorse in whipping me into action. Just like a peasant beating his horse to carry a heavy weight regardless of season, you too push and shove me ahead cruelly. What do you care if I am able to bear this burden or not…?"

Doina gulped but said nothing. The comparison instantly filled her with guilt. She remembered how one winter's day, she had witnessed her neighbour, Mos Vasile, whipping his frightened and exhausted animal into pulling a cart full of logs. The roads were icy, as well as covered in snow. The horse was not fitted with any shoes and frothed at the mouth, struggling to move. The old man carried on with the abuse until the animal dropped dead in the middle of the street. The memory sent a chill down Doina's back.

"I am sorry. I really am."

Nadea ignored the apology.

"I'll go to file that report with the police in Italy but I want you to leave me in peace after that. Forever. I want you to forget me, do you understand?"

Doina nodded in silence.

Nadea left and Doina found herself in an empty restaurant. The establishment's policy was to stay open until the last client departed. However, the three

278

hovering waiters looked at her accusingly and she rose to leave, tipping them generously.

Once outside, she tried calling Larisa. Unable to reach her, Doina Skyped a message that she'd try again in the morning.

However, at five a.m. London time, well before Doina got to message her, Larisa called.

"Ksenia tried to make contact with me."

"When? How?" Groggy with sleep, Doina was even more confused by the news.

"Just now, a few minutes ago."

Doina took some time to process the information.

"What did she say?"

"Not much…She used Skype to text me but never got my replies…" Larisa's sobs acted as a cold bucket of water and Doina jumped out of bed.

"What do you mean?"

"My messages went to whoever's phone the Skype account was registered to and not to Ksenia. It didn't occur to me what was happening until it was too late, the idiot I am…Ksiusha got caught…"

"How do you know?"

"Somebody texted back, swearing and threatening us…"

"Hey, please don't cry…"

"What if they've killed her?"

Doina didn't know how to react. She was also worried that Ksenia might have to pay for her audacity but she had to calm Larisa somehow.

"Let's not forget – she brings them money and they are greedy people. I don't think they'll take it so far. Besides, there's nothing we can do about it now and speculating is only going to make us sick. We'll get her out very soon. I've got some good news – Nadea agreed to go to Milan. I'll get her tickets booked this morning."

"When can she travel?"

"She will take time off work next week. I'll give you more details once I've sorted her flight. Promise me you won't do anything stupid before Nadea gets there."

"Don't worry, I won't go to the house by myself, much as I'd like to. I'll keep a safe distance away, I promise."

"I will also try and see if I can get in touch with Boris and tell him the good news."

"Have you heard from him recently?"

"Not really. I called a few times but couldn't get hold of him. I'll try again tomorrow."

The last time Doina had spoken to Boris was a few days before she came to England. He said he still hadn't heard anything about Ksenia. Doina tried to reach him from the UK too but her calls went unanswered.

Dog-Violet

Boris looked at Ksenia as if trying to recognise someone from long ago. The deep furrowed lines crossing his narrow forehead were new to Ksenia. This Boris seemed a hostile stranger.

Ksenia felt her insides inflate and expand, one by one, until her windpipe seemed squashed tight and she was convinced she'd burst open.

Boris puffed his cheeks out audibly and left the room without a word. Ksenia's breath was still suspended. However, the inner shock stirred deep. Her knees crumpled and she slid to the floor.

"Perhaps my nerves are packing in. I'm just seeing things. It's just a fabrication of my feverish brain. I need to calm down."

Yet when she opened her eyes again, the young woman dumped on the couch, just as she herself had been nearly two years ago, was the irrefutable proof that she hadn't imagined things. The sleeping beauty had her head turned up with her hair swept to one side, revealing a long, pale and gracious neck. The stranger was wearing Ksenia's peacock earrings. She stood there transfixed. Ksenia was assaulted with flashbacks from the past and seemingly random comments and images pushed to the surface of her memory.

"It's not the real thing, I know, but it doesn't need to be when it looks it, right?"

She suddenly understood why the remark from the good old days, when Boris gave Ksenia a ring, had not sat right with her. A sinking feeling hit her in the pit of her stomach. She realised he had revealed his true character through that ambiguous comment, yet at the time, she had disregarded it as a clumsy choice of words, rather than a timely Freudian slip.

"That bastard...How stupid am I...? They've all abandoned me: my boyfriend, that bitch Nadea, even my blood sisters...Abandoned by all, by fate and life itself, it seems – with my own sanity threatening to follow suit."

Ksenia remembered the games of musical chairs she played as a child with Doina and Larisa. The speed and agility of her friends always won them a seat while Ksenia was perpetually left standing.

"Why do they say there is a place for everyone under the sun? For me – there isn't and there has never been one."

Ksenia sat absentmindedly on the living-room floor. Madame came in followed by a skinny stranger with a dog-violet face, wearing a Hawaiian shirt. He looked at the sleeping beauty lying half naked on the sofa, nodded with the mindless excitement of a deranged beast drooling over its helpless pray and promptly unbuttoned his trousers.

Pink-Peach

Waiting for Nadea to arrive in Milan, Larisa spent every day parked outside the house where she had spotted Ksenia. Yet she hadn't seen her a second time. It worried her.

"Hi Doina! Has Nadea got her tickets yet? Hello, can you hear me?"

"Yes, meet her at Malpensa Airport next Tuesday. She is on the ten past ten EasyJet flight from London Luton."

***

Once she had arrived, Nadea wanted to get everything over and done with as soon as possible and get the hell out of there. Larisa's sudden change of plan threw her completely.

"I've been watching the house day and night but haven't see Ksenia again. We can't go to the police yet."

"What do you mean? You are not telling me you begin to doubt you've seen her at all, are you?"

Larisa hesitated.

"Oh man, don't tell me I came here for nothing."

"Of course you didn't. Look, we'll contact the police but first I want you to identify Ghena. I think I've seen him going in and out of the place a few times but I can't be sure it's him."

"What do you mean you can't be sure it's him? The guy's got one fuckin' eye, for God's sake…"

"I know but he doesn't exactly flaunt it. If you can confirm that he is who I think he is, then we can go straight to the police station."

"Hang on a second. This wasn't part of the plan," Nadea stuttered. "Doina promised I wouldn't have to face those bastards again."

"You won't. Look, it's simple. We drive to the address, we park a safe distance away and you point Ghena out to me. No one will see us, I guarantee."

"Oh man, I knew I shouldn't have come here…"

"Please trust me."

Larisa drove them to the narrow street close to the Ponte Lambro district, where she had caught sight of Ksenia over a week ago. Just off one of the main roads, the flat was at the bottom of the street, on the third floor of an old and bedraggled building. Larisa parked a few doors up the road, near a mattress filled skip, so that they could have a good view of the entrance while remaining sheltered from prying eyes.

"I'm very nervous," fretted Nadea. "What if we don't get to see the One-Eyed Monster?"

"We will. I've seen him loads this past week."

People went in and out of the building but Nadea didn't recognise any of them. It wasn't until late in the afternoon when a familiar figure finally emerged. Ghena had a couple of rubbish bins in his hands and was walking towards the skip, right next to their parked car. Realising what was about to happen, Nadea paled. She bent forward in an attempt to hide.

"Stay there and don't move," Larisa commanded and got out of the car.

Nadea hardly breathed in fear and trepidation.

"Where is she going?"

Nadea had learned not to trust anyone ever since her godmother sold her to a trafficking gang in Turkey. On top of that, the backstabbing and betrayals she had experienced and witnessed in the brothels she'd worked in had taught her that friendship was just another commodity that could be bought or traded. Larisa was, of course, trying to rescue Ksenia, but at what price? Who could tell? Nadea was certain she'd been duped again.

"What if she's struck a deal with the One-Eyed Monster to swap Ksenia for me? It wouldn't be the first time that happened."

A year before, one of the girls in the house – Liliana – had befriended Monica, who was free to come and go as she pleased. On hearing how much money there could be made on the street by doing it willingly, Liliana voiced an interest. Monica lobbied Madame to release Liliana. The deal was that if they could bring another girl in her place, they would agree to it. Monica duly recruited Olga, a whiney-voiced sixteen-year-old, freshly released from the Belti orphanage and a month later the barter was done.

Nadea was convinced she was being traded in for Ksenia.

"That's why they pushed so hard to get me to come to Italy. I can't believe I didn't see it coming. How stupid am I! Should I jump out of the car and run for my life?"

Nadea would have bolted if only she could move. Paralysed with fear, she shrank into a ball in the foot well of the passenger seat. Larisa hardly recognised the dishevelled figure when she returned to the car.

"Please don't do this to me," a crazed look glistened in Nadea's bulging eyes.

"Don't do what?"

"Please don't trade me in for Ksenia. Don't commit such a sin. No matter how much you care for your friend, I am human too. I beg you to have mercy on me." She broke down in utter desperation.

Larisa was dumbstruck.

She held Nadea in an attempt to stop her convulsions, all the while trying to understand what she was saying. In her panic, Nadea didn't make much sense, speaking the words through sobs and hiccups.

"Don't be silly – I would never do that to you. What's got into you? Please stop crying."

"Why did you go to meet the One-Eyed Monster then? Don't lie. I am sick of lies."

"What are you on about? He was coming our way and I didn't want him to spot you. I thought that if I got out of the car, it would distract him. He doesn't know me, remember?"

Nadea was inconsolable and Larisa didn't quite know how to handle the situation. Stroking Nadea's back, she repeated words of assurance:

"Please don't worry. You are safe."

Larisa was shocked and taken aback to see the sudden and utmost transformation Nadea had undergone. In the span of five minutes while she had been absent, Nadea had become a totally different person. Despite wishing to offer her more comfort, Larisa was also aware that somebody else might pass by and recognise Nadea. Staying there any longer was asking for trouble.

"Please stop crying and let's get out of here. Let's get you as far away from this place as possible."

Nadea looked up still distrustful and tried to wipe away her tears. She nodded, still hiccupping and Larisa started the car.

Once at the hotel, Nadea took a hot bath and by the evening felt better enough to apologise.

"I'm sorry about earlier."

"That's OK, I understand, but please, trust me – I'd never do anything to harm you in any way whatsoever. I am so grateful to have met you. It's all thanks to you and your will to help out."

Nadea attempted a half smile and said nothing.

"Once we report everything to the police tomorrow and they've taken all the details they need, you can return to London."

"I hope this all gets sorted sooner rather than later."

After countless knocks on doors, streams of interviews and statements, the police finally took the case up and put the house under surveillance. Nadea was able to go back to London on the promise that she return to Italy as a witness, should any arrests be made and charges brought forward.

Larisa suspected that would be the last they saw of Nadea, arrests or not. She had seen more than raw fear in that girl's eyes.

Larisa remained in Italy. The Milanese police had her details as Ksenia's next of kin and, in any case, she was determined to stay there until her friend was in her arms. Larisa was nervous about the whole rescue operation even though things were out of her control. The entire following week, she kept the mobile phone on her at all times, tucking it under her pillow at night and watching it constantly during the day.

"Let me know as soon as you hear anything," Doina told her every day as she hung up the phone.

Finally, on Sunday morning, the phone rang with the much awaited news. A raid had been carried out successfully and nine girls were rescued from the brothel, amongst them one Ksenia Robu.

"Is she OK?" Larisa breathlessly asked the officer who called her.

"She seems fine. They will all be taken to a special recovery centre until the embassy provides them with the necessary documentation to be repatriated. Take the details down and you can visit her there."

"Would you please let her know that I am here?"

"Will do," and the line went dead.

"Thank you, officer," Larisa whispered, still holding the phone to her ear despite the dialling tone at the other end.

***

Every sort of emotion assaulted her senses. Sinking to the floor, she burst out crying shamelessly, melting into tears and becoming one with them, flowing deeper and deeper into the furthest crevices of her being. All the frustration, anxiety and fear that had heaped up over the last twenty months came gushing out and Larisa made no effort to stop it.

She surrendered.

Totally.

***

After some time, still curled up on the floor, Larisa tried calling Doina but her phone rang unanswered. For the first time in her life, she realised there was a difference between being on your own and feeling alone. Sadly for Larisa, this was a state she'd soon grow all too familiar with.

Early the next day, Larisa went to the address given to her by the police officer. She held it dearly to her chest as if it were a family heirloom.

After a long and humiliating check-in procedure where her identity was painstakingly verified and her body stripped, she was finally escorted to a tiny bedroom on the top floor of a four-storey house.

In front of the room, Larisa stopped to compose herself. Anticipation, tension and nerves robbed her of all breath. She swallowed hard and knocked on the pink-peach door.

There was no answer and she let herself in.

Ksenia was watching out the window.

"Ksiusha!" Larisa called and bit her lip to stay strong.

Ksenia turned around slowly. Until now Larisa had been just grateful that her friend was still alive; however, she was now shocked to see what that survival entailed. Ksenia looked like she had lost half of her weight. Her pride and joy – her long and luxurious mane – had been clipped untidily close to the scalp. A gaunt figure stared back. Ksenia was a mere spectre of her former self.

Swaying, Ksenia seemed unable to hold her balance and instead of trying to come forward to meet Larisa's stretched arms, she slumped on the sofa.

Larisa dashed forward and hugged her long lost friend so tightly that the other started to cough. Tremors rippled through Ksenia's weak body and Larisa felt burning tears trickling down her spine.

"It's OK, Ksiusha. It's all over now. You are safe, sweetheart."

Stroking her tormented body Larisa tried to comfort Ksenia – her blood sister, a third of her soul. Trying to absorb the shocks ravishing her dear friend, she cradled her flimsy frame with boundless love and care.

Time stood still.

Lavender

After three days, Ksenia was repatriated along with the eight other Moldovan girls rescued from the brothel. The representatives of the International Organisation for Migration met them at Chisinau airport and took the girls directly to their headquarters, where the rehabilitation process began with a psychological assessment.

"Your name?"

"Ksenia."

"Ksenia what?"

"Robu."

The psychologist paused writing, adjusted the collar of her white coat and looked at Ksenia with probing eyes. She had picked up on the meaning of Ksenia's surname – *the slave* and given the circumstances, she didn't know what to make of it.

"I know what you are thinking but my name *is* Ksenia Robu," she sneered at the irony of her appellation.

Ksenia comes from the Greek word *Xena* – meaning hospitable, or *Xenios* – foreigner. Thus, a literal translation of her name would be either *hospitable* or *foreign slave*, or including both possible translations – *a hospitable, foreign slave*.

Ksenia's desolate and angry tone of voice made the interviewer uneasy and the psychologist resumed her questions with increasing uncertainty.

"Are you single, married or…?"

"Debauched," Ksenia cut in.

"Sorry, did you say divorced?"

"Debauched. I said I was debauched."

"I know what you've been through but we need your cooperation to be able to help." The psychologist put down her pen.

"Too late."

Ksenia stared at the lavender walls and refused to answer any other questions.

The young psychologist recognised that Ksenia was going to be too difficult a case for her level of experience and decided to call Antonia Ivanovna – a senior consultant.

Thanks to her many years of dealing with trafficking victims, Antonia Ivanovna managed to coax Ksenia into admitting it was her boyfriend who had sold her out.

"Ahh – the ubiquitous Boris Undescu," Dr Ivanovna exclaimed knowingly. "That guy is as free from guilt as a frog from feathers. Six other girls – that we know of – fell for his charms. We've filed lawsuits against him on dozens of occasions but every time the victim changed her mind and dropped the charges. Are you willing to see him punished? It won't cost you anything. We'll take care of absolutely everything and make sure you are safe."

Ksenia left the room vowing never to return to the humanitarian NGO. An amalgam of fear, anger, shame, guilt, nausea and a great deal of confusion fogged her mind and she couldn't explain why she refused the attempts to help or the offer to take Boris to court.

"It'll help prevent other abuses." Larisa tried logic to encourage Ksenia to go through with it.

Larisa and Doina had flown over to Moldova temporarily so that they could be with their friend and spend some time together. They also had reported Boris to the police but the authorities said they couldn't do anything until the victims came forward. Angry that he'd fooled the three of them so easily, Larisa was determined to get justice.

"We'll support you all the way, Ksiusha. This man needs to be locked away so he cannot harm anyone else."

"It's all my fault," Ksenia started crying.

"No, it's not. He has lied to you and sucked you in. You can't blame yourself for what happened."

"Are you scared?" Doina held her hand.

Ksenia nodded and lay down, facing the wall.

Upon her return, only two members of the village treated Ksenia as they always had: Laika – her dog, a black mongrel with white patches and two identical tan marks above its eyes. Catching sight of her long lost owner, the dog grew very excited and dragged the kennel a couple of metres despite the tight grip of a thick chain around its neck. Laika jumped up and down, waving her tail non-stop and licked Ksenia's hands joyfully.

The only other person who had no reservations whatsoever in welcoming Ksenia home unreservedly was Zuzu. He came shyly to her house on the first day, bringing a jar of honey as a gift. Judging by the amount of bites all over his limbs and face as he scuttled off, he must have been chased by a thousand bees.

The rest of the village avoided Ksenia. Everyone kept at a safe distance, looking sideways and gossiping on all Marani's street corners. They did not take any time to ponder the moral implications of being trafficked, nor did anyone bother to seek the truth. It was much easier to condemn and accuse her of *selling herself* abroad.

For the first few weeks Ksenia could not bear solitude and sought company day and night, yet she didn't want to leave her parents' house. Neither did she want to speak about her torments.

"Don't take it personally. It's not that I don't want to talk to you – it's just a weight I wouldn't want to put on anybody's shoulders, that's all."

"This is Doina and me you are talking about. Do not worry about the weight – it's certainly easier to carry if split between three."

Ksenia decided to change the subject.

"Enough about me. How is it going with you two? It's been so long. I'm sure your lives have been far more interesting than mine."

Larisa exchanged worried looks with Doina but said nothing. She told Ksenia about the magazine project.

"We are working on the fourth issue and it's going really well. Our people have welcomed the idea and it's proving very useful."

"If you only knew how many appeals for help to find you Larisa has printed in the paper…" Doina tried to bring the subject back to Ksenia but she bluntly interrupted.

"What about you? Larisa mentioned you've set up a cleaning business. How's that going?"

"It's going OK, I'm pleased with it. It's funny, you make all these detailed business plans but just leaving a bunch of fresh, colourful flowers on the table works magic. Clients love it."

Ksenia choked on her cherry compote.

"How thoughtless," she coughed.

"Pardon?"

"I am happy for your success but not at the expense of flowers. I feel the same way about flowers as vegetarians do about animals. If I had the power, I'd

293

make all flower shops illegal. They are just like abattoirs and nothing less."

Doina was taken aback by this sudden diatribe and Larisa tried to appease the situation.

"Hey c'mon – that's taking it a bit far."

"Why? Because flowers don't scream with pain? Or because you can't hear it? Is that why?" she burst out. "If people love flowers so much, why don't they plant their own or if they don't have the space, why not buy pots with flowers and enjoy their beauty that way, instead of maiming nature and causing pain in the name of aesthetics? Why cull them? Culling flowers is just like culling seals. Actually, if you ask me it's even worse than that. Growing flowers only to cut them in their prime for selfish human delectation – is absolutely barbaric. All people who claim to love flowers while accepting or supporting their culling are hypocrites and liars, and…and……and nothing else. Brutes!"

The uncharacteristic tirade left the other two aghast. Larisa and Doina stared at each other.

"Look, Ksiusha," Doina spoke softly. "I am sorry, I didn't know you felt that way. How about I promise to stop buying fresh flowers from now on? My clients may think I have stopped caring about them but if it means so much to you, I won't do it any more, promise. I certainly never imagined that going a little further to make others happy could upset someone like that but it doesn't matter. I will think of something else."

Ksenia studied Doina's face suspiciously trying to work out if she really meant it. However, she also knew their word to each other was sacred and she slowly relaxed.

"The business won't suffer, don't worry. You can replace the gift of flowers with another one, I am sure."

Doina nodded reassuringly and smiled:

"I'll leave fresh fruit instead."

"There you go – we don't call you Frizzy for no reason," Larisa teased. "Your brains are always on fire with new ideas."

Auburn

Following her rescue, Ksenia went through a prolonged period of withdrawal and aloofness, painting when she wasn't sleeping. She refused to see anyone other than her parents, Zuzu, Doina and Larisa. Even Maya, her trusted landlady from Chisinau, was excluded from visiting her.

Larisa was able to coordinate the *Diaspora* magazine from Moldova by the use of phone and internet, connecting with all those involved in it. She worked a few hours every day taking care of that, after which the rest of the time was spent with Ksenia.

Doina was able to be even more flexible. Figuring it was hardly rocket science, she had left one of her employees in charge of the cleaning business and kept in touch with her via emails, mainly to give strict instructions for the replacement of fresh flowers with fruit.

Before leaving London, Doina tried contacting Nadea to tell her about Ksenia's successful rescue. Nadea, however, had left her job at the tapas restaurant and her number was dead. Larisa decided to honour her promise and leave Nadea alone to find her peace.

Larisa and Doina watched Ksenia paint in silence.

"You will soon run out of space," Larisa commented dryly, assessing her friend's creative clutter spread over her room.

"Are you jealous?" Ksenia became unexpectedly defensive.

Ksenia lived through painting – touching on a variety of subjects, starting from rural life, traditions and superstitions to mythology and mysticism. She had started sketching in her notebooks during the early days at school. Over time the work became more complex, even though she still used to draw on pads well into her teenage years before she moved on to canvasses and oils. Many of them were playful representations of her inner–outer world, filtered into each other or combined, to the point where her philosopher-butterfly identities became revolving doors.

Larisa, on the other hand, documented her experiences and inner demons by putting pen to paper. What it took Larisa pages to describe, Ksenia was able to do on one single sheet simply with colour, shape and symbol.

Larisa was startled by Ksenia's comment. She had always been proud of her friend's talent and hard work.

"Not at all. You know I love your art."

Ignoring this mollification, Ksenia continued:

"Of course, working with images and colour offers more freedom of expression than the medium of words."

Larisa agreed and not only to please her friend; still Ksenia's unusual standoffishness was disconcerting.

"You are right. Communicating an idea in silence, undistorted by the limitation of words, preserves its entirety."

"That's the trouble with words: they simplify complexity and complicate simplicity. The power of words is limited while the power of images can be absolute."

Despite the categorical tone of Ksenia's delivery, the message resonated with Larisa. No matter how long she spent writing about something, she knew it could never be described or expressed completely.

"Tell me about it. I could spend ten lives writing about one experience and it would still be a work in progress. You are lucky. With images, forms and symbols, the essence of it – whatever IT may be, a whole universe of possibilities and interpretations is present in that combination of chosen shapes and colour."

This seemed to relax Ksenia and returned to the canvas.

Doina came back with some hot tea. She poured it into the ornately patterned, auburn ceramic cups always proudly on display in the Robu's family kitchen. Ksenia's mother had received them as part of her dowry from her father, a potter, when she married Petru.

Doina handed the steaming brew to her friends and asked:

"Don't take this as a criticism but it was easier to work your themes out when your paintings were closer to real life. These are much more abstract. Where do you get your inspiration from?"

The question surprised Ksenia.

"I don't search for it. It comes to me in lonely moments or through dreams, which, by the way, are not only for analysis and interpretation, as Larisa thinks. They also provide for an inexhaustible spring of raw and original ideas. The frustration is, though, that my drawings never quite manage to reflect the perfection of those images or the intensity of colours presented to me in sleep."

"At least you two remember your dreams. You are lucky. I never do." Doina sounded disappointed.

"Kabbalah says *'Un-understood dreams are like unopened letters'*," Ksenia replied with detachment.

"Uh well, in that case – I guess my divine post gets lost continuously."

"Dreams are great for art. They break away from chimerical reality and help us enter a dimension alien to our five senses. It's like tasting the magical realm mentioned in fairytales. It only exists in that dimension, which sounds so far fetched to our logical minds it had to be mythicised and interpreted figuratively, if it could be shared at all. It's a great place to be. When I'm immersed in my work I sense that dimension and quake. It's expanding and experiencing a different plane, depending on the level of concentration."

Larisa exchanged anxious glances with Doina. Ksenia never used to talk like that and she had certainly never mentioned Kabbalah before.

Doina seemed just as confused by her friend's rhetoric and tried changing the subject.

"How come there is so much fire and flames, sparks and smoulders in your work these days?"

"The fire is very powerful, both visually and metaphorically," Ksenia carried on oblivious to how she sounded. "Human potential, like the land's – is stimulated by fire. One has to burn in order to regenerate."

"But some of them give me the creeps." Larisa shuddered exaggeratedly.

"That's your interpretation of them, maybe the critic's words are never anywhere near to the artist's heart and intention. Fire is the Great Stimulator, the Great Creator of everything."

Doina was concerned.

"Where do you come up with all this stuff? Why are you suddenly talking like a professor?"

"I take my art very seriously – us nutjobs do." She finally cracked a smile and the other two almost sighed with relief.

"It's kind of weird."

"It must be a delayed reaction to all that toilet reading you used to do, remember?" Larisa said trying to lighten the mood.

It worked – they all laughed.

"Exactly – where do you think I read about Kabbalah...?"

During her teenage years, Ksenia spent hours in the outdoor latrine, which her father had built at the bottom of the garden. In the absence of toilet paper and in common with the majority of households in the village, their family used books and newspapers. Despite their tree-bark texture, they were the only materials available during those late Soviet, early post Communism times. People destroyed periodicals and literary masterpieces alike, guiltlessly. But not Ksenia. She didn't want to carelessly dispose of them in this way and insisted on reading every page before using it.

"I felt guilty wasting books like that. Artists had poured their souls into those things."

"But you were in a stinky toilet for ages, surrounded by clouds of flies," Doina teased.

"I had to read books quickly before my parents wiped their arses with them...And I always had you two banging on the doors," Ksenia smiled.

"We were only trying to warn you about the risks of prolonged toilet-sitting," Larisa chuckled.

In those days, they used to scare Ksenia that if she spent too much time in the latrine, the worms and maggots would climb up the walls and bite her *birdie*.

"True, that usually got me out quicker. Who knows how much more I'd have learned had it not been for your scare stories. Perhaps I could have been a professor. Anyway, maybe it would have been better if those worms had eaten my *birdie* – it would have saved me from the other ones in Italy."

The jolly banter ended abruptly, followed by an awkward silence.

Musty-Jade

Doina's background in psychology gave her hope for Ksenia's recovery. She recognised that their friend's symptoms following her rescue were not uncommon in such circumstances, neither were they insurmountable. She recalled the tutorials on *flooding* therapies where the patient was to be encouraged to open up and discuss the trauma in order to release and let go of it.

Yet instead of diminishing with time, Ksenia's condition worsened. Gradually, she shut herself off from everyone, including her two friends.

Tamara's eyes were constantly bloodshot from crying all night and during the day she did her best to keep it together for her daughter. Petru dealt with his sorrow the only way he knew – by drowning it in wine and moonshine.

Ksenia had taken to climbing onto the roof. No amount of pleading by Doina, Larisa or her mother, could persuade her to come down. She did it according to whim and it could never be predicted.

Realising her attempts to coax Ksenia down were futile, Doina joined her on the musty-jade roof of the house, spending hours – mostly sitting in silence. Despite Doina's best attempts, Ksenia hardly spoke.

"It's a nice view of the village from up here, isn't it?"

No reply.

"...with the meadow stretched at the bottom of the hill and the little stream winding its way towards the pond, and the tall woods guarding the horizon...Marani is a pretty village, don't you think?"

"I feel exposed, Doina..."

"Well, we are...being perched up here..."

"Like a pair of Great Tits...?"

Doina noticed the smirk on her friend's face and she also smiled.

"I know what you mean by feeling exposed, Ksiusha, but you see, we are all vulnerable in one way or another. Life itself is vulnerability. To be alive is to be vulnerable and there's nothing wrong with that."

"You don't understand, Frizzy."

"I know I'll never know what you've been through but you are alive and that's all that matters!"

"I'm in hell. I feel ashamed, guilty and dirty. It makes me sick."

"You are not a bad person, Ksiusha, and neither did you do anything wrong. You just protected your life and did what you had to in order to survive."

Ksenia was wounded from within and Doina realised that was a lot more difficult to treat than an outer injury. Any recovery would need the patient's cooperation but this would be impossible while Ksenia was constantly torturing herself.

"So fuckin' stupid of me."

"You couldn't have known."

"Why was I so naïve?"

"Don't be so hard on yourself. It's easy to guess things in retrospect but we live life in the present. You did what you thought was right at the time and you

303

can't be sorry for that. You loved genuinely and passionately. The fact that somebody abused your trust shouldn't make you feel guilty and ashamed."

"You don't know what you are talking about. You don't know what it feels like to be humiliated 24/7 – beaten, raped, fisted, pissed on, do you? Answer me, do you?"

Their precarious positioning on the unsteady timber roof made Doina – already unnerved by her friend's distress – even more anxious.

Now, for the first time, Doina regretted not taking her degree a step further and graduating in psychotherapy. She was desperate to help Ksenia face her fears and gain a degree of control of the anxiety overwhelming her, but Doina realised she just wasn't experienced enough to succeed with those kind of *flooding* therapies. She felt painfully aware of her lack of training and was worried her attempts to help Ksenia might just make things worse.

Trying to adopt a gentler approach towards Ksenia's condition, Doina hoped to desensitise her friend to her past ordeals.

"OK, let's talk about it, Ksiusha. Tell me all, bit by bit. It will make you feel a lot better, I promise."

"How can you promise that? It's like a blind man hoping to describe the colours of the rainbow to a deaf one. Frizzy, you can't talk about hell, let alone understand it if you haven't been there."

"Our minds have a way of tricking and trapping us. All I am saying is that I may be able to help you see that for yourself. Perhaps I can give you some tips for coping with all this. It'll make everything a lot easier. Just think about it – you've made it to the other side. Isn't that empowering, for a start? You are here with friends and family. You are alive. You've gone through something I can't even begin to envisage. That's amazing in itself."

"I've made it physically but it feels like my survival is worthless. Despite the pain, my body cooperated by stretching and accommodating all cock sizes and races. But it was my mind who betrayed me in the end, Frizzy – my own mind."

Ksenia paused and Doina waited.

"Perhaps I've always had the seed of madness in me – ever since I was born…"

"Oh c'mon now, don't be silly…"

"No wonder I've always felt this need to reduce the dimensions of reality through my paintings and have searched to inflict order on things with my OCD. Perhaps this urge to bring order to a chaotic world has brought me to where I am today. I am my own worst enemy, Frizzy. My mind is my enemy. Just because it hasn't been able to militarise life, it's kicking up a fuss now. And what a fuss, I tell you…"

"You can't put all the blame on yourself."

"I guess you are right. They've made it worse. They've messed me up in there. It's like some kind of a switch has been turned on and sent me over the edge. The mind-tricks you are talking about helped me for a while but now even that has been taken away from me. I've got all sorts of voices torturing me from within. Don't talk to me about the power of the mind. I was able to use it when it was in balance. But you don't understand – it's like it's broken now. It's beyond my control. Don't give me the bullshit you learned in books. I'm talking from experience."

"I believe there are ways to treat it. With the help of medication and therapies it can be kept in control. Trust me."

"Don't ask me to do that. You think you know better, Ms Psychologist? You don't know shit. You haven't been to the dark side, you're just paying lip service. I'd like to be left alone now. Please go."

Doina descended the roof with a crushing feeling of failure. She was angry with herself for not being able to help Ksenia. All she could do was to carry on acting from the heart and be there for her friend, but Doina knew that professionally she could not be of any help. Frustrated tears rolled down her cheeks and a strong desire crystallised.

"I'll become a qualified shrink, no matter what. God is my witness, this country needs them."

Rusty

Larisa turned the street corner and approached Ksenia's house. The yard was full of commotion. Some people were shouting, others running and a few were wrestling on the ground. Through all that clamour, Larisa recognised Ksenia's howl.

"What are they doing to her?"

She rushed in and saw seven people holding a struggling Ksenia to the ground.

"Get off her! Let her go! I said, let go!" she shouted.

"Ksenia's gone crazy," a neighbour told her with bulging eyes.

"She is possessed," another one said making the sign of the cross repeatedly.

Larisa couldn't get to Ksenia, who by now was being tied roughly with lengths of rope and wire that had been scattered around the yard.

"Take them off. Let her go," Larisa pushed through the shield of people but the other villagers shoved her aside.

"Stay away, Ksenia is not well," an older man spoke sternly.

"Where is Mrs Tamara?" she asked.

"Gone to meet the ambulance."

Like many Moldovan villages its size, Marani has no street names. Why would it? Everyone knows where everyone else lives. In case of an emergency, such as when an ambulance is called from the closest town, someone has to meet it near the school grounds and direct it to the exact address from there.

Doina arrived.

"Where are you going?"

"I need to talk to Mrs Tamara and find out what happened. She's gone to get the ambulance."

Gapers gathered at the gate.

"Jesus Christ, have these people got nothing better to do? What are you staring at?" Larisa lashed out.

No one blinked an eyelid.

Larisa ran towards the school. Halfway there, she met the emergency vehicle and waved at it frantically. The car stopped with a screech, not because it was going at full speed – nothing could on those country roads – but because of the age of the rusty Soviet jalopy.

Larisa jumped in.

Tamara was crying and urgently briefing the two nurses.

"My neighbours woke me up this morning to say that Ksenia was throwing stones at their windows and cursing badly. They said she was aggressive and couldn't be approached. When I got there she had smashed all windows and was laughing hysterically. I asked her to stop and come home with me but then she started crying saying she needed to find a baby first. What for? I asked her. '*Jesus ordered me to get a small child and sacrifice it for him*', she told me.

"The neighbours called the police but when they heard what was going on, they refused to come, saying there weren't enough officers available and that they weren't the right authorities to be called anyway. It was a case for the *psihushka* to deal with, they said." Tamara broke down and her words became almost unintelligible.

Psihushka is the Russian term for a madhouse.

"Does your neighbour even have a baby?" nurse number one asked.

"No."

"Has this happened before?"

"No."

"So you are saying she flipped just like that? Is there any history of abuse or traumas in the family?" The nurse's voice betrayed a note of impatience.

A pair of small glasses rested on the tip of her nose and she looked coldly above them. Her dark-raven fringe enhanced the hard blackness of her eyes.

Tamara blew her nose on some tissue offered by nurse number two, who was quiet and seemed less officious.

"She's recently come back from..."

"Oh, one of them," nurse number one interrupted, as if that explained everything, her nose twitching disdainfully.

"One of what?" Larisa snapped.

The nurse turned to face her directly.

"I wasn't talking to you."

"No, but I am talking to you, so just you listen to me, Madam," Larisa hissed, her neck jutting forward like those of the geese who'd attacked her throughout her childhood. "Ksenia was kidnapped and held against her will. I think I know the type you have inferred but she is *NOT* one of them."

"Who's this?" the nurse asked Tamara, gesturing towards Larisa.

"I am Ksenia's best friend. I am her blood sister." Larisa didn't flinch.

Nurse number one reverted to filling some forms while nurse number two sat placidly, waggling as the old vehicle struggled with the potholed, earthen roads.

As soon as they arrived, the group of people – now doubled in number – parted to make way for the white, starched bonnets. Once in the courtyard, they acted swiftly. Taking one look at the screaming and writhing Ksenia, nurse number one administered a haloperidol injection. Slumping and drugged into tranquillity, Ksenia's tongue swelled and her body weakened. The ropes were removed and she was carried to the ambulance.

Holding Ksenia's hand, Doina asked:

"Can we come with you?"

"This isn't a bus, you know," nurse number one retorted, banging the door behind her.

The ambulance disappeared into the thick dust of the road and Doina dropped to the ground.

"I've failed Ksenia. I couldn't make her better."

"We've done all we could."

"They'll destroy her in there. They'll pump her with pills till she pops. I should have tried harder...I blew it..."

Larisa hunkered down next to Doina and they quietly watched the crowd which slowly started dispersing, speculating as to what might be wrong with Ksenia and what her cure could be.

"It's not a hospital she needs – it's a monastery," somebody said.

"Doctors can't deal with matters of this sort. Only a priest or a monk can make her better," somebody else concurred.

"So young and already haunted by evil spirits! God help her!"

Such whispers lingered on in the air long after the villagers went back to their homes.

Icterine

Ksenia was taken to Cuculeni asylum, on the outskirts of Chisinau city.

Cuculeni represents one of Bessarabia's best and most successful brands. Everyone from young to the very old knows about it. Part and parcel of an entire country, it has penetrated the social psyche like alcohol has the national liver. In a society where mental health issues are ignored, condemned or outright denied, in Cuculeni is where the insane and the inconvenient are locked.

Built in the late fourteenth century, following the prototype of western institutions of that time, such as that of Alt Sherbitz in Germany, Cuculeni was designed as a therapeutic agricultural colony. Covering an area of over 100 acres, it consists of curative buildings, diagnostic and treatment wards, a club for socio-cultural events, a food block, garages, storages and other domestic buildings.

During Soviet times, it had also been used to imprison dissidents who were harbouring *reformist delusions*. Having never faced up to its repressive past, the asylum remains a secretive institution. Belated Soviet inertia still lingers around Cuculeni, where abuse is not a thing of the past.

Neither her family nor her friends were allowed to see Ksenia for three whole days, on grounds of the severity of her case. Then it was the weekend and they were told to try again the following week.

On Monday morning, Doina and Larisa travelled to Chisinau. The roads were empty and they arrived there sooner than expected.

The main reception was on top of a hill tucked away in the greenery of a huge, lush park. It was still early and eerily quiet. Not knowing what to expect in that *crazy* place, the girls spoke softly and walked as if on egg-shells.

After many inquiries and a long procedural wait in a cold, narrow and bright, artificially lit corridor, they were finally taken to a room, where Ksenia was waiting. Her icterine figure was almost blending in with the dreary yellow of the four empty walls.

However, the first thing that struck them was the change in her eyes.

They both knew all of Ksenia's expressions by heart, learned along the many years since childhood. She looked at them, yet her glance went somewhere beyond them. This wasn't one they recognised and it hurt to notice the unmistakable change that had taken place in her demeanour. It was as though a secret chamber had opened in the light of her mind and all Doina's interaction with the world outside her, with her friends – seemed to be filtered though that cranny into the foreign sphere, which had ruthlessly claimed her.

The glint in Ksenia's eyes was alien, frightening. Like a parasite, it had stealthily crept in and was difficult to tell whether it was the cause or the effect of what was dragging her away. Her usual look –

312

powerful, focused and full of silent wisdom – was no longer there.

The vacancy with which she received her friends was emptier than emptiness.

Larisa welled up and bit her lip, giving Ksenia a long, loving hug, hoping and praying that at the end of it, her friend's old self would be back. Larisa prayed that some of her own sanity be given to Ksenia.

"*It is not fair for her to be so cruelly treated by Fate,*" she thought.

Larisa was prepared to share and offer her friend whatever it was she needed to be well again – she would jump on an operating table right there and then, if only sanity could be transplanted like kidneys.

It was harrowing to see their friend in such a way and they cut their visit short. Despite Ksenia's aloofness, they couldn't tell how much she had registered of what was going on around her.

Unable to walk very far, Larisa stopped at the first bench in the park.

Silence. Sobs. Silent sobs.

"If any of us three had to lose our mind, it should have been me," she said without lifting her head.

"Why?"

"I've always been the irrational one. Why has Fate been so unfair? Why does it have to punish Ksenia instead? Especially her, who's already suffered so much?"

"I guess our sanity wouldn't have been of much use to Fate. It went for the more functional one."

They sat in silence a little longer but the cold bench made of cobalt blue, iron pipes was neither decorative nor practical. These uncomfortable benches were dotted all over the park, yet they were mostly empty, patients preferring to sit on the ground instead.

Doina stood.

"How can anyone sit on these things? You know what? They sum this place up!"

"Yeah, it's not the big shots who sit on them at the end of the day, is it?"

Sparkling Amber

After a week, Ksenia's condition improved slightly. Although the alien mist had lifted from her eyes, her speech and reactions were thick and sluggish.

"I've got a constant headache and am always dizzy," she said.

"It's probably because of the pills. Have you seen a psychotherapist?" Doina was curious.

"Only once."

"How come?"

"She was busy with the kids."

"Kids? What kids?"

"The children being treated here."

"Are you telling me there is only one psychotherapist for the entire hospital? Kids and adults?"

"They are short of medical staff. I see a lot of people brought here every day who are force-fed pills because there are no specialists to treat them otherwise."

"How many patients are there here?"

"I don't know. However many they say there are officially at the hospital, I can promise you it won't be accurate. There's loads more who do not come forward."

"Why not?"

"What do you mean, 'why not', Larisa? They are worried of course. You know just as well as I do that anyone coming through these gates is automatically branded *crazy*."

Doina sighed.

"So much need for shrinks in this country and I am cleaning shit abroad."

"How do they treat you here?" Larisa asked.

"Like I said – as they would any other crazy people. We are all nutjobs as far as the doctors are concerned. In fact, as far as the entire country is concerned. You both know that – no need to pretend."

"I wasn't…"

"That's how we are viewed. You come here once and you are branded for a lifetime. They feed us all right, but as for our basic rights – forget it. They use us for experiments, you know…"

"What are you on about?" said Doina trying to maintain an even tone of voice.

"They test foreign medication on us."

"I hope you haven't consented to that."

Ksenia laughed.

"I'm not given the choice, I'm afraid. It is being done without our supposed knowledge."

"Hey, my mum's a doctor, remember? They are meant to inform the patients about that kind of shit. Fully explain to them what the procedure involves and what the risks are before introducing new medication – especially when it comes to new drugs."

"Not in Cuculeni, Larisa, I'm telling you. Many patients are told they are being given drugs which are new to the market. *'These will cure you'* we are told. Others are bribed into giving their consent in exchange for extra cigarettes or to be let outside more often."

"That's illegal."

"Illegal? It's diabolical," Larisa kept shaking her head.

"You must not forget the type of patients we are at this hospital. Most of us are desperate to get treated and any promise, vague or otherwise, we'll latch on to. The hospital managers and doctors take advantage of it."

"How do you know all this?"

"I play cards with an old lady, Mrs Raisa. She's been here on and off for two decades. She told me it's been going on for no less than ten years."

"At least you've got friends in here..." Doina tried to sound positive.

"I get on with many of my fellow patients, especially the ones who've been assigned my diagnosis – *unhinged by grief suffered abroad.*" She smiled wryly.

"What do you mean?"

"There are plenty of women who've been slaving abroad, be it via cheap labour or sex. Even though they've been able to cope financially, inwardly they're all a train wreck – mothers working abroad, leaving children at home, families separated for years till they grow into emotional strangers. The burden of illegal migration is a heavy burden, you know. It breaks many spirits. Lots of them end up here. What's worse – I see children coming to this hospital every day. I know my rants on this subject are probably of no interest to you but it really is disastrous."

"Hey, Freud – you are the expert. What is it with migration and schizophrenia?" Larisa asked Doina.

"I guess trauma is the common factor here. Culture shock, menial jobs, humiliation, limited opportunities because you are an illegal immigrant, isolation and the awareness that despite your loved ones waiting for you – there is no way back home because there's nothing there for you. But you've seen our people scattered around Europe, Larisa. You should know about this. When you are at the bottom of the heap, it's all too easy for the mind to go off the rails."

"Heavy thoughts are not good company at all, trust me. With time, such thoughts get darker and darker and it gets worse. I am scared."

"You won't stay here for much longer." Doina took Ksenia's hand into hers. "We'll take you home soon. Very soon."

"The doctors have said I'm going to be on medication for the rest of my life."

"That doesn't mean you have to be here though," Larisa assured her pointedly.

It was late afternoon by now and time to leave their friend to rest. Ksenia wanted to see them off. In order to stretch their time together, the three girls took the longest route back to the car park.

It was a perfect Moldovan autumn day.

The sky, which early in the morning looked bruised and battered like the bloated cheeks of someone dredged from a river, became lighter and livelier as the day progressed. The dark and ominous clouds had been pushed elsewhere towards twilight. In their wake, flocks of different clouds emerged – joyful and laced with sheer vapours, travelling lightly on the immensity of the heavenly vault.

Autumn was not going to last much longer and like everything in the world when about to perish, it was desperately trying to enhance its presence. The whole landscape was soaked in sparkling amber. The sublime autumn, like a cruel dominatrix, exploited the sun mercilessly, forcing it to pour out all reserves of light and heat. Although neither light nor the heat was strong, it was enough to add to the resplendent charm floating in the air, engaged in the perpetual dance of all things around. The foliage of the trees displayed an array of spectacular colours: from fainting green, to peroxide splashes and bleeding hues of red.

A visual delirium, deceptive by default.

With an incongruous expression, autumn induced conflicting states of mind in my people. On one hand, the girls enjoyed the fairy-tale atmosphere permeated with warmth and rich light, and on the other – they could sense the inevitable fall of the fall.

Shortly before reaching the car park, they spotted a newly renovated church.

"It's part of the hospital," Ksenia explained.

"And who are they?" Larisa asked pointing to the crowds of people hanging listlessly around the vestry – men dressed in baggy, sagging tracksuits and women wrapped in flowery robes – chatting and eating sunflower seeds.

"Patients from the drug and alcohol rehab wards. Every Sunday morning they turn up religiously, queuing for the communion wine. It's the only way to fix their craving, even if it's just a teaspoon of it. After the Divine Liturgy is finished, they participate in the sacrament of the Eucharist, which the Orthodox Church claims to represent the body and blood of Christ. Everyone approaches the priest in an orderly manner to get a piece of wine-soaked bread from the chalice."

"Ingenious."

"Indeed they are and in more ways than one," Ksenia replied.

"Does the priest know about this?" Doina asked.

"Of course he does. He just makes sure that none of them get any seconds. He's a canny one, that priest. He knows every patient at the hospital and there's no fooling him. The most desperate ones have all tried their luck and have been sent away."

"I didn't know there were drug rehab wards here too." Larisa said.

Ksenia half smiled.

"Drug addiction is just an outward symptom of soul-sickness. They're just sensitive people with an inner ache, who break under tension and stress. Instead of being brought back to the road of recovery gently, they are judged, stigmatised, abandoned and chucked to the bottom of society. What's tragic is that so many of them are gifted, artistic people. Here, let me show you something." Ksenia headed towards the church's door.

"Are we OK to go in?"

"Don't worry, Larisa. The church may be on the asylum grounds, but its door is always open for all people – even *normal* ones."

They followed her all the way to the front of the nave.

"Can you see those wooden cherubs?" she asked pointing to a whole row of them gracing the entrance to the altar.

"Yes. They are beautiful."

"They've all been sculpted by a craftsman treated at this hospital."

"No way!"

"They are incredible." Doina admired the carpentry masterpieces.

"Perhaps they are the reason he ended up here," Ksenia whispered and the other two weren't sure if they were meant to hear that.

"He certainly wouldn't be the first artist with so called mental health issues to be misunderstood by society, or the last for that matter." Larisa did her best to sound breezy and casual. "Look at Van Gogh, look at Michelangelo, look at Rothko, and that's just off the top of my head…"

Ksenia nodded.

"We judge those who are guilty only of seeing the world differently from the rest. That's our crime."

They left the church and carried on walking towards the car park. When her friends were in the car and about to leave, Ksenia stopped them suddenly:

"There's a fly in the car."

"That's OK, honey, it won't bother us," Doina replied nonchalantly.

"You may not be bothered…but perhaps the fly is," Ksenia said. "Its home and family are around here and you are taking it away. I know it's got wings and can fly but it may not be able to find its way back."

Before either of them could react, she opened the door of the car and waved the fly out. Then she whispered conspiratorially:

"It's important to be close to nature in proximity, but connecting with it is what leads to transformation."

The other two looked at each other perplexed.

Always the sensitive soul, Ksenia lived closer to the spring of life and enjoyed a better connection with the space she inhabited than most. This awareness – only accentuated by her condition – far exceeded that of her friends, bound by their denser, corporeal dimension.

Doina and Larisa said their goodbyes and drove off, asking the question they always did after seeing their friend:

"Will she be OK next time?"

It was the worst kind of place, Larisa thought, for the fragile and scared. Anybody forced to spend time here would be going home less balanced than they had been in the first place.

Chartreuse

For the entire month that Ksenia was at Cuculeni hospital, her awareness oscillated haphazardly between clear and cloudy spells. Her weight kept dwindling, rendering her body to a chartreuse shadow.

Doina and Larisa visited her regularly, never knowing quite what side of consciousness they'd find her on. The bright days, when Ksenia resembled her old self despite her slow reactions, were treasured. Not knowing when the next would come along, if at all – the three friends rejoiced in each of those precious moments as if they were the last.

However low she sank, Ksenia's illness never robbed her of her passion. She carried on living in the world of shape and colour, her drawings conveying the restless soul she had become. The complexity of her art continued until all she repeatedly depicted were flying birds and headless people.

On more than one occasion, Doina and Larisa had been turned away from the hospital because Ksenia wasn't well enough to see them.

A week before Ksenia was discharged, her blood sisters went to visit her again only to be met by a medical assistant.

"I'm sorry – she's not great today. She's been doing OK recently but she had another seizure yesterday."

"Why? What happened?"

"It was unexpected. Ksenia had been sketching quietly at the club. She'd been there since lunch, then just flipped all of a sudden. We had to drag her forcefully back to the ward. It didn't go well."

Doina and Larisa turned to leave but the nurse stopped them. She took an envelope out of the pocket of her white coat:

"Here. Ksenia gave me a letter. She wrote it a couple of days ago and asked me to give it to you if she wasn't well enough to receive you."

Eager to read it, they thanked the kind nurse and left in a hurry. Unable to sit on the masochistically designed *torture*-benches in the hospital park, they opted for the grass despite its dampness and impatiently opened the neatly folded paper:

Hello my darlings!

Do not worry that I can't see you today. Generally, I feel a lot better even though my awareness keeps on going and coming without warning. It likes to play hide and seek. ☺

This morning it woke up with me and I feel good. My mind is not the cloudy swirl I've got to know in my affliction. Today I am serene. Like I mentioned, I don't think the drugs they are giving me are helping much. If they do anything at all – they certainly throw me to the bottom of the dark pit more often these days. I can't predict when the next clear spell will bless me for who knows what the future holds – I am writing this letter for you. Even though I hope to be 'normal' when you visit me again, I am at its whim, unable to control the swaying of this delicate system. Like the rising

323

and falling of the sea, so the tides of my perception change patterns, in a rhythm all of their own.

Please do not suffer for me – I am in no pain whatsoever, apart from the fact that I cannot be with you when you are here. But then again, I am not aware of it then so it doesn't count, does it?

I know you'll probably have something to say regarding this, especially you Larisa, but I will most likely not be conscious of it. And it wouldn't be fair arguing with somebody unable to defend their position, would it? ☺

But seriously, do not mourn my physical loss. It's just a body. However complex it may be, it's still a body – just a slab of meat with an expiry date. Surely, there must be more to me than that, right? It would be a cosmic waste otherwise and totally unjustified.

More importantly: do you know the most significant thing that happened today? The Sun has risen on time this morning. And you know what? The Sun WILL rise tomorrow too. It always does. Isn't that amazing? Does anything else in our petty world matter? Does it really?

Don't worry, I may sound nuts but I'm still in full possession of my thinking faculty.

It is my wish that whenever you remember me, remember the Sun and its timeless, precise cycles.

I won't say farewell to you for I am not going too far away!

Loving you always – your soul sister!
xx

The girls' stomachs shrunk. Lumps rose to their throats.

"Is she is saying good bye to us?" Larisa chewed on her lower lip.

Cracking knuckles, Doina tried to sound composed:

"Ksenia is too young and beautiful to be leaving us."

Dingy-Indigo

The following week, Ksenia was released from Cuculeni, her responses and reactions getting progressively delayed and her meekness and weakness resembling that of an abused child.

Ksenia had been home for five days when Doina called in on the Robu household, as she and Larisa had done every morning since Ksenia's return. Pushing the dingy-indigo gate open, Doina found Petru sat on the porch, already drinking wine from a half empty clay pitcher. Neither Ksenia nor Tamara was anywhere to be seen.

"Where are they?" she asked Petru.

He didn't reply straight away so she repeated the question.

"Oh, they went to-to-to Drrrroaia Monastery," he stammered and slurred his words.

"Droaia Monastery? Why?"

Petru shrugged his shoulders.

"When did they leave?"

"At midday, I think."

"But it's only ten o'clock now."

"Oh, don't you tttry and ttttrap me. I know your lllot. Can't you see the sun is setting? You women are all the sssame, you all lie through your teeth…vixens…"

"What's up?" Larisa called as she opened the gate to the front yard.

"Mrs Tamara took Ksenia to Droaia Monastery."

Larisa rolled her eyes.

"Oh fuck, why is running to the monastery the answer to everything in this country?"

"I wish Mrs Tamara had told us about it."

"We can go after them if you wish, Doina but I'm not sure how that'll help. Mrs Tamara decided to take her daughter there and when it comes to these things, reason goes out the window, trust me. I've had my own mother do the same thing to me. Anyway, no need to worry about it – nothing really happens there apart from some girls playing possessed."

"Ksenia is in no state to be exorcised, real or not. Let's go get the bike."

Running back to Doina's house, the girls crossed paths with Baba Liuba. The old woman strolled leisurely towards the well with an empty, blue enamelled bucket, which due to a rusty handle squeaked with each of her swaying steps.

"Oh no, we haven't got time for this now…" Doina muttered. "Jesus, have you seen what she's carrying?"

"C'mon, for God's sake – an empty bucket does not mean bad luck…"

"What? Running into an empty bucket AND at a junction too? Are you kidding me? It's not just bad luck but double bad luck," Doina bristled.

Crossroads in Moldova are feared by drivers and pedestrians alike. It's where most accidents occur and many of the junctions, up and down the country, have shrines built by the side of them. Icons of Jesus and the Virgin Mary are placed there and expected to keep the streets safe, despite the widespread drink-driving and scorn of seatbelts.

In her state of panic, Doina asked Baba Liuba to turn her container upside down and pour out the last drops of water that would be at the bottom of it.

The word went that such a measure negated the ills which could otherwise befall you should an empty bucket cross your path.

"What did you say?" the old woman tilted her head, pricking up her wilting ears. "Ah, the bucket...You *thee*, I've already tipped it out for Frosea, whom I met up the road. I'm afraid it's all empty now. Anyway, where are you off to in *thuch hathte*?"

Doina didn't fancy the idea of continuing her journey having encountered an empty bucket and sulked.

Larisa apprised the inquisitive old lady.

"To Droaia Monastery. Mrs Tamara and Ksenia are up there."

"That's right." Baba Liuba lit up. "I advised her *mythelf* to give her daughter that chance. It's the last Friday of the month and the priest delivers a *thpecial* liturgy for the redemption of lost *thouls*."

"What do you mean?" Larisa asked impatiently.

Thinking back to her past experience, she did not trust Baba Liuba.

"On this day the priest chants *thpecial* prayers and removes his outer vestments to cover the sick people in order to heal them. It's an extremely powerful practice – just touching the sacred garments cures many people. I've seen it done with my own eyes. Once a young man, *paralythed* after a bike accident, was brought to the church wrapped in a blanket and soon after the Divine Liturgy was over, he walked home on his own two feet. *Kthenia* will come back all healed, believe me. You just wait and see."

Doina was filled with horror.

"Larisa, we need to run."

They both fled, leaving Baba Liuba in the middle of the road, looking confused.

"*Thith* youth have all turned away from God. No wonder the Devil nests in their *thouls*," she mumbled to herself and carried on slowly down the hill.

The girls jumped on the *Yava* bike and a bone-shaking half hour later they screeched into Droaia village, which hosted the monastery. Once they arrived at Droaia town, the girls had to stop several times to ask for directions.

Signposting is less than basic in Moldova.

"It's at the other side of the village, close to the woods," a local tried to help. "I'm taking this lot there myself. Follow me," he whipped the horses and the taxi-cart transporting five people, moved ahead hesitantly with squeaking wheels.

Doina looked at Larisa and smiled. She accelerated the *Yava* and overtook the cart with blaring noise, causing the horses to rear.

The slushy village roads made it a difficult ride as Doina tried to avoid all the muddy furrows and potholes by zigzagging the motorbike wheels. When they finally reached the monastery grounds, the bike shuddered to a halt like an exhausted beast.

"Quick," Doina said jumping off and running towards the entrance.

The Droaia Monastery was a lot smaller than the Toanca one, where Larisa had been taken by her mother the year before. This one looked like an elongated house with two towers at each end, the spires of which could easily be spotted amongst the surrounding oak treetops. Neat vegetable and flower patches lined the gardens on both sides.

The sermon was in full swing and with the door wide open, the priest's voice could be heard from the widely open gates.

The girls stopped by the door and waited for their eyes to adjust to the semi-darkness of the small hall. The only light coming in was from the few narrow windows. It was an intimate interior with traditional Bessarabian flat-woven carpets covering the floors. Their vivid colours of dense, floral sprays, garlands and vines treated in the geometric Kilim style, offset the gloomy space. Still, the room was just as stuffy as the one at Toanca, Larisa thought. The smoking candles and the burning incense blistered their lungs.

Doina and Larisa tried to make their way towards Ksenia and her mother but the crowd was thick and they had to push through. The priest was on the other side and he too seemed to be heading towards the middle, where Ksenia was.

"*He must have already been briefed of her condition,*" Doina thought. "*Oh God, please don't let this happen.*"

"Mrs Tamara, we have to get Ksenia out of here," Doina whispered anxiously as they got to her side.

"The doctors can't help my child. This is her last chance."

"It's going to make it worse. Let's get her out now and I will explain outside. Please, Mrs Tamara, this is really important, trust me."

"Shhh! Be quiet," people hushed them.

Doina touched Ksenia's elbow.

"Please come out with us."

"She's not going anywhere. Leave my daughter alone."

Ksenia's eyes were wide with confusion.

"Be quiet. This is not a marketplace," people tut-tutted from all sides.

"Come out...please...," Doina begged.

"C'mon Ksenia, it's a bit stuffy in here. Let's get some fresh air," Larisa took her friend's hand but the chubby priest began sprinkling them with holy water and prayed out loud:

"Father, physician of our souls and bodies, Who have sent Your only-begotten Son and our Lord Jesus Christ to heal every sickness and infirmity, visit and heal also Your servant Ksenia Robu from all physical and spiritual ailments through the grace of Your Christ…"

Chanting, the priest proceeded to take off his phelonion.

"No, please don't…" Doina hurled forwards. "You don't understand.. Stop it…"

The priest sprayed Doina with holy water too. Some of it went in her eyes and she span away.

He faced Ksenia and carried on with his prayers.

"…Grant her patience in this sickness, strength of body and spirit, and recovery of health.

Lord, You have taught us through Your word to pray for each other that we may be healed. I pray, heal Your servant Ksenia Robu and grant to her the gift of complete health.

For You are the source of healing and to You I give glory, Father, Son and Holy Spirit. Amen."

The priest stepped closer towards Ksenia.

He began taking off his second layer.

She screamed in horror.

"Nooooooo!!! Get away from me, you pervert! Stay away!!"

The priest carried on praying.

He removed his epitrachelion.

"Be rebuked and depart…Be afraid, come forth, and depart from Ksenia Robu … Depart to thy own Tartaros … O Satan … I command thee and all the power which worketh with thee to remove thyself from her who hath been sealed in the Name of our Lord Jesus Christ, our True God … "

By this time Tamara and a dozen other church-goers had pinned Ksenia down.

She swore.

She cursed.

She spat.

She cried in terror.

"Do you want to fuck me too? You son of a bitch…!
Don't touch me! Stay away, you filthy pig!!"

All around, people crossed themselves, whispering
and speculating about how the Devil had got inside
Ksenia Robu.

"…*Banish from Ksenia every evil and unclean spirit
hidden and lurking in her heart, the spirit of error, the spirit
of evil, the spirit of idolatry and all covetousness …May the
Lord rebuke thee, O Satan…*"

The priest bent down and touched Ksenia's
forehead lightly with his cross. He sprinkled more holy
water on her.

Doina and Larisa knelt by her side.

"You've killed our friend…"

"Not here, Larisa – she could still hear us," Doina
squeezed her hand.

"The Holy Spirit is working. We'll take her outside
and she'll be revived," the priest spoke reassuringly.
"The sacred garments that have just touched your
friend will do her a world of good. This is a very
efficient practice; we are well known for it here. Do not
worry and have faith."

"You don't understand…"

"Have faith…"

But Larisa didn't let the priest finish and further
confronted him:

"What I'd like to know is whether your lunatic
practice is endorsed by the Holy Synod? Is it backed by
the Orthodox Church or the circus?"

"That's the problem with the world today – it lacks
faith in the work of God," he replied calmly and turned
his wide back, which curved under the burden of his
big, heavy belly.

The only officially recognised practices for the effect
of exorcism in the Orthodox Church are the prayers of
Basil the Great and John Chrysostom (the Golden-
Mouthed), two Holy Hierarchs who helped shape early

331

Christian theology in the fourth century. These particular prayers should only be performed in special circumstances by trained priests who have undergone at least three days of spiritual cleansing, entailing strict fasting and the performing of secret and sacred litanies. They are powerful procedures intended to cast out evil spirits from people, places and entire regions or lands.

Larisa had been aware of these special prayers from a very young age – people speculated about them relentlessly. Yet she doubted that anyone could or should carry them out any more. By the shape of many of today's Church representatives, she felt it unlikely they knew the pangs of hunger – in her eyes making them unfit for such delicate endeavours.

"These priests, whose bellies enter the room five minutes before they do, are a far cry from the gaunt, translucent figures of the Holy Hierarchs. How can anyone perform exorcisms, belching on red wine and blood sausages? Surely, that's playing with fire…" she thought.

Tens of hands airlifted Ksenia out and stretched her on the tender grass in the courtyard.

Others stood a safe distance away, still crossing themselves. Doina and Larisa caressed their friend's forehead and held her hands, wet with holy water and their tears.

They were the first faces Ksenia saw when she recovered.

"Please take me home," she pleaded with a whisper.

Larisa couldn't help but think that this was the second time the three of them had jointly confronted the established, yet irrational practices of their world. She remembered her mother's account of what happened at their christening, when they cried non-stop and were attended to before the boys. The uncanny pattern of life was being mocked derisively – Larisa stared it in the face.

Turbid Topaz

Tamara woke up one morning the following week and couldn't find her daughter anywhere. She feared another seizure might have sent her ailing child threatening and abusing the villagers again and she duly raised the alarm. Family, friends and neighbours all came to help, scouring the entire village of Marani, but no one had seen Ksenia.

Upon hearing the news, Larisa sensed an internal tug – different from any she'd known before. This sudden and unexplained feeling, like she was in a lift that had plummeted ten floors, unsettled and frightened her. Not even when Ksenia went missing in Italy did she feel her friend so far away.

"*I'm just being paranoid,*" she tried to reassure herself, yet her fear refused the bait.

Hours passed by. Day turned into night and night into another day - yet still there was no news about Ksenia. It seemed, she had disappeared into thin air. By the end of the third day, villagers had given up on searching for her. Dispirited and worried, Doina and Larisa went home to change their clothes sodden from searching the woods surrounding the village. On the corner of her street, Larisa met a distraught Zuzu.

He had his face painted with mud, like he used to when Ksenia made him the '*warrior of the woods*' during those long gone childhood days.

Zuzu jumped up and down, pointing towards the woods, crying.

"Ooosha!!! Help Ooosha!!!"

"Ksiusha...?" she asked him nervously.

He nodded and pulled frantically at her clothes to follow him. Zuzu sprinted off and Larisa pursued. Soon she realised he was taking her to the waterside, where the girls had sealed their friendship in blood all those years ago.

Zuzu ran fast and Larisa lost sight of him. When she reached the pond, coming through the acacia grove, she saw Zuzu squatting by the shore weeping like a child.

Her heart sank.

She followed his gaze towards the turbid topaz pond and froze.

Despite the certainty of what confronted her, her brain refused to register what the floating object on the surface of the water was. Moments later the truth had sunk to her very core: the huge figure cradled by the gentle ripples was the bloated body of Ksenia, her eyes wide open.

Larisa dropped to the ground and gasped for air. Her pounding heart had risen to her throat and her head was spinning. Desperate to jump in and fish Ksenia out, she tried to get to her feet but couldn't find them. Her vision tunnelled and she staggered towards the pond. Diving heavily into the water, Larisa swam as fast as she could towards the floral dress which shrouded Ksenia's body.

***

She did die young and beautiful. The balance the three girls had been used to was damaged irreversibly. The trinity that hosted their life circle, the 'Sisterhood Dial' was no longer. Like all things under the sun, it responded to the eternal and immutable call of metamorphosis: change, it seems, is the only constant in life. The realisation of this irony was so much more painful to Larisa under the circumstances.

Captive of the inexorable law, their Dial transformed into a line, suspended in time and space by two single dots, two specks – Doina and Larisa.

Yelping-Yellow

As tradition held, the body was kept in the house for two nights and three days prior to burial.

Doina and Larisa took turns and stood vigil by Ksenia's side.

The night before the funeral they decided to stay with Ksenia together, before she was taken away from them for ever and given back to the magnificent, yet perverse powers which begat her and teased the world with her presence for such a short time.

They sat lost in thought and occasionally stood up to change the beeswax candles on the metal holder next to Ksenia's head. The amount of smoke coming from them made the room fuggy and hazy, lacing it with pungent fumes that reminded the girls of being in church.

There she lay peacefully, dressed in white like the bride she would never be. Her demeanour was serene. She could have been sleeping if it hadn't been for the intrusive, deathly yellow emanating from her bloated body.

Immersed in a drift of memories, Doina's question reached Larisa as an echo from another world:

"Do you think she is going to take one of us with her?"

Ksenia died with her eyes open.

The lore says that when the dead leave this world with their eyes open, they'll return to take someone close with them to the other side. Even though Larisa picked and chose the folk beliefs and superstitions as they suited her, this one really got to her. She had to put on a show of logic:

"Don't be silly. She's had enough of us here. I am sure Ksenia could do with some rest, away from us, in the other world. She'll certainly pick somebody else for a change of company."

It wasn't funny and Larisa knew it. Concerned that dwelling on it might give the thought power or credence, she changed the subject.

"Have you heard of Zeno's paradoxes?"

"Rings a bell."

"There is a famous one about Achilles and the tortoise."

"What does it say?"

"The argument is that Achilles – a Greek hero – can never overtake the tortoise, since he must first reach the point where the tortoise started. Each time Achilles reaches the point where the tortoise was, the reptile will always have moved a little way ahead. Because there are an infinite number of points Achilles must reach where the tortoise has already been, he can never overtake the tortoise."

"Can you say that again?"

Larisa repeated the theory.

"Well, that's assuming we can infinitely divide space and time…"

"How do you mean?"

"Think of space as the race track and time as how long it takes to run it…Are you with me?" Doina exaggerated her dismissive tone.

"Just about."

"But you see, this assumption is wrong. Turning the race track into an infinite number of steps means each step is decreasing. Right? If we try to divide space – and therefore time – into smaller and smaller pieces, that implies the passage of time slows down. And that's ridiculous!"

"Well, I suppose that's why old Zeno called it a paradox. Still, I wish it was true, you know. For Ksenia's sake. She'd still be alive, one step – however small – ahead of death."

"But, darling, where is Zeno now, huh?"

"He bit off his torturer's nose and was killed."

"There you go – he himself didn't survive his own theory, did he? Pushing up daisies with a mouthful of nose – that's how practical his arguments are. He is gone. Ksenia is gone. Time passes and things change constantly and irreversibly. Funny how people say: *'Time will come when such and such will happen…'* – how ridiculous it sounds. Time only passes – it never comes."

"But it doesn't pass per se, does it? I mean, it would be good if it did – we'd be left behind unscathed. But it doesn't. Instead it drives us from behind or hand in hand, if you want. It doesn't exist ahead of us. Tomorrow is only a probability – no one's ever lived it."

"You may well have a point there."

Shifting the sorrow of their immediate circumstances to an abstract level somehow eased their pain. Its rarefied space, devoid of emotions and suffering, offered a soothing balm to the soul, however transient that relief might be.

The etymology of *'abstract'* derives from the Latin: *'drawing away'*. Drawn away, rising above all that's earthly, in order to search for meaning and essence: a bird's eye view of all that's been, is and ever will be.

338

In and of themselves, abstract conversations do not provide hard answers to thorny questions, but if pursued, they soar to rarefied states of mind and that's where the chance to taste freedom lies. It's where carnal bondage loosens up and there is a sense of lightness – that sweet and *bearable lightness of being*.

Doina sighed:

"It's fucked up, I tell you...We, out of all people, who once took the phenomenon of death as something natural and familiar, today feel like we are encountering it for the first time, rebel against it with utter fury."

Growing up in a small community, death was all around them. The girls were accustomed to seeing people and animals being born and dying. Death was part of life's tableau. Marble faces in open coffins were paraded towards the cemetery on a regular basis and they didn't think to question it once, not in any meaningful way, at least. Immune to them from an early age, those images sank into their subconscious, forming the earliest memories the young girls had of life. Their awareness of death happened the instant they became aware of life – witnessing them hand in hand from the moment they could remember daylight.

When they were too small to see the dead in their coffins, their parents lifted the girls up to see inside, even if the short-term consequences were fear, traumas and anxiety. It was part of life as far as the adults were concerned and they had no intention of keeping their children away from it.

"It's not death that's upsetting, if we really think about it. We can never experience it ourselves. What's painful is the loss of someone close to us – that's what's hard to deal with. Isn't it strange that we are affected by something that happens to somebody else when they themselves are not affected by it?"

"That sounds so cold and distant, as if you weren't talking about Ksenia," Doina chided.

Larisa carried on obliviously:

"If the person to whom death is happening cannot be upset or hurt about it, for obvious reasons, why should we, mere witnesses, be? Isn't it because of our innate selfishness? Because we want them to be here and they are not? Because we want something that is not and we choose – most probably unconsciously – to go against the grain?"

"Your theory makes sense at a lofty level but right now your *generous compassion* is not exactly soothing, you know. We are sat here, by Ksenia's body, and you seem to be asserting that death does not exist?"

"As a personal experience, it does not. Forget about seeing it happen to somebody else – that's second-hand information. I am talking about our own individual, life-long fear of death. It's nothing but existential worry, a hypothetical affair and it should not be something to be concerned with. Life – that's what should preoccupy us – and only life."

"But aren't we confronted with the same dilemma here too? Just like we cannot tell what death is exactly, neither can we explain life. I mean, what is life? The fact that we live and experience life doesn't necessarily mean that we can understand or explain it, or does it?"

"You are right – we can only speculate, I'm afraid," Larisa said dryly. "No wonder so many people resort to mysticism. I do not remember who it was but someone wise compared life to fire:

"'…*it lights up, burns with powerful flames, brightens a portion from the eternal space and then, sooner or later it loses its strength and goes out, the wood changes into ashes, which is spread all over the earth. Earth then gets covered with grass and that grass will be caressed by that same wind, which has intensified not long ago the fire…*'"

"That might explain why Ksenia was so obsessed with the element of fire in her drawings – she was searching for the essence of life."

"Possibly…I suppose we'll never know now…"

It was well past midnight, yet noises could still be heard around the house. Ksenia's family was preparing for the funeral to take place in the morning and the food wake after it. Friends and relatives were coming in and out to bid farewell to the deceased.

Tamara had hardly spoken since the day her daughter died. Unlike her intoxicated husband, who had barely even registered the fact that his only child had died, Tamara was consumed by regret.

Her monosyllabic words were concerned solely with the planning of the funeral. Otherwise grief and sorrow claimed the rest of her attention. No amount of well meant, consoling words from family and friends were going to make her feel any better. Nor were the jabs of diazepam administered regularly by Silvia. Tamara either sat in silence or was crying.

Shortly before sunrise, the grief-stricken mother came in with an armful of walnut tree leaves and threw them on the top of the ones already on the floor. The strong smell of iodine and juglone counteracted that of human flesh in decay.

Tamara had reaped them from the tree in front of their house, which Petru planted a quarter of a century ago to mark the birth of their daughter.

Meant as a token of life, the walnut tree was now being used for rituals in death. Seeing Ksenia off on her last journey, its leaves were used to bathe her abandoned body, fight off the odour of rot, and its fruit adorned the remembrance alms to be shared shortly.

Before leaving the room, Tamara stopped to adjust the sheet covering the wall mirror.

When somebody dies, all mirrors in the house are covered with towels or sheets so that the freed soul does not get trapped into them.

From time immemorial, in various lands, mirrors have been viewed as powerful magic tools, used for purposes of clairvoyance and as means of transcending to other planes of existence.

"*The mirror facilitates the entrance to the entrails of reality,*" her grandmother used to tell Larisa, but she disregarded it as mere folklore.

Superstitions or not, she did not want to find out by lifting or removing the covers of the mirrors. It was none of her business and neither was she curious enough to lose peace of mind over it.

The girls' efforts to diffuse their pain through abstract conversations did not totally succeed – tears rolled down their faces, flouting their attempts not to cry. Still, it was this philosophical attitude, which saved Doina and Larisa from a shot of diazepam. Like a robotic anaesthetist, Silvia was on a mission to tranquilise all those unable to deal with their emotions.

"Here we are, looking at death like we have never done before. Not so long ago, the only way we had known it was as a business opportunity."

Despite the situation a sad smile wedged on Larisa's face and her countenance lightened up, if only slightly.

Many years ago, when the concepts of loss and pain were unknown to the girls, they awaited new deaths in the village with eagerness and greed.

One of the many customs when a funeral convoy passes by is that relatives of the deceased throw coins at every well and crossroad on the way to the cemetery.

The money, so the lore goes, is in aid of the soul's paying the toll at the twenty-four bridges from this world to the next – a ritual unauthorised by the Orthodox Church yet practised by many priests. It does tend to boost candle sales. During each of these twenty-four stops, a kitchen towel is laid out on the road with a cup of water, a candle and wreath bread. The deceased is meant to be carried over this so called *bridge*.

Doina, Ksenia and Larisa used to run ahead of the procession and after picking up every penny from the dust of the road – fighting and spitting at other kids who were there for the same reason – they raced to the next stop. Strategic placement around wells and crossroads was paramount – that and the star under which you were born.

Many times, spatial awareness, logistics or craftiness did not matter one bit and they were solely dependent on luck – on the caprice of Fortuna: she could be bountiful, blind or a downright shrew and the girls could only hope for the best.

Being a lightweight, Larisa never stood a chance among the sharp elbows of the other kids. Many times she ended up thrown to the ground, lost and confused in the commotion. However, she never missed a well or a crossroad. Out of selfish charity, some kids gave her their small change: one *ban*, five *bani*, ten *bani* in order to unburden themselves of excess weight. Larisa was grateful nonetheless – it was better than nothing at all.

This cynical escort of the funeral procession went all the way to the cemetery gates, at which point the three of them turned back happy and content, whatever the revenue that day, totally oblivious to the suffering around them. All that concerned them was who made how much.

Even when they didn't accrue much, it didn't matter. There was bound to be another death following soon after – there always was. The cyclic law of existence inculcated that certainty.

The best way of finding out whom the next victim in the village would be, was to cock your ears and listen out for the Little Owl, then spot the house it had chosen to sing on.

The Little Owl is a peculiar bird which, when it sings on a rooftop, foretells the death of somebody from that household. Confirmation comes when the church bells are later heard. They usually ring to announce the liturgy or mark holidays but they also notify the village about someone's death or burial. It is a double message intended for both worlds: yours – to know that somebody has left the physical plane, and the other world – to learn there is a soul on its way.

The bells' vibrations are said to be attuned to a particular wavelength, which gets picked up by the existential dimension outside corporeality, thus heralding the arrival of a new soul into the kingdom of the spirit.

None of this was of any concern to the young girls at the time. Totally absorbed in counting their swag, they were in a world all of their own.

"You always ended up with less coins than anyone else in the gang," Doina recalled.

"Someone had to, I guess."

Riddled with a mixture of emotions, neither of them could disregard the irony of fate subjected upon them. Past memories and present circumstances fused, exposing how much their present reality was entirely dependent on time and space, despite their own subjectivity.

These sweet memories made their current circumstances even more painful, highlighting their irretrievable loss mockingly, mercilessly.

"How peaceful and serene she looks, totally oblivious to our suffering and everything else around. I guess her spirit is back to bliss. I can't help thinking that while our lives are in rupture, mourning her body, Ksenia's essence is in rapture," Larisa reflected in a monotonous voice.

"How's that rapture? You are starting to sound like Ksenia, talking like this. What we don't know, we cannot tell."

"The fact that we don't know doesn't mean it can't be true."

"Perhaps you are right but please let's stop this. C'mon, don't you start going off the rails too," Doina begged.

Out the window, the first cracks of dawn were visible at the horizon and her heart raced.

"That's it, today the last of Ksenia will be taken away forever."

The unfathomable grasp of this implication of *forever* gave Larisa a feeling akin to vertigo. No matter how hard she looked for the other end of that *For Ever* – she couldn't find it, staring instead into a bottomless pit.

She went outside for some fresh air. The gates were kept open, welcoming all who wanted to bid Ksenia adieu; and there were many – the entire village in fact.

The black cloth tied at the traditionally indented cornice of the house depicting a floral pattern in the shiny aluminium was waving unaffectedly in the morning breeze. The wooden hearse that would carry the coffin to the cemetery was waiting patiently by the porch, creaking under the burden of gift alms.

Funerals in Bessarabia have become increasingly competitive affairs. What should be a time of mourning is nowadays little more than an opportunity for families to parade the depth of their grief – and their pockets. Each newly bereaved family tries to outdo the previous one – despite the hefty debt this may incur. The price tags of presents procured by the family to give away as alms to friends and relatives, the type of coffin the dead one is buried in, and how much food and alcohol is served at the wake – these are all just criteria to determine the success of the affair. Sadly,

345

funerals, christenings and weddings, have become the most profitable and thriving businesses in Moldova right now.

Tamara, however, was determined to stage an event that the whole village would talk about for years. Even if it would cost her entire life savings. All those bribes which she had stashed under the mattress along the years in order to pay for Ksenia's wedding dowry would now instead be spent on her funeral.

The grieving mother threw all her efforts into the funeral her daughter was having in lieu of the wedding she'd never have. Tamara fetched Veronica, the village seamstress, to take Ksenia's measurements and tailor her a layered, lemon-chiffon, bridal dress.

She then travelled to UNIC, the biggest department store in Chisinau, and bought her only child, now dead, a pair of gold cross earrings, a sparkly purse and matching silvery shoes.

A make-up girl from a local bridal salon was generously paid to disguise Ksenia's death pallor and under Tamara's unyielding, vigilant gaze – to apply a frosting of poppy-red lipstick on her daughter's swollen lips.

Tamara also sought out and contracted the biggest flower company in the district to provide a dozen wreaths of fresh fir branches and a mound of yelping-yellow roses for her daughter's coffin.

Consumed by the choking regret of never fully reconciling with her daughter after their row following Ksenia's refusal to become an accountant, Tamara's guilt and sorrow squeezed all sense out of her. Or perhaps all those details, however untimely and inappropriate, helped to distract her from the reality at hand.

A few hours after sunrise, the priest arrived to carry out his duties. Ksenia's body was taken out of the house and subjected to its last journey on this Earth –

slowly moving towards the graveyard. People lamented to the sad fanfare of the expensively hired funeral band.

Larisa couldn't stop staring at Ksenia's lifeless body lying in the prettified, manually sculpted oak coffin ordered from Gavril Munteanu – the finest carpenter in the district.

The abundant black lace and ribbons surrounding the rim of the wooden box offered a stark contrast to the immaculate lining of her marital attire. Larisa found it a surreal world:

"*A funeral-wedding*," she thought and quivered at the grotesque absurdity of it all.

Larisa blinked regularly to assure herself she wasn't dreaming. The cries of the village women hired to raise loud lamentations served as undoubting reminders of the macabre procession.

"Ksenia, wake up…"

"Where are you going…young lady? Have…some mercy…on your distraught parents…which you are leaving behind."

"Arise, Ksenia! Arise, young lady!" and so the cries went on, all the way to the cemetery.

These wails, accompanied by trumpets, drowned all other sounds.

Doina and Larisa trudged just behind the coffin, pale and bereft. Their eyes were long dried up and they were hollow.

The tranquillised Tamara was staring into the beyond, walking slowly, halting now and again.

Petru's alcoholic stupor caused him to miss his daughter's funeral altogether. He sobered up briefly a week later and wandered the neighbourhood, bleary eyed, asking if anyone had seen Ksenia or knew where she was.

Zuzu, who was never seen to take part or attend any events in the community, followed the cortège crying like a child and holding the coffin's supporter with an iron grip.

Gangs of street urchins waited impatiently at each well and crossroad, like the three girls had done themselves at other times. Amongst all the people present, these children were the only ones removed from what was going on, the only ones concerned with life. Those careless, happy creatures accompanied the convoy all the way to the graveyard, where the last money was thrown out. Like a flock of hungry crows, they dived into the dirt of the road, picking up the coins to the last one, before flapping back merrily and noisily towards the village.

The coffin was laid into the gaping maw of the earth and people left gradually, returning to the house for the food wake. In half an hour there was no one left, apart from Doina, Larisa and the gravediggers. The two girls watched the cemetery workers in silence as they diligently undertook Ksenia's restitution to Mother Nature – the womb and tomb of all life!

The church's bell rang out for the last time, announcing the completion of the burial. They were powerful vibrations for such a simple instrument. Its resonance and timbre relied entirely on its contour and shape of the curve. Lost to its sound and the view of Ksenia's grave, Doina and Larisa sat there long after the gravediggers had left.

By the time they got home, the food wake had ended and the crowd had dispersed. Only family and relatives stayed behind to clean tables and bring order about the house. The two friends withdrew to a corner of the veranda and watched in silence.

Larisa slumbered. Before long, she was woken up by a hefty figure bustling around her:

"*Thith* poor girl *hath* been given the evil-eye. I'll *catht* away the bad spirits" she heard someone say and felt a callous hand touch her forehead, followed by fervent whispering:

"Run away, evil eye, from between the eyes
Run away, evil-eye spell
Or my breath will catch up with you
Run away, evil-spell
Or a wild wind will get you
Run away, evil eye, from between the eyes
Or the sun will get you
And chop your legs.
Run away evil-eye,
From the cheek
From the bridge of the nose
From the bottom of the throat
From the brains of the head
From the spleen and the heart.
You will get out and go away
Because my breath has broken your spell
With my hand I have lifted you
And cast you into the wind
Leave Larisa
Clean and filled with light
Like the flower of the meadow
Like the morning dew."

Unable to remember quickly enough where she was, it took Larisa a couple of minutes to understand what was happening. By that time, Baba Liuba – her old neighbour – had managed to spit out her chant, spraying her abundantly with precipitation like she had done so many years ago.

Doina appeared in the doorway as Larisa was frantically washing her face in disgust.

"What happened?"

"I got chanted over again by Baba Liuba. She scared the hell out of me. This country and its childish superstitions…"

"Just spit in your bosom and you'll be fine."

Part Three

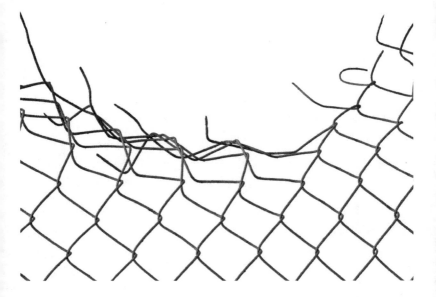

Dusty-Ash

Larisa and Doina returned to London a week after Ksenia's burial. The world seemed to have uncomfortably tilted on its axis and their entire existence had become mechanical: the dusty-ash of their present was lived through the prism of their shared, vibrant past. Things had happened so quickly and dramatically that their new circumstances still hadn't quite sunk in.

Yet Ksenia was gone.

For ever.

"I feel vulnerable," Larisa confessed. "Death has always seemed so far away – when we'd grown old, into fat and hairy *babushkas*. Now death is no longer ahead of us but right here – an eventuality at any given moment. This is terrifying."

Their sudden comprehension of that concept, however subjective, had deeply shaken their ground. Notwithstanding this, Ksenia was right – the sun did rise every day.

The fresh fruit had improved business for Doina's cleaning company still further. Despite this and following her final conversations with Ksenia, her plan was to sell it as soon as possible so that she could train to become a qualified psychotherapist. It was too late to be of any help to Ksenia but there were many others suffering back home who could still be saved.

Larisa continued publishing the *Diaspora* magazine.

They both kept busy to numb the pain. During the day this was a fine plan, but the nights were long and increasingly dreaded. A piece of them was missing and always would be from then on – a stark realisation too powerful to be ignored or forgotten.

No day passed without thinking of Ksenia. The end that Doina and Larisa were working towards was intrinsically linked with their friend's memory. They planned on selling some of her paintings to raise the funds needed to open the psychotherapy centre Doina was thinking about.

A year later she qualified as a behavioural therapist and volunteered to work temporarily at Cuculeni asylum to undertake work experience. She sought to assess the infrastructure of the institution and judge how best to fill the gap in order to help victims of the sex and slave trade.

During that year in Chisinau, she met Radu – an ambitious young doctor whose conservative appearance belied a passion for motorbikes that almost matched hers and her brother's.

He was supportive of Doina's plans to establish a clinic for returning migrants and was by her side all along. Together they had been able to lay the groundwork necessary to make her dream come true.

"We managed to get another psychiatrist interested in the project and quite a few psychology graduates from the State University," Doina told Larisa over the phone. "In the next few months I'll get the official application ready to be submitted to the government and register the organisation. As soon as they give us the green light, I'll come to London and sell the cleaning business. I am so excited. See you soon."

"That's great news. Give me a shout if you need help with anything in the meantime."

Smooth Azure

Larisa kept her habit of recording those dreams she could remember in the morning or the ones that woke her up in the middle of the night.

***

Weakness creeps in, melting my body into a pleasant mist. Like smoke I escape the house effortlessly and wander around the streets. I am searching for something. Turning corner after corner, street after street – I carry on looking. The roads become familiar and I start running. Can it be the way to take me home? I disappear into the smooth azure of the horizon. But it grows hazy, stretching itself widely ahead. The airy bubble rolls along, trapping and preventing me from leaving it behind. I can't escape the enclosing mist. The icy walls are squeezing in till the echo of growing laughter shatters the frozen hurdles. Like broken mirrors they fall to smithereens and there it is – the acacia grove. Drifting through the clump of trees, I head towards the waterside.

Doina and Ksenia are sitting next to each other on the other side of the shore. I call their names but they don't answer.

I'm shouting, getting out of breath but I realise I can hear no sound. No, that's not true – there is sound, except that it's not external. Perhaps more akin to telepathy. It feels like I'm moving through a mute environment where all sonorous vibrations come from within – and stay there.

Wanting to cross the pond I search for a bridge. There is none. Going around it, is impossible – the more I walk, the bigger it gets, stretching and hiding its end from my view. I step into the water hoping to swim over but the threatening waves push me back to the shore. I come out and call their names again. They look at me but neither of them responds. None of my frantic jumping or waving gets them to react. Ksenia and Doina carry on contemplating the waters on the other side, silently. I eddy up and down the shore in vain attempts to reach them. They remain cool and aloof.

The wind picks up and blows noisily – again – without sound. Heaps of leaves and dust swirl in the air, wheezing through the swaying branches. It gets stronger and stronger and I open my arms to meet its outburst. We become one and I bless the communion.

***

It was a year after Ksenia's death and still Larisa dreamt of her.

Fluorescent Green

After a strenuous day writing for *Diaspora* magazine, Larisa readied herself for her friend's birthday dinner party. Alison, a fellow cyclist, was turning thirty.

Larisa arrived late. The house was already full of people and dance music was turned up full blast.

Not long after her arrival, a horrible headache struck Larisa without warning. She couldn't remember the last time she had any sort of headache, probably years and there'd never been anything like this before: a sharp, head splitting, ear-ringing pain as if she'd just been hit full-on by a train at full speed. It was overpowering and she was forced to crouch down on the kitchen floor, holding her head.

A few friends gathered around.

"Are you OK? What's wrong?"

"Perhaps she's had too much to drink," somebody joked.

"What? Larisa? She hardly touches a drop."

Their voices sounded like distant noise. People's mouths opened and closed but their words did not synchronise, reminding Larisa of all those badly dubbed Soviet films she grew up with.

A few people helped her to a sofa and stretched her out.

The contusing, mysterious pain was stringent and unbearable. She could think of nothing, save for one horrifying image which kept flashing through her mind: a silhouette, dripping red, driving a *Yava* bike.

Despite it seeming like hours, after only five minutes Larisa was able to talk again and immediately reached for her mobile.

Doina's family didn't have a telephone and Larisa dialled their neighbour's number, anxiously waiting to see how she'd be greeted.

"Mos Ignat would know if something was wrong with Doina. He lives across the road," Larisa thought. *"I will be able to tell straight away by his tone of voice."*

"Hi Larisa, everything OK? You don't call often these days. Forgot all about us, have you, English lady?"

Larisa exhaled deeply.

She had a short friendly chat with Ignat, after which she politely asked him to go fetch Doina.

After ten minutes Valentin spoke at the other end:
"Hello!"

Larisa tensed.

"Valentin!"

"What a lovely surprise to have you call us, Larisa," he said joyfully.

Valentin's cheerful voice made Larisa sigh with relief a second time. Her heart, however, was still somehow tight.

"Hi Valentin, how are you? How is everything?"

"Still crawling and relying on my crutches. Apart from that, all good over here – busy as always, you know. It's autumn time and there's plenty to do. We just finished harvesting the corn and got to do all that shucking now. Planning on organising a husking social the day after tomorrow – means we should finish it in one go. Doina and Radu are here to help out and you are invited too by the way. Forget about that rainy, old England. Come home. It's more fun here."

The husking socials are an autumn fixture in the village, when there is a lot of work to be done as quickly as possible. The rains are unpredictable and everyone tries to have their harvest sheltered well in advance. Family, friends and neighbours gather in an agreed place to help each other with whatever tasks need to be done. There are usually all kind of socials happening: preparing clay and pasting it to brick walls or poles when building a house, helping with weddings, christenings and funerals. The collective work is efficient but also full of camaraderie. People tell jokes, gossip, sing and spin yarns, which get taller as the day grows older.

As children Larisa, Ksenia and Doina loved those gatherings – they got to peek into the alien world of the adults. Food and alcohol meant tongues loosened up, memories flared and imaginations soared. They were fascinating affairs and the girls used to eavesdrop, hidden in trees, behind fences or pretending to play silently nearby.

"Thank you for the invite but I don't think I can make it in time," Larisa said.

"Up to you but I guess you can always help later on with removing the kernels off the cobs," he laughed. "Or have you forgotten how delicious the *mamaliga* is?"

Mamaliga is a type of polenta, cooked out of maize and a traditional dish in Bessarabia. Corn is one of the main crops cultivated there and it has many uses. The stems are stored as fodder for livestock in winter times, in rural homes cobs replace charcoal and kernels are ground into golden flour.

"Maybe I'll visit around Christmas, we'll see. Hey, where's Doina?"

"Showing Radu around the village. I'll tell her you called."

"Is she on the *Yava*?" Larisa asked nervously.

"Oh no, the bike is broken down in my friend's shed. I don't have enough space to keep it at home."

Larisa's rib cage finally loosened, allowing her to breathe normally again.

"Can you please tell her I'll call again, same time tomorrow? I need to speak to her urgently."

"OK, will do."

"*Thank God she's safe*," Larisa thought and hung up.

"Is everything OK?" her friends still wanted to know.

"Yes, all fine, thanks."

"What was that fainting business all about? You are not pregnant, are you?" Alison quizzed and nudged, knowing full well Larisa was single.

"It'd definitely make my mother happy," she jested and returned to the living room.

Unable to fully relax, Larisa felt out of place at the party and went home soon after. But she couldn't fall asleep. Instead she found herself restlessly staring at the ceiling.

"*I should stop being so paranoid and not think I am going to lose all my loved ones now. I need to unwind. Perhaps I can talk to Doina about all these silly fears. Maybe she can help, now that she is a qualified shrink. I will ask her tomorrow. Sleep, where are you? Please come and get me…*"

***

The following day was a Sunday and Larisa went for her usual early-morning weekend bicycle ride. She chose the Box Hill route, her favourite for its spectacular views and scenery.

The three-hour unbroken journey, when most of London was still asleep, invigorated and recharged her like no other activity did. It was especially pleasant when the British weather allowed. She didn't mind the cold as long as it was dry.

Shortly before reaching the back-breaking Zig Zag Road, her phone went off.

She ignored it.

"I'm sure it can wait till I've conquered this."

But the phone kept vibrating in the pocket of her fluorescent green jacket and a memory from other times clouded her mind.

Only Bessarabians call non-stop without leaving texts or voicemails.

Larisa delayed answering her phone.

It shook incessantly.

A sudden, unexplained fear overtook her. She pulled to the side of the road and checked her phone. She was right – the prefix was Moldovan. Anxiety strangled her and in a faint voice, she spoke with a tremor:

"Hello…?"

Loud sobs could be heard at the other end and her heart sank. She felt the news before she heard it.

"Larisaaaa" and more sobs followed. "It's about Doina…She's dead…My beloved sister is dead…"

The bicycle fell to the ground and she collapsed by it. Only fragments of Valentin's further talk reached her – random, stabbing words:

"…Motorbike accident…Died instantly…Radu survived but is in a critical condition…"

Larisa sat in shock, dizzy from the sharp zigzags of events set in motion the night before and now culminating in such a terrible blow. Her brain refused to process any information and nothing made sense any longer. She lay in a heap by the side of the road, gaping into the void.

Strangers, kind English people, stopped, to try to help.

Dandelion

L arisa made it in time for the funeral.

An overwhelming feeling of déjà vu suffocated her.

She felt empty.

"It's all my fault," Valentin cried bitterly. "I provoked Death by asking her to take my father and she's come back to haunt me by robbing me of my young sister…"

Death in Bessarabia is feminine.

Valentin refused to come and see his dead sister. What there was to see.

Doina's body had been broken to pieces.

There would be no open casket for Doina.

***

Wishing to ingratiate himself with his presumptive brother-in-law, Radu had been attempting to fix Valentin's *Yava* since he arrived in Marani with Doina. However, unfamiliar with the workings of a mongrel bike, Radu overlooked the soft brake lever pull

Valentin had salvaged from an ancient *Dnepr* military motorbike.

Pleased with himself, he allowed Doina to take him for a ride and show him the countryside around the village. As they pulled out of the yard, neither of them noticed the front brake lever bolt drop into the dust of the road.

When they reached the top of the hill close to Doina's neighbourhood, she shouted *"Hold on tight"* and dived down the road with the wind whipping her hair against Radu's freshly shaven face.

At that moment Baba Liuba appeared as if from nowhere, crossing the junction with a lazy waddle – an empty, blue enamelled bucket, swaying in her old bony hands.

Doina hit the brakes.

Nothing happened.

She swerved sharply to avoid the half-deaf, half-blind woman totally oblivious to the desperate honking of the *Yava*, which stirred martins in their nests and caused dogs to howl.

The *Yava* took the bend too quickly and crashed into a concrete, bulbless lamp post.

There was an abrupt silence.

The motorbike lay crumpled on its side, its wheels spinning.

The dogs resumed their wailing.

***

Valentin withdrew to the bottom of the garden and let out his pain the only way he knew how. Words could not translate the agony he was going through but like a barometer for human emotion the accordion expressed the extent of his torment. His entire body was frozen, save for the flying fingers and the slow-rolling tears.

Larisa sat next to him. His melodies were full of guilt.

"It's my fault that she is dead. Please forgive me," he repeated in broken, choking sobs.

In the throes of regret, he carried on playing the accordion and the harrowing tune, like heavy smoke, whirled around and imbibed their world fully, before rising gently towards the sky.

***

Doina was buried next to Ksenia.

The inexorable Arrow of Time continued its one-way journey. Larisa's belief in a cyclic existence, inculcated by her rural upbringing, made no sense any longer. The accelerating and devastating events proved otherwise to Larisa and she came to abhor the linear curve of entropy.

On the last Sunday before returning to London, Larisa spent the entire day sitting with her friends. Lying down between their graves, she talked and laughed and cried. It was hard to believe they were both dead, when their presence was so vibrant.

"Instead of blood sisters we should have called each other soul sisters," she thought. *"Blood is confined to life while the soul transcends it."*

The two blue crosses marking the graves were proof enough that her soul sisters were underground. Larisa hated those symbols of death – they stirred a memory in her.

The whole cemetery was full of crosses and many were blue but the ones on her friends' graves reminded Larisa of another place from another time. The park benches at Cuculeni psychiatric clinic were made of the same cobalt blue, metal pipes.

"Perhaps," Larisa thought, *"I should have been more alert at the time and seen what was coming."*

Destiny, in her view – was not something prescribed at birth with an immutable course. Larisa had always believed it to be fluid, like the energy the world is made of. She thought it could be moulded and shaped according to one's heartfelt desires: dancing and taking the form of people's visions. But having witnessed the death of her closest friends at such proximity, she began to question her fundamental beliefs.

"What if I was wrong? What if we can't change our destiny, after all?"

Lost in her own thoughts and arguments, Larisa couldn't be certain what she thought any more. There was only one certainty: the order of things could not be tinkered with.

"I always thought life was all about 'how you are' rather than 'what you are'. If you follow your passions and live beautifully – you create your own destiny. But perhaps doing that, we just end up fulfilling it?"

The dazed, dandelion autumn sun was coming down and the coolness of earth ascended Larisa's body. It was time to leave the cemetery but she wouldn't move before scolding her friends for leaving her behind.

"Ksenia, you left with your eyes open and took one of us with you soon after. Doina, you on the other hand, weren't so compassionate. I feel abandoned, you know. It feels like you've both conspired against me."

Larisa wiped her eyes carelessly with the back of the hand.

Before leaving their side, she picked something and put it in her pocket.

"Peace to your souls and to your memory!" she whispered through sobs and turned to go.

Night was fast approaching and Larisa headed towards the exit of the cemetery.

Perched on top of a hill – closer to heaven – the graveyard watched over the world beneath, with a mixture of detachment, irony and eternal compassion. A community within a community, this place was on its own – cold and far away from mundane trivialities. The living tried to avoid it, apart from obligations such as All Souls Day and tending the graves of loved ones.

For Larisa, though, it was no longer an alien world. Her blood sisters were resting there and part of her was buried with them too.

The crushing weight of mind and soul increased her density and she descended towards the village with dragging feet.

Dull Charcoal

The Southbank breeze caressed Larisa's cheeks and played joyfully with her hair. London was no longer the place she wanted to be. Floating without reason or direction, she felt trapped. The triangle of her existence, which had rested on Ksenia, Doina and herself ever since she could remember, had gone and Larisa was riddled with despair.

An inner and obscure hum quivered unexpectedly, striking a familiar chord.

"A homecoming call," she thought. *"So soon?"*

She leant over the metal fence and stared into the dull charcoal waters of the old Thames. Too dark for any scrying, the moving water was hypnotic and seemed to beckon her.

"But death can be an option at any time," Larisa thought.

Despite the alluring call to relinquish all to nescience, she opted for life.

"Perhaps it's the homecoming call I am dreading? Jeez, I'm more scared of going home than I am of dying," she shuddered. *"Returning to the world I was so desperate to escape, to the superstitious customs and daft traditions –*

what a joke! What was the point of the fight I put up all this time and the journey I undertook, if I am to give up and go back now?"

Yet something kept tugging at her. Larisa couldn't figure out what it was about her origins that had such a strong pull.

"It certainly can't be of a spiritual nature – spirit is universal and it doesn't care where in the world it resides. The only answer that makes sense is that my memory is playing tricks on me."

A person who remembers nothing of his or her past has no identity. But if memory were the source of personal identity, it would belong to the cerebral dominion, and if that were the case, Larisa would be able to understand, analyse and deal with it. The issue was that she felt it was something much more powerful than that, even though she couldn't locate or explain it.

"Memory is deceiving."

To carry on, sincerity and acceptance were needed. She scanned her depths and assessed the wreck she had become: a heap of shards – pieces of broken recollections, broken dreams and broken hopes. There was no running from it and neither was there a way to make it whole once more. Despite outer fragmentation, deep connection with all loss and gain could be sensed, or perhaps imagined? What did it matter, if it was enough to save a soul?

"Am I going forward or backwards? But one is the other at the end of the day. The English had a phrase for it: 'this is doing my head in'."

A new identity emerged – a kaleidoscopic figure propped up and held together by pieces of different shape and colour. Choosing to treasure those smithereens more than anything else in the world, Larisa learned who she was. Their individual reflection and spark was enough to make her want to quit; but looked upon as one – they were acceptance, mystery, peace and wonder.

The hum persisted, rippling steadily – upwards or outwards she couldn't tell. Even though it was only slightly perceptible, Larisa was able to recognise her song, the one her grandfather hinted at all those years ago.

She felt in her pocket for the two walnuts she'd taken from the tree watching over her sisters' resting place.

She turned and looked east.